An LR Publishing Book

SPORTS OFFICIATING: CAREER HANDBOOK

Second Edition
1999

LR Publishing Staff

Roger E. Perlmuter, President and Publisher
Jeannine Dreimiller, Editor
David Dreimiller, Writer and Research Coordinator
David Perlmuter, Director of Sales and Marketing

Production Staff:

Len Bergenstein
Laurie Fischer
Carol Yehl

LR Publishing Company
Cleveland, Ohio

Cover photos, front: Center, Michigan High School Athletic Association; clockwise from top right, National Federation of State High School Associations, Roger Perlmuter, Michigan High School Athletic Association, Michigan High School Athletic Association; **back:** Top to bottom, Michigan High School Athletic Association, Tom Lowry, Whistle Stop, Roger Perlmuter

©1999 by LR Publishing Co.
Cleveland, Ohio

Library of Congress Catalog Card Number: 99-71520

ISBN 0-936217-49-9
Printed in United States of America

We welcome all comments, suggestions, updated information
and photographs for future editions:

LR Publishing
4555 Renaissance Parkway, Suite 101
Cleveland, Ohio 44128
(216) 591-1492 • Facsimile (216) 591-0265
www.sportsref.com

Printed on recycled paper

FOREWORD

by Bob Rice,
NFL Assistant Supervisor
of Officials, 1987-95

I love sports. As a gym teacher, coach and official for over 40 years, I have been involved in the sporting world in many different capacities. Due to hard work, lots of enthusiasm and a little luck, I was fortunate enough to turn my love of sports into a personally satisfying and financially rewarding career. In fact, I was able to put four children through college with the money I earned as an NFL official, working only on Sundays!

As I worked my way up the officiating ladder, I met a lot of interesting people. When I attained my goal of becoming an NFL referee, the excitement of the people involved was truly incredible. Some of my co-workers were top business executives who would rather give up their entire fortunes than miss the chance to call a professional football game. Sports is that addictive, whether you're an athlete or one of the people wearing black and white.

Most of the time, officials are the forgotten people of the sports world. We are vital to the operation of the game, but often go unrecognized until a *bad call* is made. It takes an incredible amount of self-confidence and patience to become a successful official, to say the least.

Life has rules. People are constantly judged by their ability to perform within the guidelines. And someone has to enforce the regulations or else there would be total chaos! Sports officials are like the justice system – the judges and police of the sporting world. Whether you are a line judge at the tennis finals during the French Open or calling balls and strikes during the World Series, or simply a Pee Wee football referee making some extra money while your kid plays on the team, you call the shots! And that's what makes sports officiating so exciting.

Sports Officiating: Career Handbook is a terrific new guide on how to become involved in officiating, in the sport you love, in the state where you live. The book is loaded with practical information that not only tells how to get started, but also gives a realistic picture of this career and whether it's the right choice for you. It's your call!

TABLE OF CONTENTS

SECTION III: OFFICIATING IN THE MAJOR SPORTS

The Track & Field Official

The Volleyball Referee

The Wrestling Official

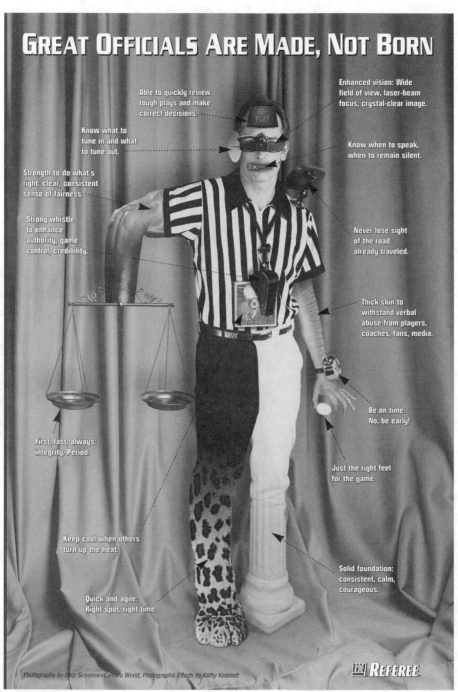

Introduction

With interest in both professional and amateur sports at an all-time high, opportunities abound for prospective officials in a wide variety of competitive sports. Often understated as a career path, sports officiating can be an exciting, lucrative, and personally satisfying experience. The first book of its kind, Sports Officiating: Career Handbook is a comprehensive reference on all aspects of sports officiating in virtually every sport and every level of competition. While information on rules interpretation and the mechanics of officiating in specific sports is readily available, the goal of this book is to go beyond the technical issues and focus on the career-oriented aspects of officiating. Whether you're a prospective official looking to break into the business, or a working official seeking career advancement, the Handbook is your source for practical, up-to-date information that can give you a definite advantage.

A career in sports officiating is just that – a career. No one walks onto a field to officiate a major sporting event without considerable training and experience. Of course, like some athletes, certain officials have a knack for the job, and superior officials tend to advance more quickly than others. For most officials, however, advancement to the high profile level of the professional sports arena is earned through hard work, dedication, and years of work at lower levels of competition. Sports Officiating: Career Handbook shows you how to acquire the basic certification and training you need to get started at the interscholastic level, how to establish yourself as a local official, and how to maximize your chances of advancement to higher levels of competition.

As any veteran official will tell you, sports officiating requires much more than familiarity with the rules. The sports official is

part police officer, part safety monitor, and part diplomat. Successful sports officials share several common personal qualities, including the ability to communicate well with others, resolve conflicts, make instantaneous decisions, and cope with pressure and stress. No one can hope to advance as a sports official without a complete mastery of these skills. Sports Officiating: Career Handbook confronts the psychological aspects of sports officiating head-on in an article guest-written by noted sports psychologist Robert Weinberg, Ph.D. Dr. Weinberg's text provides a comprehensive and much needed analysis of the psychological aspects of sports officiating that is a *must read* for novice and veteran officials alike.

Sports officials are expected to work within accepted norms of behavior. Chapter 8 takes you through the issue of conduct and demeanor and helps you understand what's expected of you when you take the field as an official. This chapter also provides practical advice on how to look, act, and respond like an official.

For any official, a thorough familiarity with the rules of the sport is essential. Section III points the way with information on obtaining the official rules book for the sport of your choice and a detailed discussion of officiating in each of the major sports. Informative background information is provided for each sport, along with an overview of the role and duties of the official(s). Also featured are sections on attire and equipment, compensation, levels of competition, and detailed resource listings for officials which outline regulatory bodies, professional associations, and key contacts. Because certification requirements vary by state, a complete directory of state high school athletic associations is included to help you focus on your geographic area. Each listing outlines registration information and eligibility requirements, classification of officials, levels of competition, and key contact information.

Make no mistake – sports officiating can be a physically challenging and exhilarating career. Indeed, officiating in many sports requires a degree of physical conditioning equal to that of the competing athletes. For those who rise to the challenge, sports officiating can be a financially and psychologically rewarding career.

Get in and study refereeing
Do your favorite thing
Though not playing basketball anymore
Lots of fun it still will bring

Obey the tenets, make the best call
And of course speed the blessed day
When you graduate from the little leagues
And become an official in the NBA

Section I:
The Profession
of Sports Officiating

AP Wirephoto

Sports officials often are subjected to spirited challenges of their calls. Here, Chicago White Sox manager Chuck Tanner strikes an animated pose as he implores umpire Art Frantz to reverse a call. Veteran sports officials have learned to take arguments such as these in stride.

CHAPTER 1:

LET THE GAMES BEGIN
Career Orientation

THE SPORTS EXPLOSION

There has been a veritable sports explosion in the United States over the last few years. Competitive sports permeate virtually every aspect of modern life. High-profile athletes are constantly in the news; mass television audiences gather for everything from Olympic competition and championship games to local coverage of high school football games; new sports are continually emerging while old mainstays remain as popular as ever; and sporting goods manufacturers load the airwaves and print media with advertisements, symbols, and sports icons. In short, America is nuts about sports, and not just as spectators. Participation in sports is at an all-time high, particularly at the youth and high school levels. The widespread growth of participant sports has spurred an urgent need for qualified officials, particularly at the local level. Now, more than ever before, there is an abundance of opportunities for prospective officials to break into the business.

THE OPPORTUNITY

Outside of the sports industry, few people realize just how widespread officiating jobs have become. A recent poll of state high school athletic associations, conducted by *Referee* magazine, indicates that in the states of California, New York, and Pennsylvania alone, nearly 49,000 officials are certified to work at the inter-scholastic level. An estimated 300,000 officials work nationally, with as many as 30,000 new positions opening each year. So great is the need that many state athletic associations must constantly recruit new officials just to offset the loss of experienced officials that results from normal attrition. At the interscholastic level, which encompasses officiating at the junior and high school levels, there is a very high turnover among certified officials. In fact, the Kansas State High School Athletic Association estimates that 20 percent of their recently certified officials (those with four years or less experience) leave the profession each year. And every year also sees the retirement of veteran officials, further increasing the need for new officials at the local level.

The high turnover rate has resulted in a continual need to recruit new officiating talent, thereby greatly increasing the chances of a newcomer gaining acceptance. And for anyone who aspires to the collegiate or professional levels, interscholastic officiating is the first step in gaining the practical skills and work experience that are required for advancement. For those already knowledgeable in a particular sport, but new to officiating, the process of becoming a state-certified official is surprisingly easy. By following the basic steps outlined in Chapters 2 and 3, you quickly can attain state certification and begin officiating interscholastic-level competitive sports in short order.

UMPIRING

The North Shore Umpire Association school for new softball umpires, Sunday and Wednesday evenings starting Jan. 19 at St. Mary Byzantine on State Rd. OHSAA, ASA and NSA accreditations.

Meeting of the Parma Heights Senior Umpires, 7 p.m., Jan. 17 at City Hall. No experience necessary. If you are interested in umpiring but unable to attend,

Ralph Zarzycki

There is an urgent need for qualified officials at the youth and interscholastic levels. Some leagues have resorted to newspaper ads and roadside billboards like those above to attract officials.

While interscholastic officiating is perhaps the most common entry point for novices, it is certainly not the only game in town. In many areas, recreational sports leagues sponsor athletic programs for children including softball, soccer, hockey, and many other sports for boys and girls. Another sport that has seen tremendous growth in recent years is adult softball. In both cases, it is possible for the novice official to get involved with minimal effort and pick up some spare cash in the bargain. Children's leagues, in particular, are an excellent means of getting involved in officiating.

DEVELOPING SKILLS FOR A LIFETIME

Parents looking to steer their children into part-time employment would do well to look at sports officiating. For most kids, officiating at an athletic competition is far more enjoyable than flipping burgers or delivering newspapers. And in cases where a young person's desire to compete is stronger than his or her physical ability, part-time work as an official, or even as an event statistician or timekeeper, is a viable alternative to actual competition. More importantly, the skills and experience a young adult will acquire as a sports official will help him or her excel in virtually any career that he or she may ultimately pursue. Looking beyond the technical aspects for a moment, officiating requires concentration, decisiveness, clear articulation of thought, a sense of fairness, and an ability to keep one's emotions in check. It is difficult to imagine any other part-time job for a 13 or 14 year old that would stress (and help develop) these skills more than sports officiating.

NOT JUST FOR KIDS

Sports officiating is by no means the exclusive domain of the young. Officials come from all walks of life and from many disciplines. Some people use officiating to round out another part-time job, while others are millionaires who take time off from running corporations in order to officiate. Many officials work on a part-time basis to augment their monthly incomes. The trend toward part-time employment is by no means unique to officiating. As many workers know, the American economy no longer guarantees job security. Companies routinely are bought and sold, and jobs once thought secure oftentimes are eliminated as a result of corporate restructuring. It is little wonder that temporary work agencies represent one of the fastest growing business segments in America today. In fact, the single largest employer in the private sector is Manpower, Inc., which employs over 500,000 part-time workers.

Whether through choice or necessity, workers increasingly are choosing employment that involves job sharing, independent contracting, temporary, and freelance work assignments. The prevalence of part-time occupations has allowed many people the luxury of pursuing careers they love while protecting themselves from sudden job upheavals. In addition, you often can choose a schedule that best suits your needs.

The *be your own boss* concept truly applies here. And you can begin to take charge of your life working in a field you enjoy. Given these factors, exploring a career in sports officiating makes good sense and explains why so many people do. If you would like to get off the corporate treadmill, seize control of your life, supplement your income, work with athletes, and become involved in a fulfilling career, you should take a look at officiating.

An Opportunity for Everyone

Sports officials increasingly come from diverse groups. Those who picture an official as a white male might be surprised to learn that the modern official is as likely to be a female, a member of a minority group, or an elderly person. The explosive growth in popularity of women's sports over the past several years has resulted in numerous opportunities for female officials. In some states, participation of female athletes in interscholastic athletic programs is estimated as high as 50 percent, and state and regional athletic associations are in desperate need of female officials for their events. At the interscholastic level in particular, athletic associations increasingly are aware of the importance of presenting positive female role models in the arena of competitive sports. Sports officiating presents an excellent opportunity for women to act in the capacity of role models for the many female student athletes who compete at the interscholastic level.

At the college level, the National Collegiate Athletic Association (NCAA) has long advocated the involvement of women and minorities in all levels of intercollegiate athletics. The NCAA Women's Enhancement Program offers, among other services, a Vita Bank program to assist individuals and organizations in identifying qualified applicants seeking careers in college sports programs.

For those who are nearing or have reached retirement age, sports officiating is a great way to keep active while earning some extra money. While workers once looked forward to retirement at the age of 65, this is no longer practical for many people. In addition, senior citizens today are increasingly looking for ways to remain active and maintain a sense of vitality.

OFFICIATING AS A CAREER CHOICE

Note from the publisher: In many sports, at the professional level of competition, officials' salaries reach into six figures. In terms of income, Major League Baseball umpiring ranked 8th of 250 jobs in a recent survey, outpaced only by such jobs as President, surgeon, Indy car driver, and major league athlete. Survey results were included in the Jobs Rated Almanac (Wiley & Sons, Inc., 1995), a joint project by Les Krantz, the Wall Street Journal, and the National Business Employment Weekly. The book provides a fascinating comparison of various occupations and includes job rankings by such factors as salary, stress level, and working environment. Presented here are excerpts from the study that pertain to baseball umpiring. Although specific to work at the major league level, this information offers an overview of the duties, benefits, and income potential for those who reach the top.

Major League Baseball Umpire

Outlook
Ranking: 134/250
Job Growth: 11%
Promotion Potential: Low

Promotion Opportunities: Experienced umpires occasionally advance to administrative positions within the Baseball Commission. Employment opportunities for major league umpires are expected to remain constant through the next decade, unless a rule change permits an increase in the size of the league and in the number of games.

Physical Demands
Ranking: 238/250
Basic Day: 6 Hours

Though major league umpires are not required to be as well-conditioned as players, they must nevertheless run, throw, and stand for long periods of time. Unlike players, umpires are on the field for the entire game, which can last over three hours. Umpires must be quick and agile enough to achieve proper positioning to make calls and to avoid batted balls. This job requires excellent eyesight and quick judgment. Extensive travel, combined with night games, can be fatiguing for umpires over the course of the season. In the summer months, games may be played in extreme heat and humidity. In the spring and fall, night games in Northern cities are often played in the cold.

Security
Ranking: 228/250
Job Growth: 11%
Unemployment: Low

Major league umpires enjoy good geographic freedom. Employment opportunities for umpires are expected to increase only slightly over the next decade. The pool of umpires will remain relatively small and very competitive.

The National Business Employment Weekly Jobs Rated Almanac (Third Edition), © 1995 Les Krantz.
Reprinted by permission of John Wiley & Sons, Inc.

Environment and Job Description
Ranking: 199/250
Hours Weekly: 30

Duties: Referees monitor play in a major league baseball game, making judgments on pitched and batted balls, and on the legality of plays. Major league umpires are employed by the National and American Leagues in professional baseball. In a regular-season game, four umpires are used, one behind home plate and one located near each of the three bases. Foursomes normally work together for a series of games and rotate positions game to game. The primary responsibility of the home plate umpire is to determine balls and strikes on pitched balls. He also keeps the pitcher supplied with new balls, rules on fair and foul batted balls, and keeps play moving. Umpires in the field make calls on plays at their respective bases and in the outfield. Umpiring requires good eyesight and quick judgment, as well as a thorough knowledge of baseball rules. Players and managers occasionally engage umpires in heated arguments over disputed calls, and umpires are subject to jeers and taunts from fans. In important games, umpire decisions sometimes come under intense media scrutiny. This profession involves extensive travel during the baseball season. Most games are played outdoors, and weather conditions vary. In addition to players and managers, umpires regularly come in contact with league officials and media personnel.

Income
Ranking: 8/250
Starting: $60,000
Mid-level: $140,000
Top: $175,000
Growth Potential: 192%

The earnings of major league umpires are exceptionally high, relative to the modest educational requirements of the field. There is little distinction between the income and benefits of novice and experienced workers in this field.

Stress
Ranking: 207/250
Hours per Day: 6
Time Pressure: Low-Moderate
Competition: Moderate

Baseball umpires need to be in good physical shape, as they must stay on their feet throughout the game and work in all weather conditions. They must remain constantly alert and make hundreds of decisions quickly and accurately. Other stress factors include working erratic hours, being in the public spotlight, and dealing with players, managers, and fans who disagree with their decisions.

Travel
Style: First Class
Frequency: Very High

Baseball umpires work in crews of four, and crews travel from city to city to work three to five games in a series. Umpires, like players, normally are provided four-star (top-of-the-line) accommodations in the major cities which house big league baseball teams.

JUST DO IT . . .

There is a job waiting for you in major sports as an official. The perceived *Hollywood* lifestyle of the professional sports athlete is the rainbow many individuals chase. However, sports careers do not begin and end with the athlete. Successful competitive sports requires dedicated officials at all levels. And frankly, the average person has a much better chance of becoming a good sports official than a star athlete.

Top NFL officials earn $250,000-plus a year along with a host of perks for what amounts to a few hours of work each week. At the other end of the spectrum are volunteer officials who preside over youth leagues. While these two groups are miles apart in terms of salary and prestige, they both share a love of the sport and the ability to work with people. While officials work with little notoriety in the shadow of the athletes, they derive tremendous satisfaction from being involved with the sport, doing the job well, and

earning the respect of the athletes and coaches. In addition, officials often get the opportunity to travel and always enjoy the camaraderie of fellow officials. No matter what level you work, you'll find motivation in the power the official possesses in the competitive arena and the sheer adrenaline pump of working the big game. An anonymous softball umpire sums up the mentality of officiating: "Sure, I enjoy the bucks . . . but I enjoy much more the respect I get from fellow officials, coaches, and players who see my true reason for officiating . . . teamwork, self-respect, staying consistent, a chance to travel, an opportunity to work the best ball in the country (which, by the way, does not always pay the most), and lastly, an opportunity to achieve my goals and make some lasting friendships."

In the chapters ahead, you will learn more about what's involved in breaking into the business, how to establish yourself as a local official, what you can do to advance your career as an official, and what's in it for you if you apply yourself. You'll also learn more about what it takes to become an effective official, along with the specific requirements for officiating the sport of your choice.

The starter's gun signals the start of the race. Just like the athletes, sports officials must train and prepare long before the competition begins.

Chapter 2:

On Your Mark, Get Set, Go!
Getting Started

Children's Leagues

If you think you might want to be a sports official, try offering your help in children's leagues. Although there might not be much pay, you can get onto the field of play many times without the commitment of taking tests, having previous experience, or registering with your state athletic association. Try it. If you enjoy it, if it feels right, then maybe this great career is for you. Officiating at this level is generally limited to recreational sports and little league games. The action and emotions at these events are often just as intense as those found in higher levels of competition. Officiating for children's leagues is often performed on a voluntary basis, although in many areas you can expect compensation for your effort. Many officials at the children's level get involved for the pure satisfaction of working with youth, particularly in the capacity of a role model. In many cases, parents get involved in officiating as a way to participate in sports with their own children. Officiating children's leagues is also an excellent way to stay involved with a sport you love, or to simply help convey the importance of sportsmanship and fairness to children.

Officiating children's leagues is not a prerequisite for inter-scholastic officiating; in fact, anyone seriously pursuing sports officiating as a career path would be well advised to apply directly for state certification as interscholastic officiating will ultimately prove more beneficial in terms of advancement.

Certification requirements for youth league officiating vary widely by league and locale. As a general rule, state certification is not re-quired for officials at this level. In many cases, your knowledge of the sport and a willingness to work are all that are necessary. Many youth leagues openly recruit officials, either through word-of-mouth or advertisements in local newspapers. Watch the sports section of your local paper for announcements, or contact the di-rector of the appropriate league for officiating opportunities in your area.

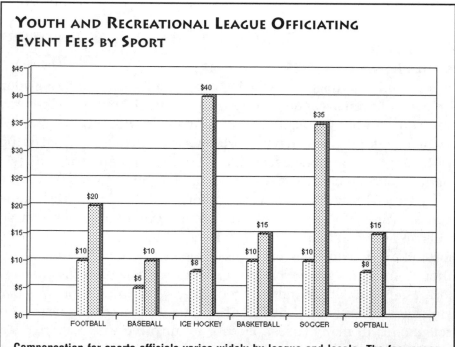

YOUTH AND RECREATIONAL LEAGUE OFFICIATING EVENT FEES BY SPORT

Compensation for sports officials varies widely by league and locale. The fee ranges presented here were compiled from a nationwide review of officials' earnings in both large and small cities. However, this information is intended only as a general guide. Contact your league or athletic association for information specific to your area.

OVERVIEW OF INTERSCHOLASTIC ATHLETIC PROGRAMS

Interscholastic athletic programs encompass sporting events played at the junior high and high school levels. In most states, interscholastic sports programs include separate divisions for boys and girls, and these are broken down by age or grade level. Typically, interscholastic competition includes junior high for grades 6-8 and high school for grades 9-12. The principal team or squad at each level is referred to as the varsity team and generally is composed of the best athletes in a given sport. A junior varsity team typically fields younger athletes or those whose skills have not yet reached varsity standards. Just like the athletes, interscholastic officials tend to begin their careers at the lower levels of competition and work their way up to the varsity level.

Most schools offer a wide range of individual sports in their interscholastic athletic programs, which affords prospective officials many opportunities to get involved at this level of competition.

Jody Schroath/Weekly Villager

Youth and interscholastic sports offer numerous opportunities for officials to gain invaluable on-the-job experience.

Table 2:1 outlines the officially sanctioned interscholastic sports typically offered to student athletes, along with the number of officials required at the varsity level and the seasons of play for each sport. This list was compiled by reviewing athletic programs from across the country and may vary somewhat from region to region. However, it will give you a good idea of the types of sports officials most often required in interscholastic sports.

Interscholastic sports normally are scheduled for specific seasons. This policy encourages athletes to participate in more than one sport and ensures that sporting events are scheduled throughout the academic year. Likewise, many interscholastic sports officials take advantage of seasonal sports schedules by working more than

Table 2:1
INTERSCHOLASTIC SPORTS OFFICIATING

SPORT	OFFICIALS REQUIRED	SEASON PLAYED
Baseball	2	Spring
Basketball	2	Winter
Cross Country	1	Fall
Field Hockey	2	Fall
Football	4	Fall
Gymnastics	2	Winter
Ice Hockey	2	Winter
Lacrosse	2	Spring
Soccer	2	Fall
Softball	2	Spring
Swimming/Diving	2-3	Winter
Tennis (Boys)	1*	Spring
Tennis (Girls)	1*	Fall
Track (Outdoor)	1	Spring
Track (Indoor)	1	Winter
Wrestling	1	Winter
Volleyball	2	Spring & Fall

*Varies by locale

SEASONS OF PLAY

Fall: September 1 - November 30*
Winter: November 15 - March 31*
Spring: March 8 - June 30*

*Dates are approximate

one sport. For example, an interscholastic official could work the fall football season through Thanksgiving and then pick up again in March with baseball. Working a second sport helps you maintain your overall proficiency and also increases your earning potential.

Table 2:1 provides a working time frame for interscholastic sports within the academic year; actual time frames may vary slightly from state to state.

STATE CERTIFICATION

You must be certified by your state athletic (or high school athletic) association to officiate interscholastic sports in most states. Your state athletic association is responsible for regulating, certifying, licensing, training, and testing prospective sports officials in accordance with the guidelines set forth by the National Federation of State High School Associations. Earning certification as a new official is a relatively easy matter. It's even easier if, like most applicants, you're already knowledgeable about the sport for which you are registering. Once you receive certification and an officiating license, you can begin gaining the practical experience and developing the professional relationships so necessary for career advancement.

The following sections lay out the basic steps involved in obtaining an interscholastic officiating license from application to certification. While the information presented here provides a general overview of the certification process, the requirements of individual athletic associations do vary. A directory of the individual state athletic associations is included in Section V, complete with current classification, registration, and certification requirements. Prospective officials are urged to contact their state or high school athletic association for specific information on the certification process in their state.

CONTACTING YOUR STATE ATHLETIC ASSOCIATION

The first step on the road to a career in sports officiating is to contact your state athletic association and request a registration information package as it relates to your sport. This package usually contains information on the application process and an official application form. Be sure to request a copy of the current rule book for the sport(s) you are applying for, unless this is supplied in the information kit. In some cases, a nominal fee is required for the rule book. Most state athletic associations impose time limitations on when you can register. Specific time frames and cut-off dates normally are included as part of the information package. Registration within the allotted time frame ensures that you can start officiating as soon as possible.

ELIGIBILITY REQUIREMENTS

To meet basic eligibility requirements in most states, you must be at least 18 years of age and a high school graduate at the time of application. In addition, some states require personal references to process your application. Individuals with criminal records are automatically excluded from the application process in many states. In some states, attendance at a training session and a written examination also may be required.

Although you may apply at any time after you reach age 18, anyone considering a career in sports officiating should file his or her application as soon as possible after reaching the minimum age. Experience is everything in sports officiating. The length of your tenure as an official will weigh heavily in any future decisions regarding advancement. Therefore, the sooner you begin, the sooner you'll have a respectable number of years of professional association membership under your belt.

APPLICATION FORM

The application form typically will require that you provide your name and address, date of birth, occupation, and the sports in which you plan to officiate. Be sure to furnish all the required information or your application may be delayed or even rejected. Normally, a separate fee is required for each sport you wish to officiate and is payable at the time the application is submitted. Application fees generally are non-refundable.

FRONT

OFFICIAL REGISTRATION CARD
(This application must be signed)

Name (Print clearly)   Date of birth

Mailing Address (RR, PO, Box, Street, etc.)   City   State   Zip + 4

Occupation   County   Home Phone   Business Phone

I hereby agree to abide by rules and regulations as determined by the Executive Board and to cooperate with the KSHSAA in every way.
I certify that I:

1. Agree to be bound by the applicable provisions of Rule 11 of the KSHSAA and any amendments thereto;

2. Am not presently subject to a suspension or revocation of my ability to act as an athletic official at the high school level in Kansas or another state; and

3. Have not been convicted of a misdemeanor or felony within the last five (5) years.   **OVER →**

Applicant's Signature   Date

BACK

KANSAS STATE HIGH SCHOOL ACTIVITIES ASSOCIATION
520 SW 27th Street, PO Box 495, Topeka, KS 66601-0495

I hereby apply for registration as an athletic official in the following sport(s) for the KSHSAA: Amount enclosed: $_____
Check the desired sport(s) below:

Sport		Were you a registered official with the KSHSAA last year?		Have you registered with the KSHSAA in another sport this year?		
☐ Football	☐ Girls' Gymnastics					
☐ Basketball	☐ Baseball	YES	NO	YES	NO	
☐ Wrestling	☐ Soccer	☐	☐	☐	☐	**OVER →**
☐ Volleyball	☐ Softball					

The registration fee is $30 for one sport and $10 for each additional sport. ANY **FUTURE REGISTRATION WITHIN THE SAME SCHOOL YEAR IS $30 FOR ONE SPORT AND $10 PER ADDITIONAL SPORT.** If you were registered last year, you must register **prior to May 15** *(February 1 for Baseball or Softball).* Registration **after the deadline includes a $10 late registration penalty.** If you have been registered 21 years or more and register prior to May 15, the fee is $30 for one sport and $5 for each additional sport.

FOR OFFICE USE ONLY			
ACCOUNTING	REGISTRATION	PACKET MAILED	NEW ☐

Above: Sample official's application form, Kansas State High School Activities Association

WRITTEN EXAMINATION

As part of the application process, you will need to take a written examination in the sport of your choice. The focus of the exam is to test your knowledge of specific rules of the given sport, and the official rules book will be your primary study guide. Although such examinations often are *open book* exams (you may bring your rules book along for consultation), generally lasting an hour or less, do not assume you can pass the test without studying the material in advance. You must score at least 70 percent or better in most

Sample License

KANSAS STATE HIGH SCHOOL ACTIVITIES ASSN.
OFFICIALS LICENSE

9999	**FEE**	**DATE**	**EXP. DATE**
	$50	4/29/95	JUNE 1, 1996

Rick Bowden
520 SW 27th St.
Topeka, KS 66601

is an official in the sports indicated below and may contract for games with K.S.H.S.A.A.
members.   **KAYE B. PEARCE, Executive Director**

BASKETBALL - Jeff T. Stromgren
VOLLEYBALL - Gene Valentine
BASEBALL

Left: Sample official's license as issued by the Kansas State High School Activities Association

states for your application to be considered. A thorough review of the official rules book beforehand will greatly increase your chance of success.

The examination for a particular sport usually is administered only once each year. The date and location of the examination are set by your state athletic association.

YOUR OFFICIATING LICENSE

Once you have successfully completed the written examination, you will be issued an officiating license listing your name and address, the sports in which you are certified, and the expiration date. This is your ticket to officiate, and you should be proud of it. Keep in mind that your license is subject to annual renewal. Assuming you have attended the required rules meetings throughout the year and your status as an official is in good standing, you need only submit the appropriate fee within the allotted time frame in order to have your license renewed.

COMPENSATION

At the local junior high and high school level, compensation normally is set on a per-event basis, with the actual rate of pay and number of games set up on a contractual basis. A typical sports officiating contract will outline exactly when and where you are expected to officiate and how much you will be compensated. In other cases, there is no formal contract. Typically, an official is assigned to a specific number of games or events and a standard officiating fee is set for each. Table 2.2 presents various high school level competitive events and an average event fee range for each. The actual event fee varies widely, and your earnings may be higher or lower, depending on where you officiate. In some states, uniform fee structures are established by the state athletic association; in other states, the fee amount is determined by school administrators. Keep in mind that officiating post-season events generally will yield a substantially higher rate of pay than games played during the regular season. In some areas, you also can claim reimbursement for mileage in addition to the event fee.

Regardless of the event fee, your actual gross income will depend entirely on the number of events to which you are assigned. Interscholastic sports programs generally consist of separate leagues or divisions for junior high, freshman, junior varsity, and varsity teams, with games or events scheduled on different days of

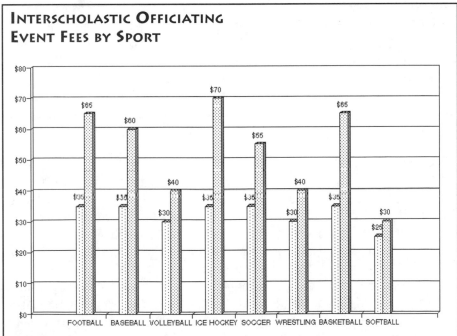

INTERSCHOLASTIC OFFICIATING EVENT FEES BY SPORT

Compensation for interscholastic sports officials varies widely by league and locale. The fee ranges presented here were compiled from a nationwide review of officials' earnings in both large and small cities. However, this information is intended only as a general guide. Contact your local league or state athletic association for information specific to your area.

CLASSIFICATION OF OFFICIALS AT THE INTERSCHOLASTIC LEVEL

State athletic associations classify officials in accordance with the experience and training they have received. Newly licensed officials are classified at the lowest level and may advance to higher levels as they gain experience. In some areas, a point system is used to determine eligibility for advancement; in other areas, eligibility is dependent on the number of years in service. The exact number of classification levels and the terminology used to describe them varies widely. The classification system used in your area will normally be provided in the official's handbook issued by your state athletic association. Regardless of which system is used in your area, the primary purpose of the classification system is to match an individual's experience with the level of competition. In most cases, the two basic classifications are described.

ENTRY-LEVEL RATING

Upon successful completion of an open-book test and a mechanics examination for some sports, your state athletic association initially will certify you as a novice or entry-level official. This license, akin to a temporary drivers permit, allows you to officiate subject to certain restrictions. For example, you may be prohibited from officiating at the varsity level, or restricted to officiating specific sports. These restrictions are dropped as your classification advances, which greatly enhances your ability to gain essential experience.

ADVANCED RATING

Advancement to the more prestigious advanced status requires two or more years of practical experience gained in each sport in which you hold a novice rating. In addition, you must pass a closed book test covering the rules and regulations of the sport. For some sports, including football and basketball, a mechanics examination is required in addition to the written portion. The mechanics examination is used to judge your ability to position yourself in the correct location to be able to make a call and requires thorough familiarity with the tempo and flow of the game. In both cases, a higher passing score is required than for a novice rating. You may also be required to submit two or more favorable field evaluations from other advanced officials. Those officials must physically observe your performance during a scheduled event and may not themselves be participating in the event, as either competitors or acting officials.

the week. This schedule allows officials to work many more games within a single sport than would be possible if they worked at only one competitive level. For example, a high school football official at the varsity level would average only eight or 10 games in an entire season. However, that same official could also work junior varsity games on Saturday mornings and perhaps even pick up junior high or high school freshmen games played during the week, thereby doubling or tripling his earning potential. From a career standpoint, it certainly helps to exhibit a willingness to work as an official, and the experience gained will be invaluable for future advancement.

You also might consider becoming certified to officiate in sports that are played in the off-season of your primary sport. This will help increase your earnings and can help eliminate or at least reduce the number of months of down time experienced by officials who work only seasonally in one sport.

ATTENDANCE AT PERIODIC MEETINGS REQUIRED

In order to keep up with new rules and regulations and to maintain your standing as a state-certified official, your athletic association usually asks you to attend periodic rules interpretation meetings. While requirements vary, you can expect to attend approximately four such meetings per year for each sport in which you are licensed and, in some cases, many more. In some states, newly licensed officials need to attend more meetings than experienced officials.

Certain officials may be exempt from meeting attendance if meetings are not held in their area. However, no matter what the sport, keep yourself apprised of the dates and times of scheduled rules meetings. As a general rule, consider attendance mandatory. Often, failure to attend or even tardiness may result in a suspension of your officiating license. In cases of emergency or extreme hardship, your state may allow you to attend a makeup meeting; however, such cases normally are reviewed on an individual basis, and there is no guarantee that you will be permitted this option.

In addition to rules interpretation meetings, you may be asked to attend one or more of the following: annual training clinics or camps, a regional officials meeting, and/or a pre-season officials meeting. While these meetings are primarily designed for the benefit of officials, coaches often are welcome to attend as well. The meetings provide a unique opportunity to compare the different perspectives of coaches and officials.

TRANSFERRING YOUR OFFICIATING LICENSE

The sports officiating license issued by your state athletic association entitles you to officiate in your state only. In the event that you relocate to another state, you need to contact the athletic association in your new state to determine whether a reciprocity agreement exists with the state from which you moved. Reciprocity agreements recognize your status as a working official and permit you to waive the examination process for new officials when applying in a different state. If a reciprocity agreement exists, you need only submit verifiable evidence that you hold a valid officiating license in your former state along with an application form and filing fee for the new state. In most cases, you will be issued a new officiating license which allows you to begin the process of scheduling work. However, if no reciprocity agreement exists between the two states, you will have to repeat the entire licensing process, including the written examination, regardless of your previous officiating experience.

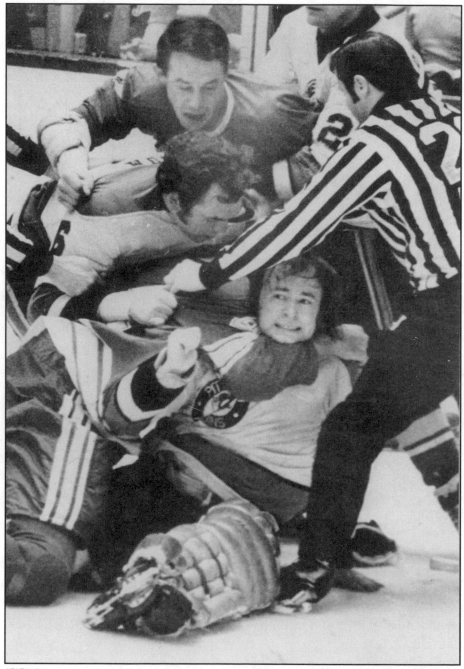

UPI Telephoto

Competitive sports tend to bring out the best and worst in people. An intrepid ice hockey referee is shown here attempting to break up a brawl involving players in a 1971 game in Pittsburgh, PA. Officials must maintain control and prevent emotions from boiling over.

CHAPTER 3

SAFETY FIRST:
Sportsmanlike Conduct and Safety Issues

Although the word *fan*, as in *sports fan*, sounds harmless enough, keep in mind that fan is derived from the word *fanatic*. Sometimes sports fanaticism leads to safety problems, such as objects thrown onto the field of play. This is the point where the official must draw the line. Heckling is one thing, but any action on the part of the fans that physically interferes with play or player safety must be brought under control immediately. You must not allow the game or event to continue when the safety of the participants (and this includes you) is on the line. In extreme cases, you may even have to resort to your ultimate power: *forfeiture*. It's an ugly word, but no game is worth jeopardizing safety.

THE WEATHER

Art Treuman, a high school football referee in Alabama, told us: "Before I leave to officiate, I always check the local weather report." Being aware of the weather is yet another officiating responsibility and one that must be taken seriously. Sports played outdoors often are subject to extreme weather conditions. In many sports, the officials are responsible for deciding if and when a game must be called as a result of weather. Lightning is a very dangerous situation. Professional golfer Tony Lema was killed by lightning during a match that was not postponed soon enough. Every year, players are seriously hurt or killed because of poor weather judgments on the part of officials. Weather considerations apply both during the game and during pre- and post-game travel.

Any decision regarding a delayed start of a game as a result of unsafe weather normally is dependent on the league rules, and suspending play altogether is sometimes the only solution. As a game official, your primary concern will be weather events that develop once the event gets underway. High winds and fog can be hazardous. These *Act of God* situations are outside your control, but your reaction to them is critical and necessitates a sense of good judgment on your part.

INJURIES

Injuries to players necessitate game stoppage. Your league normally will have rules governing this type of situation. If you notice a player is injured you should call immediate attention to him or her. However, as an official, it is not your duty to treat the player. Your job is to ensure the player receives prompt attention. In a recent game, an official noted that a particular athlete exhibited excessive sweating, heavy breathing, and dizziness. He stopped play to advise the coach. Later that night, doctors discovered that the player had developed a form of asthma. Both the coach and the athlete subsequently thanked the official. Sadly, there also have been numerous occurrences of players competing under the influence of alcohol or drugs. These matters should be reported to coaches and the league.

An athlete rendered unconscious is a very serious situation. Many athletic associations maintain so-called *unconscious rules* that require the official to temporarily stop the competition and rule the athlete ineligible from further participation. In most cases unconsciousness is not limited to a total black out but also includes situations in which the athlete is incoherent or unable to answer simple questions. Nonetheless, at all times the official should be vigilant in watching for any signs that a player has sustained an injury or is not in full control of his or her faculties.

Bleeding on the field of play has become a hot topic because of such blood-borne diseases as HIV and hepatitis. New rules have been promulgated and specific policies and guidelines have been instituted to reduce the risk of infection to others. In general, any bleeding athlete must be removed from the field of play until bleeding stops. Competition should be brought to a halt until the situation can be assessed.

EQUIPMENT

Protective equipment is required in most sports to prevent injuries to the athletes. It is your job to ensure each player is utilizing the proper equipment. As an official, you need to be aware of the type of equipment required for your sport so that you will be able to recognize an unsafe situation the moment it develops. In most cases,

THIS IS A PUCK GENTLEMEN—
IT'S THAT HARD ROUND RUBBER THING
THAT YOU HIT WHEN YOU MISS EACH OTHER!

you must call a halt to the action the minute you spot something that may result in injury. For example, a cracked face guard or helmet could result in irreparable injury or even death. Players sometimes lose their mouth guards or forget to put them back in place after a play. If you notice this, you could save a player's teeth or jaw. Although watching for illegal or unsafe equipment may sound like nitpicking, compare the task to that of the policeman who enforces seat belt laws; someone has to protect people from their own carelessness.

There are also rare situations in which players use illegal equipment which could cause injury to others or affect the outcome of the game. This brings to mind the 1995 incident involving Cleveland Indian Albert Belle's *corked* bat which was discovered in a game against the Chicago White Sox. The cork presumably gave Belle an unfair equipment advantage.

Another incident involved a case of *fanaticism* which translated to the playing field. Allegedly seeking revenge for an aggressive tackle sustained in another game by his son, a high school football player's father was accused of sharpening a fastener on his son's helmet. Numerous players and a game official sustained lacerations as a result.

EJECTIONS

As an official, there may be times when you will have to reprimand an athlete or coach. Allowing unsportsmanlike conduct to go unchecked almost always results in the development of an even uglier situation. The best way to avoid this scenario is to rule decisively at the first sign of inappropriate behavior. It must be made clear that unsportsmanlike conduct will not be tolerated. Set the tone early to establish control of the playing arena.

Although ejections are extreme occurrences, to be effective as an official you need to take your power as an official very seriously to protect yourself and others. In many cases, you may have no alternative but to eject a player or coach who disrupts the event. Of course this calls for patience, fortitude, and a cool head on your part. It takes very little effort to set off a coach or athlete who is already emotionally charged. However, no matter how tense the situation, you never want to exhibit any sign of unsportsmanlike conduct while ejecting someone else for exhibiting the same sort of behavior. When the offender is an athlete, it is your responsibility to inform the player as well as his or her coach as to the reasons for the ejection (even if it is blatantly obvious). Your task is to assess the situation, then provide a concise and well-founded explanation for the benefit of the coach and the player. In extreme cases, you might be required to make a written statement after the event has concluded. There should be no room for debate or second guessing in cases of ejection.

CHAPTER 4

ESTABLISHING FIELD POSITION:
Obtaining Work as an Official

The first step in obtaining work as an official is to identify the key decision makers responsible for assigning officials to specific games in your area. Depending on where you live, these decision makers may include recreational or league directors, coaches, school officials, sports commissioners, or regulatory bodies. Once you've familiarized yourself with the system by which assignments are made in your area, you'll want to let the right people know you're available to officiate. Send a brief note indicating your interest in officiating their events. Be sure to include your name and contact information, availability, and the sport(s) in which you are qualified to officiate. Some athletic associations employ local or regional supervisors who act as a liaison between the schools and prospective sports officials. If a supervisor is assigned to your area, be sure to let that person know of your availability as he or she frequently is contacted by schools seeking qualified officials. In addition, be sure to review the specific rules set by your athletic association regarding whom you are permitted to contact to obtain officiating work. For example, in some areas, you may be prohibited from initiating direct contact with a coach or school official.

In many areas, officials are contracted to work through a local officials association. Although membership in these organizations may not be mandated by your state athletic association, in many cases you will not obtain work as an official unless you enroll. Local officials associations often wield tremendous clout in terms of hiring officials; often, an Assignment Chairman acts as a liaison between schools and qualified officials. Your membership places your name in the pool of available officials and greatly increases the chances of your being hired to officiate. Membership in a local officials association allows you to attend periodic rules interpretation meetings. Some have dues. However, the up side is that you will be able to interact with veteran officials, which is invaluable for the novice. At present, there are literally thousands of such organizations throughout the country. Your state athletic association should be able to provide a list of the associations in your area.

At this stage in your career, your motivation should be acquiring experience as much as monetary gain. Even though you are certified to officiate at interscholastic events, you should also consider officiating in children's leagues whenever the opportunity presents itself. There are a wealth of officiating opportunities at this level, including little league games, intramural competitions, pre-season scrimmages, church leagues, and recreational sports. In some cases, you will not even be compensated for your efforts at this

---

SOLID ADVICE
for getting work as an official includes:

Sell yourself to league officials and athletic directors.
Observe as many games and officials as you can.
Learn the rules.
Identify the people who hire officials.
Desire all the work and experience you can get.

level. Nonetheless, your involvement will provide invaluable practical experience that can only enhance your career. In addi tion, you will begin to make acquaintances with coaches, athletic directors, and other officials that can lead to vital personal references which are required for advancement. Working alongside more experienced officials will also help you hone your practical skills as you observe them in action.

You should try to work every game or event that is offered to you. Consider it an honor that they have selected you. At this point, you need to acquire as much practical experience as possible and develop a steady history of employment as an official. Moreover, you want to give the impression that you can be counted on to do the job.

As with any job, you can increase your chances of getting additional work by performing competently on every assignment you are given. This means thorough advance preparation is a must.

You might also consider watching a few games at the level at which you will officiate to get a feel for how other officials work. Try to observe the event not as a typical sports fan but as a trained observer concentrating on your officiating counterpart on the field of play. For example, pay careful attention to how the official acts on the field and interprets the rules as different situations arise. In sports that involve mechanics, there is much to be learned on how an experienced official positions himself or herself in various situations in order to be able to make a call. Have a copy of the rules book handy so you can follow along as the action unfolds.

Arrive promptly to your assigned games. As an official, the game cannot begin without you. Advance preparation pays big dividends. Be sure you know exactly where your events are scheduled to occur ahead of time. You can't always find a site simply because you know where the school or facility is located. When operating in unfamiliar territory, it's a good idea to travel to the site ahead of time to familiarize yourself with its location, the proximity of parking, and any other details. Veteran officials often arrive a half hour or more before the competition begins in order to get oriented, meet with other officials, team captains, or coaches, and, much like the athletes, begin to mentally *psych up* for the event.

In order to advance as a sports official, you must impress people with both your knowledge of the game and your ability to control the competition. Your appearance and demeanor go a long way toward making a favorable impression (see Chapter 8 for additional information). To this end, it is important for you to maintain a professional appearance at all times while in the public eye. Your uniform should be clean and neat and in good repair. Your shoes should be polished. If your sport requires a team of officials, be sure that everyone else is uniformly attired. Your personal grooming habits also reflect on your professional officiating image.

POST-SEASON OFFICIATING

In many sports, more financially rewarding officiating opportunities exist in the post-season when playoff and championship events are held. In most cases, these positions are filled from the ranks of more experienced officials; in other cases, post-season officials are selected on the basis of recommendations made by schools or coaches. In nearly all states, post-season officiating is limited to officials who have achieved certified status, which will likely preclude the novice from participation. You should consider attending the event as a spectator in order to observe other officials in action in what is almost invariably a higher level of competition than the regular season.

EMPLOYMENT CONTRACTS

Your employment as a sports official will be regulated by a written contract in most states. Such contracts typically lay out the name of the school or organization for which you will officiate, the dates and times for the scheduled events, and the amount of your fee. Review your contract carefully for any potential scheduling conflicts and be sure to sign and return a copy within the allotted time frame. In many areas, verbal agreements are used in place of written contracts to schedule officials. In such cases, be sure to write down all pertinent information and treat such an agreement as if it were a written contract.

Many an official has found himself or herself in the situation of being offered an officiating slot at a high paying or prestigious event that conflicts with a previously scheduled event of lesser caliber. However, no matter how much money is involved or how big the game is, you stand to lose more by breaking a contract than you could ever gain by officiating the other event. In cases of illness or extreme necessity, such as a death in the family, it is often possible to get out of a contractual obligation. In most instances, you will have to notify the organization that contracted you, advise them of the problem, and offer to locate a competent official to act as your substitute. Don't send a substitute official without prior approval, but you can suggest one to the proper people.

TAX CONSIDERATIONS

As an independent contractor, your income as a sports official normally is considered as part of your taxable income. Keep in mind that no deductions will be made from your officiating fees, and you will be responsible for any and all income tax requirements. Like any other employment, it is essential to keep accurate records of all financial transactions that take place over the course of the calendar year, including fees paid to you and any expenses that you incur as a result of officiating, such as travel and mileage. In some cases, these expenses may be allowable as deductions. It is highly advisable to consult a tax preparation expert to ensure you are in compliance with applicable tax codes.

LIABILITY INSURANCE

Sports officials and, for that matter, anybody dealing with public life should have insurance coverage. Although you already might have health insurance coverage, keep in mind that such policies cover only those injuries that you personally sustain. As a sports official, you also should have liability insurance to help protect against lawsuits that might arise if participants or spectators are injured as a result of your actions. This type of insurance covers damages that might be levied against you in civil court if you are found negligent. Even if you are not negligent, liability insurance could help cover the cost of your legal defense. Fortunately, liability insurance coverage for sports officials is a service offered by many officials associations as part of their annual dues. Check with your local association to see what type of coverage is available.

MAINTAINING GOOD STANDING AS AN OFFICIAL

Your conduct as a state-certified sports official is regulated by the state athletic association. Specific rules regarding your conduct and demeanor typically are set forth in the official's handbook that is provided to you as part of the registration process. The official's handbook includes policies and by-laws with which you are expected to conform and often lists the sanctions you will face for infractions and violations. Although policies and regulations

concerning an official's conduct vary by state and locale, some of the more common elements include:

Conduct/Demeanor of the Official
Uniforms/Appearance on the Field
Contractual Obligations for the Official
Adherence to Sportsmanlike Conduct
Guidelines for Officiating in Specific Sports

A general discussion of each of these topics is provided in subsequent sections of this book. It is important that you familiarize yourself with the specific policies and by-laws issued by your athletic association. Even relatively minor violations can result in potentially severe sanctions such as probation, suspension, written or verbal reprimand, and even monetary fines if the infraction warrants. In most cases, you can be sanctioned for improper conduct (both on and off the field), consumption of alcohol prior to or during an event, demonstrated biases or lack of impartiality, or a deterioration in your mental or physical health. You can also face sanctions for nonpayment of fees, failure to attend the prescribed number of rules meetings, use of non-regulation or inappropriate attire, or even failure to notify the association in the event that you move from one district to another.

State athletic associations typically encourage feedback on the performance of officials (both positive and negative) from coaches and school officials. In many cases, a report form is provided to facilitate the process of filing complaints or grievances and to minimize the chances of an open confrontation on the field of play. Therefore, you cannot assume an event was trouble-free just because complaints were not lodged on the field of play.

Sanctions act as a blot on your record and are counter-productive to your career goals. As a sports official, your advancement depends heavily on the integrity and moral character you demonstrate both on and off the field. As a representative of your state athletic association, it is essential that you be aware of any and all rules that pertain to your conduct or actions as an official and comply with them at all times.

Referee Hue Hollins gives a *thumbs up* signal prior to the start of an NBA game. For many officials, advancement to the professional level is possible only through hard work and dedication at lower levels of competition.

Chapter 5

Moving the Ball Downfield:
Career Advancement

Advancement at the Interscholastic Level

Your goal as a new official is to obtain a certified rating (or the equivalent) from your state athletic association. This rating allows you to officiate at all high school events, including the varsity level. The state high school association is your key to unlock the door of officiating opportunity.

Establishing Professional Contacts

Once you achieve the Certified Rating, officiating opportunities will abound. Officiating at this level likely will bring you in contact with a whole new group of professionals including coaches and officials with far more experience than you. This is a golden opportunity to add depth to your roster of personal references by courting professional relationships, establishing rapport, broadening your knowledge of the sport, and sharpening your officiating skills. The *Lone Ranger approach* will not work here; this is yet another area where your social skills and your ability to interact well with others really come into play. Even though your newly achieved

Certified Rating confers on you the same status as more experienced officials, do not let it go to your head. You should always accord a more experienced official the deference and respect he or she has earned. In general, you'll find that long-time officials will be more than happy to work with you by answering your questions and generally encouraging your career development and personal growth.

OFFICIATING LOG

As you gain experience as an official, it's a good idea to keep track of your work history by maintaining a log of the games or events you have worked in. You should record the date and type of sport, the names of the teams and league involved, the nature of your officiating duty, the number of hours worked, the amount you were paid, the location of the event, and any pertinent details regarding your performance. You might also list any expenses you incurred such as travel or mileage.

In sports involving a team of officials, you also want to record the names and telephone numbers of the officials you worked with as you might need to contact them at a later date. Your officiating log

---

OFFICIATING WORK LOG

Date: _____

Place: _____

Position Officiated: _____

League: _____

   Team #1: _____

   Team #2: _____

Miles to: _____

Miles from: _____

   Total Miles: _____

Other Significant Details: _____

_____

_____

. . . we are, by nature, pro-active, if our lives are a function of conditioning and conditions, it is because we have, by conscious decision or by default, chosen to empower those things to control us."

The 7 Habits of Highly Effective People
Stephen R. Covey

will help you reconstruct your career when the time comes to prepare a professional resume and will also serve as a personal yardstick to compare one season to another. Your log may also prove useful in reviewing event fees and the frequency of work with a particular school or league.

In some states, a complete log of your officiating duties will be maintained for you by the sponsoring league. In other cases, no official record will be kept. In either case, you should maintain your own log as you are likely to include much more detail than the league.

PROFESSIONAL CRITIQUES

A professional critique of your performance is an excellent way to sharpen your skills as a sports official. In fact, such critiques are generally required for interscholastic advancement. However, at this point, you should be looking beyond satisfying minimum requirements with an eye toward getting as much feedback as possible. Invite an experienced official to watch you in action through an entire game or event. Often, he or she can point out problem areas that you might not be aware of and help you focus on becoming a better official. You should keep an open mind throughout and try to remain receptive to comments and suggestions. In fact, an official who becomes resentful of such critiques is probably not a good candidate for advancement anyway. Many a veteran sports official owes his or her success to the guidance received from more experienced officials during these early years.

SELF-CRITIQUES

In addition to professional critiques, you might also consider a self-critique. While it is often impossible (and nearly always inappropriate) to preoccupy yourself with a self-critique during the actual competition, many teams videotape the entire event for the benefit of the athletes. As an official, you might be able to view these tapes after the event. By studying a game tape, you can determine how you look in action, whether you are positioning yourself properly within the competitive arena, and perhaps most important, gauge the accuracy of your calls with the added benefit of hindsight. If team-sponsored game tapes are not available to you, or if the tapes that are available do not present enough information, consider having a friend or family member videotape your performance for you. Be sure to discuss your needs ahead of time so that your videographer knows exactly which camera angles will best suit your needs and what to focus on during the event.

ADDITIONAL TRAINING

Once you achieve certified status, it's time to seriously consider enrolling in any of the numerous officials training clinics, seminars, and classes offered across the country. While such courses may not be mandated by your state athletic association, they are an excellent method of demonstrating initiative and interest in your work, not to mention an outstanding opportunity to rub elbows with other officials with an eye toward career advancement. It has often been said that an official who stops learning is an official whose professional skills are deteriorating. All things being equal, the official who goes the extra yard in terms of receiving additional training will likely move ahead of the official who meets only minimum requirements.

Another definite plus in terms of career advancement is your membership in national officials associations. Just as your long-standing membership in the state athletic association will figure in any future decisions regarding your advancement, the same applies for affiliation with officials associations. Officiating associations exist for the sole purpose of encouraging the professional development of their members. Your membership opens vital access to the latest rules changes, training seminars and workshops, books and publications, and a virtual network of other sports officials which can help sharpen your skills and make you a more effective official. At the interscholastic level, membership in the National Federation Interscholastic Officials Association (NFIOA) is highly recommended. In most states, a portion of your high school athletic association's annual license fee covers membership in NFIOA; therefore, you automatically are enrolled as a member. In states that do not have automatic enrollment in NFIOA, you are encouraged to apply directly to the National Federation for membership. In addition to the services and benefits outlined above, NFIOA offers liability insurance coverage to its members as part of the annual dues.

Roger Perlmuter

Communication among sports administrators and officials is essential for successful competition. Here, a high school athletic director meets with the officiating crew prior to the start of a football game.

You also should consider membership in the National Association of Sports Officials (NASO), a non-profit educational association. Established in 1980, NASO offers a wealth of benefits and services for the sports official. NASO membership dues include liability insurance coverage, toll-free access to the sports officials *hotline* for quick answers to your officiating questions, a periodic newsletter on officiating, along with a subscription to the monthly *Referee Magazine, The Magazine of Sports Officiating.* Membership in NASO is open to any official, regardless of competition level.

Roger Perlmuter

DEVELOP YOUR OWN STYLE

An important aspect of an official's career advancement is the development of a unique officiating style. Most successful sports officials bring to the competitive arena a distinct style, certain mannerisms, and a personality which help distinguish them from other officials. Although the prescribed method of giving signals is dictated by the rules book, there often is some latitude in terms of the actual mechanics involved. For example, observe the subtle variations in the way major league baseball umpires signal a strike; although they all conform to the rules book, virtually no two give the signal in exactly the same manner. The goal is to display a style that conveys your interest and enthusiasm in the competition and perhaps introduces a bit of your own personality to the game in the process. At the same time, remember that the best officials are those who do not draw undue attention to themselves, either through their actions or their demeanor.

STAY ON TOP OF THE LATEST INFORMATION

Another excellent method of ensuring career advancement is to keep up with the latest news and information for sports officials. A large number of books and publications have been written over the years specifically for sports officials – everything from training manuals to monthly magazines devoted exclusively to the science of officiating. Such publications can lead you to training clinics, camps, seminars, how-to articles, national officials associations, equipment suppliers, and much more. In addition, the tremendous growth of the Internet in recent years has led to the development of a host of sites on the World Wide Web dedicated to sports officiating. (See Appendix III for additional information.) Many web sites give you the ability to network with other officials, check out employment opportunities, and review the latest rules changes.

In short, advancement from high school varsity-level officiating hinges on how well you laid the groundwork up to this point. Hard work, perseverance, drive, ambition, and initiative are expected norms; anything less is counterproductive. You should be mentally and physically prepared to work as an interscholastic official for five or more years. For those who tough this period out, the potential reward – advancement to collegiate or even professional sports – can far outweigh the effort.

ADVANCEMENT TO COLLEGIATE & PROFESSIONAL SPORTS OFFICIATING

Advancement to collegiate and professional-level officiating usually is achieved through years of dedicated effort at the interscholastic level. Overall, there are fewer officiating opportunities at the collegiate and professional levels than at the interscholastic level. Your advancement depends on your effectiveness as an official, your professional bearing on the field, your ability to maintain the flow of the event, and equally important, your professional contacts and references. This is not to say that employment prospects outside of interscholastic competition are bleak. Indeed, college athletic conferences and most amateur and professional sports leagues actively recruit across the country in order to meet the demand for qualified officiating talent.

Although college level officiating is not regulated by your state athletic association, most officials maintain their standing as state-certified officials even as they advance through the college level. In some cases, it is possible to officiate at both levels, at least in the preliminary phases when college level work may be limited. As always, your goal is to maintain proficiency and a steady record of employment as an official. Allowing your state certification to expire while you search for college level work is not a good idea.

Not every sports official aspires to career advancement. Many officials are perfectly content to work the interscholastic level throughout their careers, while others stop at the collegiate level. In other cases, otherwise qualified interscholastic officials simply lack one or more of the skills required for advancement, and thus must be content with their current status. Any official considering the move should carefully review his or her performance over the years in order to meet the challenges of the job. The following sections are designed to show you the basic procedures involved in advancement at these levels, along with some tips on how to increase your chances of acceptance. You should also review the various Official Profiles that appear throughout Section III to learn how other officials achieved their status.

The Perfect Ref

The perfect ref let us praise
He's never sick on Saturdays
In fact this wondrous, welcome wight
Is dressed to the t's, what a sight
He studies hard to learn the motions
Not for money, but for sports devotions

He's on each play without fail
At the end of the game, the ref they hail
With coaches he is kind and stern
He gladly listens, then waits his turn
And even others I have heard it said
Say he's so kind with an even tempered head

He takes advice, but calls it fair
He's never late and always there
This officiating wonder doesn't get old
He's even got a heart and a pot of gold
He has but one small fault I'd list
He doesn't (what a shame!) exist.

A college basketball referee stands courtside during a pause in the action. Most collegiate-level sports officials are drawn from the ranks of talented high school officials.

Chapter 6

First Down:
Officiating Collegiate, Amateur, and Minor League Sports

The next step in your career advancement is officiating at the college and amateur levels. You need the background and continuing participation at the lower levels to advance. At the amateur and collegiate level, athletes are still competing for the love of the sport and not remuneration. The crowds are larger. Some teams are vying for bowl game opportunities that can mean up to tens of millions of dollars in income to their schools. Many officials prefer this level to all other levels as do many fans. George Becker of Hudson, Ohio notes: "Collegiate sports are my favorite; the college atmosphere can't be beat." Paul Meyers, a veteran official, recently posted the following observation to an Internet Newsgroup devoted to sports officiating: "I've been officiating college football for over 30 years after I was cut from the freshman team. I've worked games for free, for beer money, for travel money . . . and for a pat on the back and a thank you."

Because the competition is more intense, you need to hone your skills to increase your chances of success. Those who excel at the college and amateur levels are the ones chosen to work the major league.

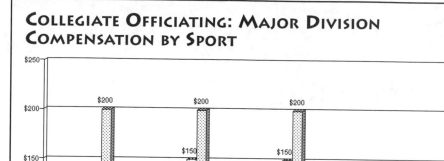

COLLEGIATE OFFICIATING: MAJOR DIVISION COMPENSATION BY SPORT

Compensation for college sports officials varies widely by conference, division, and locale. Top earnings occur in Division I, while smaller divisions tend to pay lesser amounts. The fee ranges presented here were compiled from a nationwide review of officials' earnings in Division I competition. This information is intended only as a general guide.

There is no single regulatory organization or uniform method of certifying sports officials for college and amateur athletic programs. In fact, organized competitive sports is highly fragmented in nature outside of the interscholastic level. Eligibility requirements for officiating vary widely, depending on the league or conference that regulates the sport for which you are applying. As a rule, the more advanced the level of competition, the more experience and skill are required of the official.

Your earning potential as a sports official increases in direct proportion to the level of competition. At the collegiate and amateur levels, you can expect a higher per-event fee. Although potentially more lucrative than officiating interscholastic events, collegiate officiating entails more extensive travel and often much more in terms of training and attendance at rules meetings than in high school sports. In most cases, you will be reimbursed for mileage and travel expenses, but even so, it may be difficult to fit the demands of extended travel and training into a schedule that involves full-time employment elsewhere. Collegiate officiating also requires membership in professional associations, so you can expect to add annual dues to the list of expenses. Table 6.1 presents some typical event fees for NCAA officials.

An overview of the major college and amateur athletic organizations is presented in the following section. Additional information on collegiate and amateur sports officiating in a particular sport, complete with contact information, may be found in Section III of this text.

NATIONAL COLLEGIATE ATHLETIC ASSOCIATION (NCAA)

One of the nation's largest regulatory organizations for intercollegiate sports competition, the NCAA maintains committees on 36 individual sports and encompasses more than 1,200 member institutions and conferences. The primary goal of the NCAA is to promote post-season competition for college athletes.

NCAA competition consists of Divisions I, II, and III with Division I being the most advanced level. Separate programs are conducted for men and women, and officiating opportunities exist at each level. The NCAA does not certify or hire officials; however, the organization does sponsor annual training clinics for some sports, attendance at which is mandatory for officiating NCAA championship games. In addition, attendance at these clinics is absolutely essential to be considered by the larger college athletic conferences for regular season work.

In most cases, officials who work in NCAA sports are hired by individual colleges and athletic conferences. Therefore, the first step in obtaining officiating work at this level is to contact the appropriate conference or organization. They can provide additional details on the eligibility and certification requirements for officials in their league. In general, you will be required to submit letters of recommendation from your professional contacts in order to be considered. Your references can include athletic and recreation directors, fellow officials, league officials, and coaches. A typical letter of recommendation should stress your moral character, the skill and ability you have developed as a sports official, and also include some mention of your work experience. You should also consider preparing a professional resume detailing your work experience as an official, including any related activities and/or special training that might help your cause.

No matter how much experience you have acquired as an interscholastic official, you will most likely have to start out in small conferences or schools and advance your way to higher levels of competition. As a rule, the larger Division I conferences, such as the Big Ten, Pac Ten, and the Atlantic Coast Conference, hire only the best and most experienced officials. In most cases, an official

Table 6.1

NCAA CHAMPIONSHIP COMPETITION
Event Fees for Head Officials

SPORT	NCAA DIVISION I	NCAA DIVISION II	NCAA DIVISION III
Baseball	$1500	$1000	$1000
Basketball	575	115	91
Cross Country	100	100	100
Football	350	137	88
Gymnastics	150	n/a	n/a
Ice Hockey	300	175	175
Soccer	140	140	140
Softball	750	810	630
Swimming	300	300	200
Tennis	1000	500	500
Track	100	100	100
Wrestling	90	90	90
Volleyball	475*	600**	375**

*Per match, men's competition
**Flat rate, finals competition

may have to work as long as three to five years in Division I competition in smaller conferences before becoming eligible to work the large college conferences. Officiating Division I competition at smaller conferences, in turn, requires experience in Divisions II and III.

NATIONAL CHRISTIAN COLLEGE ATHLETIC ASSOCIATION (NCCAA)

The National Christian College Athletic Association is the primary regulatory body for athletic competition at religious and private colleges. NCCAA competition consists of two divisions; Division I encompasses 48 institutions, most of which maintain dual affiliation with the NAIA. NCCAA Division II includes 53 non-scholarship colleges which offer a minimum of 20 hours of Bible or religious course work. The NCCAA also includes ministry and community endeavors in its post-season championship games. The goal is to instill better moral values in college athletes.

Officials for NCCAA championship games are selected on the basis of recommendations from their host colleges and conferences. As a rule, NCCAA officials are selected from the ranks of talented interscholastic and junior college officials. Although the NCCAA does not certify officials, the organization does sponsor periodic training clinics for officials, attendance at which is mandatory for officiating at NCCAA national events. The NCCAA adheres to the NAIA's schedule of event fees for its officials.

NATIONAL JUNIOR COLLEGE ATHLETIC ASSOCIATION (NJCAA)

The National Junior College Athletic Association is the primary regulatory body for sports competition in junior, two year, and community colleges. NJCAA competition includes Divisions I, II, and III and sponsors post-season competition at all three levels. The NJCAA does not certify officials; NJCAA national competition officials are selected from the ranks of qualified NCAA officials.

NATIONAL ASSOCIATION OF INTERCOLLEGIATE ATHLETICS (NAIA)

The National Association of Intercollegiate Athletics is the regulatory body for intercollegiate sports, primarily at the Division I and II levels. As with the other associations listed here, the NAIA was created to offer post-season opportunities for college athletes by sponsoring a series of national events for their affiliated athletic conferences. Officials for NAIA national events are selected on the basis of recommendations from individual conferences; the conferences, in turn, seek their officials from the ranks of outstanding interscholastic officials. Sports encompassed by the NAIA include football (Division I and II), basketball (Divisions I and II, mens and women's), soccer (men's & women's), volleyball, cross country, wrestling, swimming/diving, indoor track, outdoor track & field, golf, and tennis.

AMATEUR ATHLETIC UNION (AAU)

Founded in 1888 in response to widespread abuses of amateur athletes by unscrupulous promoters, the AAU is dedicated to the promotion and development of amateur sports in all age groups. With an estimated 300,000 participants nationwide, the AAU encompasses a wide range of sports and physical fitness programs. The AAU regulates amateur athletic competition in several Olympic sports and is perhaps best known for its Junior Olympics program which sponsors contests for youths from ages 8 to 18.

The AAU consists of 58 state and regional association offices and coordinates athletic competition at the state and local levels. The AAU does not certify sports officials; individual association offices typically hire qualified interscholastic varsity-level officials for their events. To get involved with AAU officiating, it is essential to attain the highest rating offered by your state high school athletic association and maintain your status as a working official. The AAU relies on recommendations from their member associations for national tournaments, and these recommendations are invariably based on the skill and ability demonstrated by the officials employed during the regular season.

OFFICIATING MINOR LEAGUE SPORTS

Officiating at minor-league events is similar to collegiate officiating in many respects. The pay is comparable; you get to travel extensively; and the intensity of the competition increases dramatically. The big difference between minor league and college sports is that minor league athletes get paid for their efforts. Officiating a game in which athletes get paid for competing is serious business. Joe Sharp, a minor league baseball umpire from Florida, recently told us: "I had to live up to my name (Sharp) when I started working minor league games because so many of the athletes' careers were on the line."

From a career standpoint, those who aspire to professional and major league officiating are likely to spend at least a portion of their careers officiating at the minor league level in order to develop the experience necessary for professional advancement. However, as a minor league official, you are only one step away from the big leagues.

There is no single regulatory body or league governing all sports at this level of competition. In most cases, individual sports or groups of sports fall under the auspices of one or more sports associations or competitive leagues. In baseball and hockey, the farm team system is used to develop both athletes and officials for the major leagues. Regardless of the sport involved, in order to get started, you must identify the regulatory body or league for your sport and then contact that group to determine eligibility requirements. In general, each organization maintains a staff or department expressly dedicated to the recruitment and development of officials. In most cases, there is no formal certification process for officials as is used in interscholastic officiating. However, you will need letters of recommendation from recognized sports authorities and plenty of experience as an official in order to officiate at this level.

Reuters/Mike Blake/Archive Photos

The image of professional tennis as a courteous sport was jolted in the late 1980s when the explosive outbursts of American player John McEnroe took center stage. McEnroe is shown here in September, 1992, demanding the removal of a courtside photographer at the U.S. Open in Flushing Meadows, NY. At the professional level, sports officials must learn to deal with controversy involving high-profile athletes.

Chapter 7

Touchdown!
Officiating Professional/ Major League Sports

The pinnacle, the top, the *cat's meow*. All of these superlatives are necessary when discussing the major league official. Your outstanding ability has finally been recognized, and the pay is commensurate with the responsibility. Only the cream of the officiating crop is even considered for work at this level. In addition, the total number of officiating berths in professional sports leagues is extremely limited. For example, in major league baseball, there are only 64 full-time umpires in the entire league. Major league officials tend to hang onto their jobs as long as their health and age permit, which further limits your opportunities for advancement to the big leagues.

Eligibility requirements of professional/major league officials vary depending on the league and the sport, but most boil down to experience. As a rule, you'll need at least 10 years of practical work experience as a sports official with at least five or more years at the collegiate or semi-professional level to even be considered for the pros. A lengthy record of work experience alone is not enough here; the professional sports leagues look as much at the quality of your work as the quantity.

I was fortunate enough to turn my love of sports into a personally satisfying and financially rewarding career. In fact, I put four children through college with the money I earned as an NFL official, working only on Sundays. And the people I met along the way have been incredible . . . some were top business executives, millionaires, who would rather give up their entire fortunes than miss the chance to call a professional football game.

Bob Rice, NFL Assistant Supervisor of Officials, 1987-95

Simply working a long string of regular season games will not suffice; the Big Leagues also take into consideration your involvement in post-season championship competition and the professional accolades you have received as evidence of your officiating ability.

You can increase your chances of acceptance by enrolling in one or more sports officiating camps or training schools. These camps are often visited by major league talent scouts and recruiters seeking top-level officiating talent. In some cases, talent scouts look to the camp director for recommendations of potential candidates for professional advancement. As with other levels of competition, letters of recommendation are absolutely essential for career advancement. At this level, your references must have somewhat higher professional stature than those required at the collegiate and semi-professional levels. At this level, you'll want team managers, collegiate-level athletic directors, sports commissioners, and referee supervisors to act as your references. These recommendations will factor heavily in the league's determination of your suitability to work as a professional sports official. Assuming you pass muster, an application will be provided for your completion. Once your application is on file, a talent scout or observer will be assigned to conduct performance evaluations of your skill and ability at an actual game or event at your current level. The results of these evaluations will ultimately determine whether you are accepted at the professional level, but don't expect immediate results. In many cases, it can take as long as four or more years from the time your application is filed before you are accepted as an official.

The pinnacle of a major league official's career is involvement in prestigious post-season competition. Only the most experienced, effective, and dedicated officials are invited to work these events, so even those who arrive at the major league level have something to shoot for.

From the standpoint of compensation, officiating at the major league level is the most lucrative of all. Although seasoned sports officials routinely claim that money is not a motivating factor, annual salaries for major league officials can easily run into six figures, which is not bad for part-time or seasonal work. Post-season playoff and championship games, in particular, can yield enormous paychecks; a veteran official working the Super Bowl, for example, can earn as much as $10,000 for that game alone. Of course, this is the high end of the compensation spectrum. Less experienced officials, and those new to the major leagues, will earn proportionately less. For additional information on sport-specific compensation at all levels of competition, refer to Section III.

I DON'T DESERVE THIS HONOR—
BUT I HAVE ULCERS, AND I DON'T
DESERVE THEM EITHER.

SECTION II:
THE PSYCHOLOGY
OF OFFICIATING

Jet Media

A baseball team manager gradually closes the distance between himself and the home plate umpire during a heated discussion over a judgment call. Effective sports officials are polite but firm in their dealings with participants. Notice how the umpire's hands remain virtually motionless throughout the sequence, while his body language in the final frame shows he has no intention of backing down.

CHAPTER 8

YOU MAKE THE CALL:
Conduct and Demeanor
of the
Sports Official

As a sports official, the way you act in the competitive arena is just as important as your ability to interpret the rules and regulations. Consider the impression conveyed by a judge in a court of law.

Everything from the judge's robe to the way he or she acts must impart authority, confidence, and, above all, impartiality. The judge does not expect the attorneys to agree with every decision made, but attorneys are expected to respect his or her rulings. However, no matter how well a judge knows the law, credibility suffers upon failure to both act and look like a judge.

As a sports official, you are a judge of sorts, and the players are like the lawyers who are there to present their respective cases. The players have worked hard to prepare for the game you are about to judge and are counting on you, as an official, to hold up your end of the bargain. Like the lawyers in our courtroom analogy, they expect you to be fully versed in the rules and regulations. And like the judge, anything you do that brings your ethics or impartiality into question will immediately undermine both your credibility and authority.

Learning to focus on the play at hand, maintaining control of your ego, and learning how to look, act, and respond like an official are all essential elements of quality officiating. In this chapter, we'll explore each of these issues, and how they affect you in your choice of becoming an official.

Focus

Have you ever been caught asking someone to repeat a question because you weren't listening to what they were saying or, frankly, weren't really interested? This inattentiveness indicates a lack of focus, and in sports officiating, it can be a problem.

Consider the typical sporting event. Whether you are an athlete or a fan, you know how emotionally charged a game can become. Imagine yourself officiating in this atmosphere in a decisive game,

Feeling the pulse of the game.

Observing all extraneous activities.

Controlling your ego.

Utilizing your concentration skills.

Sensing the flow of the game.

when suddenly you are distracted by something that takes your attention away from the action. Perhaps your mind wanders to a gaggle of geese flying over the stadium the day before hunting season or to the cheerleaders on the sidelines; maybe a piece of paper blows across the field or someone shouts something from the stands. Then you look back to discover you've missed a key play. How awkward is this for an official? Very . . . so to avoid distractions, you need to focus on the action as much or more than the competing athletes.

Focus ensures that you won't miss a key play, and you will perform much more effectively as an official. In addition, a constant level of alertness will greatly reduce the chance that you will unconsciously transmit a negative body language signal such as placing your hands in your pockets, standing with your back to the field of play, or just yawning and looking bored. What would happen if you missed a play because you weren't paying attention to the action? You would alienate the players, coaches, and fans alike. In a close game, a lapse in your concentration could affect the outcome of the game, particularly if you make a bad call. After all, if you didn't see the play, how can you judge it?

Your interest and enthusiasm during the game is critical to your success as an official. That is why officiating in a sport you already love is so important. It helps you keep interest during the game.

CONTROLLING YOUR EGO

A great deal of our personal development involves building self-confidence. It is a natural human tendency to take pride in one's work. Perhaps we even show off a bit when performing a job we know well. However, the sports official walks a fine line between exhibiting self-confidence, and acting *cocky*. Successful sports officials are careful not to cross this line. They have learned the art of subordinating their desire to feel important while officiating.

Keep in mind that fans come to a sporting event to support their team. They are not there to watch you officiate. Your job is to blend into the background. Do not let your ego control your desire to be

the focal point of the game. Grandstanding is unacceptable; upstaging the action is unthinkable. To be effective as an official, you must control your temper, avoid arguments with athletes and coaches, and not allow your judgment calls to be influenced by negative reactions from the fans or participants. Truly, maintaining a low profile makes you a *big-time* official.

Have you ever watched an athletic event during which the official became the main attraction (or distraction) of the game? Comments such as *the referee lost the game for us* or *the referee had it in for our team* suggest that the official influenced the outcome of the game. Every official will blow a judgment call sooner or later. However, an official who deliberately makes a bad call in an attempt to even up a lopsided score or penalizes a player or team for a prior mistake is unacceptable. The contest must be decided by the athletes on the field of play; your sole function is to ensure that the event is played by the rules.

In short, it is wrong for you to inject yourself into the competition by using your status as an official to sway the outcome of the event. This can be a difficult trait to develop, especially for former athletes who become officials, as it runs contrary to their previous experience as players. However, no matter how knowledgeable you are in terms of the rules of competition, or whatever your former status as an athlete may have been, exhibiting conduct that draws attention to yourself detracts from your professionalism.

As an official, you must also learn to control your ego after the event has concluded. New officials always have some difficulty controlling their excitement after a game. It is a natural tendency to want to congratulate the athletes, console the losers, or offer public commentary on the game. After all, you love the sport, and post-game analysis is an American tradition. However, as an official, it is a good idea to leave the facility promptly at the conclusion of the event. Post-game interaction usually detracts from your hard work during the game. Any attempt to interject yourself into post-game activities usually results in negative consequences.

Appearance

As an athlete, you no doubt wore a bright and colorful uniform that was designed to be an attention-getter on the field. Your uniform also helped convey a sense of enthusiasm and excitement for the team. However, when you take the field as an official, you exchange your bright colors for a staid, somewhat monotone look typically consisting of black and white. In most sports, officials wear shirts of alternating black and white stripes. This distinctive patterns allows the official to stand out on the field of play. It also helps minimize any confusion with the players.

Most officials probably never give a second thought to their *stripes*; however, there are some subtle symbolic aspects to your uniform that you should keep in mind as you pull on that uniform before every game. Consider the fact that black and white are both neutral colors. Black and white can make other colors look better, rarely causing a clash. When you think of the *other colors* as the athletes on the field, you get a clearer picture of the role you are to play as an official. Your job is to complement the competition by making the athletes look better, without causing a clash. In a larger sense, you are the neutral *buffer* between the colors.

Consider also the psychological message conveyed by the colors of your uniform. Black conveys a sense of power, authority, and respect while white imparts a sense of fairness, wisdom, and decency. Perhaps it is no accident that an official's uniform includes alternating stripes in these two colors. Think of those stripes as a balance between authority and fairness as you consider your actions on the field. Even if your uniform shirt is solid gray rather than striped, remember that gray is nothing more than a mixture of black and white.

For many people, the mere act of putting on a uniform affects the way they think and act. Sports officials are no different than anyone else. Their uniform represents their dedication and commitment to the job. It also reflects the responsibility that comes with it. It has been said that clothes don't make the person, but the person makes the clothes. This is profoundly true when applied to the sports official. So often, it's not the uniform itself that conveys respect, but rather the way you present yourself in uniform. A dirty or frayed uniform conveys a lack of interest on your part that tends to undermine your credibility before you make the first call. After all, first impressions are lasting; the manner in which you keep your uniform usually is the first measure of how you will do your job. Always check your uniform before every game. It should be clean and in good repair. Also, be sure your uniform fits properly, as nothing looks worse than an ill-fitting uniform. Even your hat should be fitted (rather than adjustable) for the ultimate professional look.

Your physical condition is also a critical component of your image. You should try to stay in good shape. Beyond the physical difficulty of keeping up with the action, overweight officials are often subject to ridicule by athletes and fans alike. Obesity suggests you may be slower to react than other officials, lackadaisical, and, at the very least, out of touch with the athletes. This poses an obvious credibility problem that can be difficult to overcome no matter how skillful you are as an official. Likewise, being flat-footed suggests you never played the sport. It can also give spectators the sense that you may not always know what is going on. Your personal grooming habits are equally important. Your hair should be neatly trimmed and combed. Long hair is frowned upon; most officials are clean shaven.

Any display of jewelry by an official (other than a simple wedding band) is distracting. Gold chains and religious artifacts tend to distract the players. Although veteran officials often receive

commemorative pins or emblems from local community groups as an expression of gratitude for their service, displaying such insignia on your officiating uniform generally is not allowed. Any distinction like a button would make you more obtrusive, standing out from the crowd. If you are better than the other officials, an emblem will not be the measure of your skill. Rather it is your actions on the field that will serve as proof of your ability.

BODY LANGUAGE

Someone once said that 80 percent of interpersonal communication involves body language. According to Dr. A. J. Johnson, people are so sensitive to body language that after meeting somebody, they know in the first eight seconds whether or not they will like them, all before the other person utters a word. Part of the reason is that through body language, we often unconsciously betray our true feelings.

As a sports official, you need to be aware of the nonverbal signals you transmit with your body. You should try to exhibit the most positive image possible. Sports officiating is, by nature, a highly visible position. Add to this the fact that all eyes are upon you at key moments to watch for the first sign of your reaction. Your every move will be watched by coaches, players, and the fans. The slightest miscue on your part can lead to negative reaction. For this reason, you should strive to give signals and calls in a uniform manner. For example, if you display any sign of pleasure when one team scores against another, you instantly convey a signal that says you're rooting for one side. Likewise, excessive zeal in calling a foul on one team suggests you favor the other.

94

Even between plays and during timeouts, you can bet at least someone in the crowd is following your movements. Just because the action has momentarily stopped is no reason to lower your guard. For example, a simple pat on the back while talking to a player may convey favoritism. Do you have a special relationship with that player? Are your calls going to favor that player or his or her team? These are the kinds of signals you are sending out, and they are all wrong. Remember, you are not the player's coach, team trainer, or fan. Your position as an official should always be one of neutrality.

Other unconscious body language signals have nothing to do with favoritism, but look equally bad. For example, constantly rubbing itches, scratching, or fussing with your uniform can detract from the image of alertness that you try to project as an official. In a recent football game played in a driving rainstorm, the referee was observed spending most of his time attending to his wet hair and uniform. He was perceived as completely distracted by the downpour. His attention was totally diverted from the game, and the fans noticed and complained.

Sometimes, an official gets so wrapped up in the moment that he or she completely forgets the role that is to be maintained. In one high school football game, the umpire began to sympathize with a quarterback who was being blitzed on nearly every play. The umpire got so involved that he actually began helping the quarterback to his feet each time he was tackled. By outwardly protecting a player in this manner, the umpire's conduct could be construed as favoritism. Equally important from a career standpoint, it could also be perceived as unfair. Any official who singles out an individual player or team, even within the context of the rules, will ignite a negative reaction from the fans and participants. No matter how lopsided the score, it is not your job to even things out. In a recent Internet Newsgroup discussion, a youth soccer official observed, "I've been in several of these situations and haven't seen much luck with blatantly slanting calls to even things up. The kids on the winning team smell you are doing it, get resentful, and play even harder. You also need to call dangerous fouls on the losing team because to ignore them lets the game get quickly out of hand."

PERSONALITY

Becoming an official does not mean you need to alter your personality. By nature, some people tend to be more matter-of-fact or strict than others. Others tend to be more easy-going and tolerant. If you are a strict disciplinarian and adhere to letter and intent of rules, it is likely that your on-field body language will reflect this mentality. Coaches and athletes likely will get the impression that there is going to be a no-nonsense, no argument kind of atmosphere during the games you officiate. A more easy-going official often will allow the game to unfold on its course and will not adopt a stern approach unless it becomes necessary. Neither approach is right or wrong, and most officials tend to come down somewhere in the middle. All in all, the key is adopting an officiating mentality that suits your personality. Samuel Johnson once said, "The fountain of content must spring up in the mind, and he who hath so little knowledge of human nature as to seek happiness by changing anything but his own disposition will waste his life in fruitless efforts and multiply the grief he proposes to remove."

As a sports official, you should try not to get frustrated by circumstances and must never respond to heckling or obscene gestures on the part of fans and spectators. Sometimes it seems like fans purposely try to make officials angry. And such criticism is not limited to advanced levels of competition. In fact, many a youth league official has seen first hand just how emotional parents can become when their children are involved. A youth hockey official recently recalled one such occasion: "I can still remember a Pee Wee game where I was refereeing; one of the parents got so irate that they actually tossed pop at me. And I've seen far worse." As an official, you need to rise above the name-calling and heckling. If you react negatively to criticism, you will merely exacerbate the situation.

The avoidance of visible reaction is a difficult task for sport officials to learn. While one can reasonably expect the athletes and

National Federation of State High School Associations (NF)

All sports officials make unpopular calls at one time or another. No matter the fan or player reaction, you need to avoid visible emotion in order to officiate effectively.

coaches to afford the officials a certain level of respect, the fans are as fickle as the wind when it comes to voicing opinions. The larger the crowd, the greater the chance you may be heckled or challenged. No matter what the reaction to your calls, try to be

mindful of the emotion that sports engender and the fact that otherwise normal individuals can turn into screaming lunatics at a sporting event. Also, keep in mind that the level of hostility you encounter is directly proportional to the way you handle yourself on the field. Your actions can do much to dispel an image of vulnerability. If you are nervous or unsure, it will show. Certain gestures will give you away and you need to learn to avoid them. When all else fails, remember that seldom is it a personal matter; it's your uniform the fans are yelling at.

COMMUNICATION

The way you call your signals is very important. Any pet owner knows how important tone and inflection are in communication. For instance, dogs know *good dog* sounds and normally respond with a wagging tail that indicates trust and a sense of well being. On the other hand, dogs react strongly to stern voice tones such as the *what did you do?* voice. People's reactions are no different; pleasant tones tend to put people at ease, while stern tones tend to put people on the defensive or drive them to anger. As an official, you need to be aware of the weight your voice carries and the effect your intonations are likely to have on others.

The official's calls are his or her primary means of communicating with the participants. When making calls, the best approach is to sound decisive, articulate, matter of fact, and devoid of emotion all at the same time. It may sound difficult, but it comes with practice. Your speaking voice should also be used in a uniform manner. It is unwise to bark at one team while speaking softly with the other. As noted previously, excessive zeal on critical calls can convey a lack of impartiality which will open you to criticism. If your position requires the use of a whistle, keep in mind that it is an extension of your voice and should be treated in the same manner.

Keep in mind, what you say is just as important as how you say it. Many times, some off-the-wall comment by an official is remembered long after the game. In a state championship football game in Indiana in the 1980s, a wide receiver continually asked a side judge to check if he had lined up off-sides. The side judge eventually voiced his frustration with the player, telling him in effect that after the preceding 12 regular season games, he should know damn well whether he was off-sides. No doubt after the game, the player's memories were of the official rather than the results of the game.

AP Photo

Referee Denny Freund calmly restrains Iowa State Coach Tim Floyd following Floyd's ejection from a college basketball game. Successful officials have learned that a calm demeanor is an effective means of diffusing emotionally charged situations.

CHAPTER 9

TIMEOUT:
Psychological Qualities of the Successful Sports Official

by Robert Weinberg, Ph.D.

A Note from the Publisher . . .

While experts readily agree that the psychological makeup of a sports official has much to do with his or her ultimate success, the subject has not received the same level of coverage as the mechanics of sports officiating and the interpretation of rules. In order to round out our discussion of sports officiating as a career choice, LR Publishing is pleased to present a chapter on the psychological aspects of officiating which has been guest-written by Robert Weinberg, Ph.D., Professor and Chair at the Department of Physical Education Health and Sport Studies at Miami University of Ohio. As a veteran sports official, past president of the Association for the Advancement of Applied Sport Psychology (AAASP), and highly respected sports psychologist, Dr. Weinberg brings a unique perspective to this vital subject. Dr. Weinberg's book Psychology of Officiating (Leisure Press, 1990) is recommended reading for anyone embarking on, or currently working in, a sports officiating career.

INTRODUCTION

When most people think about being a good sports official, the first things that come to mind are the technical aspects such as rules, regulations, and the mechanics involved. To the uninformed observer, officials seem to act as robots, stepping in to make the call, and then retreating to the background until needed. But anyone who has ever officiated knows that nothing could be farther from the truth as officials face many of the same emotions and performance anxieties as the athletes and coaches themselves.

As a former basketball, tennis, and football official, I have always felt that the psychological or mental side of officiating was more important than the physical or mechanical aspects. The numerous research studies and interviews with top officials I have conducted over the years conclusively support the idea that qualities such as confidence, judgment, communication, and decisiveness often spell the difference between an average official and one who is outstanding.

Although sports officiating is considered a science, there is definitely an art to becoming an effective official. Indeed, a large measure of the art of officiating is dependent on the personal qualities that you bring to the competitive arena. The purpose of this chapter is to provide a brief overview of the key mental skills and abilities most important to a sports official. The text is augmented with self-tests to help determine how well your present psychological makeup is suited to officiating. Even if you score lower than you expected on these tests, do not despair. Just as the technical and mechanical aspects of officiating must be acquired through study and experience, so too must the psychological skills be developed and honed in order to excel.

OVERVIEW

The game ended more than an hour ago. You no longer need to be extremely alert, or prove yourself to the players, coaches, and fans. You feel drained both physically and emotionally, so you sit back with a cool drink, put your feet up, and try to relax. But for some reason, you can't unwind. In your mind, you keep replaying every call you made. You worry that you may have blown some calls and can still hear the criticisms of spectators ringing in your ears. You wonder what the other members of your officiating crew think of your performance. You seek to console your mind by reminding yourself that you were prepared for the game, worked well with the other officials. Yet the lingering self-doubts persist, despite your best efforts to toss them aside.

This post-game self-analysis is common for officials across all levels of competition. What causes such inner turmoil? Much of it stems from the unique role that sports officials fill in the competitive sports arena. While officials work in the public eye, and their actions are subject to constant scrutiny, they receive no accolades for their efforts. In essence, officials have to be content to feel good about their performance and their contribution to the competitive event and not rely on positive feedback from coaches, spectators, or the media as such compliments are usually few and far between.

Without question, good officiating adds to the event and ensures that the outcome is dependent upon the skills of the athletes. Indeed, when a game goes smoothly, few people even notice the official. Conversely, poor officiating detracts from the contest, decreases the enjoyment of the event for participants and spectators alike, and increases the likelihood of negative feedback for the official. In a very real sense, doing a good job in officiating means not being noticed. It is difficult to imagine any other profession where this holds true.

On what basis, then, should officials judge themselves, or be judged by others? There seems to be little doubt that there is a strong relationship between psychological skills and physical performance. Therefore, an official's success or failure can be measured by the extent to which he or she has mastered the physical skills (conditioning for the demands of the particular sport, techniques and mechanics, visual acuity, etc.) and mental abilities (self-confidence, concentration, emotional control, etc.). No critique of an official's performance is complete without examining both sides of the coin.

The relationship between the physical and psychological aspects of officiating is an interesting one. In the sports world, mental skills more than physical ability are the topic of conversation among veteran officials – making the unpopular call, not allowing the event to get out of control, communicating effectively with irate coaches and players, keeping your cool and not allowing yourself to be rattled. In fact, veteran officials report that psychological skills account for 50 to 70 percent of an official's success. Similarly, supervisors of officials in various sports tasked with evaluating the work of referees and umpires emphasize consistency, fairness, mental fortitude, the ability to make quick and accurate decisions, and a relaxed demeanor as important assets for successful officials. Indeed, when it comes to sports such as tennis, track, and volleyball, in which the physical demands are minimal, the mental aspects may be the only assets that really matter.

Thus, it seems strange that training camps, clinics, and seminars for sports officials place so much emphasis on physical technique, rules interpretation, proper attire, and written and practical testing, with relatively little attention to the development of psychological skills. In many circles, there is a belief that psychological skills are innate: you either have them or you don't. However, just as physical ability can be acquired, so too can the psychological skills. The ability to concentrate, relax under pressure, maintain confidence, and relate well with others needs to be systematically practiced just as the physical skills of positioning, signalling, and rules interpretation.

Beyond question, a certain combination of physical and mental characteristics is all that separates the mediocre official from one who is superior. Based on my personal interviews and research studies, I will now present some of the significant mental skills that are essential to good officiating. I have made no attempt to rank these in any particular order, as opinions on which are most important are varied and subjective at best. In each section, I will present the specific characteristic in terms of how they relate to sports officiating, and then follow up with a discussion of how best to develop that characteristic. As you read this section, you might take a look at yourself to determine whether you already possess these skills, or are inclined to acquire them.

CONSISTENCY

It is expected that an official's decisions remain consistent and evenly applied to both sides. Not surprisingly, inconsistency on the part of officials is the most frequently raised criticism by coaches and players alike. Inconsistency creates a variety of problems including second guessing on the part of athletes as to what is and is not allowed, frustration and lack of trust on the part of coaches, and a tendency for officials to "even up" calls, thereby punishing a team or athlete for previous officiating errors. Athletes simply do not know what to expect when a sports official vacillates in making decisions. Confusion reigns when an official ignores a foul one time but then calls a foul for a similar infraction later in the game. This uncertainty often leads to anxiety, frustration, anger, or negative physical expression by those who perceive they are being cheated. In most cases, the level of frustration experienced by the participants is in direct proportion to the level of confusion created by the official's actions.

Achieving consistency is the result of applying the correct rule interpretation in each situation. While no two competitive situations are exactly alike, the official who makes each judgment according to the rules will in fact be consistent because the correct rule interpretation is unchanging. For example, if a basketball official calls a hand checking foul on a defensive player early in a game, players should expect to be called for similar infractions throughout the game. This type of within-game consistency allows both players and coaches to adjust to the official and carry out their game plan accordingly. Achieving this level of consistency requires complete mastery of the rules governing the competition, correct interpretation of those rules, and the mechanical skills necessary to be in the proper position to make the call.

COMMUNICATION SKILLS

Circle the number that best reflects your behavior for each statement. Refer to **scoring the test** to measure your communication abilities.

Communication Traits	Never	Seldom	Usually	Always
1. I like listening to others	1	2	3	4
2. I state one thought at a time	1	2	3	4
3. I pretend I'm paying attention	1	2	3	4
4. I use sarcasm	1	2	3	4
5. I repeat key points	1	2	3	4
6. I respect others' right of expression	1	2	3	4
7. I am easily distracted	1	2	3	4
8. I listen to all of another person's message	1	2	3	4
9. I finish the other person's thoughts	1	2	3	4
10. I listen actively	1	2	3	4
11. I keep an even pitch in my voice	1	2	3	4
12. I shake hands firmly	1	2	3	4
13. I look directly at people when talking	1	2	3	4
14. I walk slowly and hunch my shoulders	1	2	3	4
15. I use my hands to augment my words	1	2	3	4

SCORING THE TEST:

Calculate your score by adding the numbers you circled on lines 1, 2, 5, 6, 8, 10 through 13, and 15. Then, for lines 3, 4, 7, 9, and 14, reverse the order of the numbering system. For example, if you circled "4" for line 3, you would score it as 1; if you circled "2" you would score it as a 3. Add your reverse-scored sum to your previous total to calculate your total communication score.

RATING SCALE:

Total Score	Rating
51 and up	Clear Connection with Others
40 to 50	Mixed Messages
39 and below	Tongue Tied

Keep in mind that an official's between-game consistency is equally important as his or her within-game consistency. Just as the best athletes are seen as those who perform at high levels over the course of the competitive season, so should good officials be expected to maintain high performance standards every time they officiate. Peaks and valleys in performance are often directly related to psychological inconsistencies. If you feel tired and stressed out, your ability to concentrate on the game or event will be hindered, and inconsistency will almost certainly result. Therefore, the ability to get in the proper psychological frame of mind, and maintain it throughout the contest, is essential to becoming an effective sports official.

COMMUNICATION

Outstanding sports officials recognize the importance of effective communication, both on and off the field of play. How you communicate your message conveys a great deal about your overall level of confidence, self control, state of mind, and objectivity. On the field, clear communications instill confidence in the coaches, athletes, and spectators and facilitate their acceptance of your style and the amount of cooperation that you will receive. Off the field, seasoned officials recognize the importance of clear communication with fellow officials, administrators, and the media.

Keep in mind that communication is a two-way street; effective communication involves your ability to listen as well as your ability to convey a message.

In many respects, good communication skills are an essential part of establishing rapport. In its simplest form, rapport refers to the ability of relating well with others. Good rapport is a desirable quality in any line of human endeavor, perhaps even more so in the field of sports officiating. As an official, you are not trying to win a popularity contest, but, at the same time, you don't want to make enemies of the participants. From a career standpoint, there is certainly nothing to be gained by alienating coaches and administrators. Sports officials can improve rapport by treating coaches and athletes with courtesy and respect, and officials, in turn, have every right to expect the same kind of treatment. While it is important to be personable in your officiating capacity, you must maintain a proper distance from the competitors so as not to appear biased. You should be approachable and willing to listen to questions and complaints; however, you should not allow the flow of the event to be interrupted by continued questioning. You should avoid lengthy debates and restart the action as soon as possible to preserve the continuity of the event.

Improving your communication skills is a matter of assessing where you stand now and focusing on those areas that are preventing you from communicating effectively. To this end, Self-help Test 9.1: Communication Skills was devised to help you evaluate your current ability and point out areas that you might need to work on. Complete this test now and total your score in each category. The lower the total, the more you will need to work on your communication skills; likewise, the higher you score, the more likely that you are already an effective communicator.

DECISIVENESS

A sports official's decisions should be made simultaneously with the action, or as soon thereafter as possible. This is not to say that the actual call or signal should be made without hesitation. In fact, a slight pause may be needed to fully comprehend what has occurred. For example, a home plate umpire might want to take a long look at a close play to make sure the catcher has held onto the ball and determine whether or not the base runner stepped on the plate before actually signalling the call. This greatly reduces the chances of having to change an erroneous initial call.

However, a lengthy delay in signalling a call gives the participants the impression of uncertainty, and a delayed call is far more likely to be questioned. Judgment calls, like the play at home plate noted above, are generally not subject to formal protest, and controversy can oftentimes be avoided by quick and decisive rulings. And the closer the action, the more important decisiveness becomes. Hesitation will only bring controversy, and clear and decisive action is imperative. When making such a call, an official must give the impression of being absolutely certain of what occurred. Being timid or hesitant will invite questioning of your calls, so it is essential to be strong, clear, and decisive on close calls.

POISE

Competitive sports is often fast-paced and rapidly changing and can result in a highly-charged emotional atmosphere that envelops the participants, coaches, and spectators. This is particularly true in the latter stages of a close contest, or other moments of high tension when fights, fouls or other violent outbursts are likely to occur. However, no matter how tense the situation becomes, the sports official is expected to remain calm and poised at all times. Although you cannot necessarily control the emotions of others, you are expected to remain in control of your own emotions regardless of what is happening around you. One hallmark of the successful official is the ability to remain poised and in control, while asserting authority by keeping critical situations from escalating into ugly incidents.

When asked about the pressures and stress associated with officiating, a veteran official noted: "Trying to be a successful official is just like preparing for war. You don't know who's going to fink out when you come face to face with death." Although it might sound far-fetched to equate sports officiating with a battlefield, officials have been seriously injured, or, in rare circumstances, even killed, by rioting fans or overly aggressive athletes. Although these examples may be extreme, officials are routinely subjected to verbal harassment by unruly spectators, agitated coaches, and belligerent athletes.

The level of competition has little to do with the level of stress experienced. Whether you are working Game 7 of the World Series, or the finals of an intramural basketball tournament, you are under enormous pressure to perform at a high level of proficiency. Making a call on a close play at home plate in the bottom of the ninth inning with the score tied, dealing with an irate coach, coping with an unruly crowd, calling for a penalty shot at the end of a soccer game, or simply the feeling of being constantly evaluated by everyone in attendance are just a few of the situations that can put pressure on officials. Coping with stress requires fortitude and conviction. As football referee Kelly Nutt observed, "You can bring your whistle and you can bring your flag, but if you don't bring your guts, you might as well stay home."

Coping with stressful situations calls for more than self-assurance. By the same token, it is not enough to know the rules, regulations, and mechanics involved as these skills will quickly go by the wayside if you lose your cool. What is required is the ability to manage stress when faced with a difficult situation.

Veteran officials consistently report performing better when they are able to remain clam and relaxed. Of course, this is easier said than done. In fact, for most officials, the ability to manage stress comes only with experience. Ron Luciano, a former major league baseball umpire and coauthor of The Umpire Strikes Back, described the difficulty he had relaxing at the beginning of his career:

> "I was trying too hard to run the whole show," said Barney Deary, a minor league supervisor of umpires. "Let the other umpire handle his own problems," he said. "I've watched you work, you've got enough of your own." We talked a long time and he turned me around. "Baseball's a great game," he said, "but you're not enjoying it at all. Just relax and have fun out there." I took his advice and began easing up a bit.

Part of remaining calm in difficult situations is not being fearful of making mistakes, disappointing people, or losing control. Seasoned officials are able to focus only on the task at hand and are not preoccupied with the negative consequences of failure.

Remember, no matter how well you perform as a sports official, 50 percent of the coaches, athletes, and fans will be unhappy with your decisions. Putting additional pressure on yourself to make all the *right* calls will only increase your chances of burning out and becoming too self-critical.

INTEGRITY

Integrity is defined as an adherence to a code of moral values that prevents one from being corrupted by outside influences. As a sports official, you are expected to perform your duties in an unbiased manner regardless of the reactions of the participants or spectators, time remaining in the event, score, previous calls, or any other potential sources of influence. In other words, you must block out all distractions and focus on making the proper call to the best of your ability.

It is vital that your integrity as a sports official be protected both inside and outside of the competitive arena. Seasoned sports officials keep their personal opinions concerning players and teams to themselves and never wager on the outcome of any game they officiate in. Likewise, it would be imprudent at best to accept an officiating assignment that might compromise your integrity, such as when a family member or close friend is involved as either a coach or player. As with politicians, even the appearance of impropriety must be scrupulously avoided.

JUDGMENT AND CONCENTRATION

Good judgment in officiating begins with a thorough and complete understanding of the rules and regulations governing your particular sport. Once established, knowledge of the rules serves as a guide for determining the legality of the play. After that, sound judgment, gained through experience, allows an official to apply the rules consistently over a wide variety of individual circumstances.

Understanding the rules of the sport involves attending workshops and clinics, reading trade journals, and networking with other officials to keep pace with the latest developments and rule changes. Just as an athlete must practice techniques to develop the requisite skills, the sports official must do likewise in order to develop good judgment.

Exercising good judgment in sports officiating also requires that you be totally focused on the event at hand while simultaneously blocking out distractions and not worrying about previous calls or the negative reactions to those calls.

A college-level soccer official sums up the importance of being focused during the competition:

> When the game gets under way, I just try to block out any thoughts that are not related to the game. I am interested only in doing my job in an effective and efficient manner. When I am doing my job well, it's as if I have tunnel vision as I focus solely on the players and the court. I am not distracted by the crowd; in fact I sometimes don't even hear them. I have only one thing on my mind and that is to focus on the action and call them as I see them.

Similar comments are echoed by a volleyball official:

> The most important thing for me when officiating a game is to maintain my concentration throughout the course of the contest. The old adage that "it's a game of inches" can often be true, and I want to make sure that I'm there and ready to make the call when the situation arises. A lapse of concentration can result in missing a key play which may help determine the outcome of the game. I always want the player to determine who wins and loses. I work hard all the time to keep up my concentration regardless of the score or level of competition involved.

While these statements underscore the importance of concentration in sports officiating, many officials cling to the belief that concentration can be turned on and off like a faucet. Some officials believe that, when they really need to concentrate, they can automatically tune in to the action at hand; others feel that if the score is lopsided or the quality of play is poor, their full concentration is not needed. Neither scenario, however, could be further from the truth. These attitudes not only cheat the athletes and coaches, but also the official who subscribes to them. This is not to say that officials shouldn't take a mental break during a time out or other

CONCENTRATION SKILLS

For each of the following statements, circle the number in the right-hand columns that most closely corresponds to your reaction in that situation. Rank your answers according to the following scale.

1 = Almost Never 2 = Rarely 3 = Sometimes 4 = Frequently 5 = Almost Always

I have difficulty putting a blown call out of mind.	1	2	3	4	5
I can easily analyze what I need to do before an assignment.	1	2	3	4	5
While officiating:					
I can quickly analyze what's happening.	1	2	3	4	5
I keep irrelevant thoughts from entering my mind.	1	2	3	4	5
I am good at blocking out the noise of spectators.	1	2	3	4	5
I get confused when many things happen quickly.	1	2	3	4	5
I find myself distracted by my own thoughts.	1	2	3	4	5
I am good at prioritizing what I need to focus on.	1	2	3	4	5
I am not distracted by what has or might happen.	1	2	3	4	5
I can concentrate despite hassles with coaches or players.	1	2	3	4	5
I focus on my assignment and forget my other problems.	1	2	3	4	5
I can keep my concentration, even when I get anxious.	1	2	3	4	5
I maintain my concentration if a fellow official is doing a poor job.	1	2	3	4	5
I easily maintain focus on the action throughout the event.	1	2	3	4	5
I have trouble regaining my concentration after a break in the action.	1	2	3	4	5

SCORING THE TEST:

Add your circled numbers to determine your total concentration score. The highest possible score is 75, and the lowest is 15. The closer you score to 75, the better your concentration skills. If you score 40 or less, you need to work on your concentration skills.

break in the action. However, it is critical that the official maintain continual vigilance while the competition is underway.

Concentration, as it relates to sports officiating, is most often defined as the ability to focus on the relevant cues in the environment and maintain that focus over the course of the contest. The first part of this definition refers to focusing on the most important cues in the official's environment. The exact nature of these cues is determined by the sport or event you happen to be officiating, as well as your specific responsibilities within that event. For example, a home plate umpire in baseball requires a different attention focus than a second base umpire.

While it may appear relatively easy to focus on the action of the event, inevitably a wide variety of irrelevant mental and visual cues will compete for your attention. Such things as the antics of coaches, a hostile crowd, or a complaining athlete, compounded by your own thoughts about the game, a previously missed call, or anything else your mind conjures up, can all conspire to divert your attention from the action at hand.

Although it is important to selectively focus on the proper cues in order to maximize your chances of making a good call, you must also learn to maintain this focus through the course of the competition. Keep in mind that many sporting events take two to three hours to complete. Just like athletes, officials can become mentally and physically fatigued over the course of a long contest. And once fatigue sets in, it is very easy to lose your concentration and make a mistake.

The following quote from a veteran basketball referee emphasizes the difficulty involved in maintaining one's concentration:

Staying interested in a game from an official's standpoint is a lot harder than many people think. It's sometimes hard to stay motivated and focused when the game is lopsided, or of seemingly little importance in terms of team standings. I would have to fight really hard to keep my mind from wandering. It was sometimes a little scary when I realized that I wasn't giving the game my full attention, and thus missed a call. But I have come to realize that every game is important, and that I owe it to the athletes to be at my best throughout the game.

In order to focus on the relevant cues in the competitive environment and maintain that focus through the course of the event, it is important to assess your current attentional strengths and weaknesses. This can be accomplished by completing Self-help Test 9.2: Concentration Skills. This will give you a starting point to see how well you concentrate while officiating and point out areas in need of improvement.

CONFIDENCE

One of the most important aspects of effective sports officiating is self-confidence. In fact, many of the officials I have interviewed believe that self-confidence is second only to a thorough knowledge of rules and techniques for effective officiating. This belief transcends any particular game or situation. A confident official remains in control during adversity and is not rattled by a bad call or other setbacks. Every sports official has experienced games they would rather forget; but good officials do not allow a bad experience to undermine the underlying belief that they are competent in the performance of their duties.

The following observation from a seasoned high school basketball official demonstrates the central role that confidence plays in effective officiating:

If you are not confident in yourself, you might as well not show up. Coaches and players will quickly notice an official who lacks confidence in his or her calls and try to take advantage of the situation. I always try to convey a confident attitude and approach to my officiating. Without confidence in yourself, it is hard to get the respect of the players, coaches, and fans.

CONFIDENCE INVENTORY

Read each of the following statements carefully, and consider your level of confidence over the past year with regard to each. For each statement, indicate the percent of time you have had too little, too much, or just the right amount of confidence. The total percentage for any one statement should equal 100, however, you may distribute lesser percentages as you see fit. For example, you might assign 100 percent to one category, or split it between two or three columns.

With respect to your ability to. . .	Under Confident	Confident	Over Confident
Keep calm under pressure	___%	___%	___%
Maintain self-control	___%	___%	___%
Relate successfully with other officials	___%	___%	___%
Communicate with coaches and athletes	___%	___%	___%
Concentrate throughout the competition	___%	___%	___%
Make tough calls decisively	___%	___%	___%
Make critical decisions	___%	___%	___%
Put forth the effort to succeed	___%	___%	___%
Persist to achieve your goal	___%	___%	___%
Improve your technique	___%	___%	___%
Control your emotions	___%	___%	___%
Handle irate coaches or athletes	___%	___%	___%
Be assertive in making calls	___%	___%	___%
Maintain a high level of physical fitness	___%	___%	___%
Be mentally prepared for assignments	___%	___%	___%
Deal effectively with an unruly crowd	___%	___%	___%
Total Score	___%	___%	___%

SCORING YOUR CONFIDENCE INVENTORY:

Add up the percentages in each of the three columns, and then divide each sum by 16. The higher your score in the "Confident" column, the more likely you are to be an effective official. However, high scores in the areas of "Under Confident" or "Over Confident" suggest some potential problem areas.

A high school volleyball official notes:

> The difference between feeling confident when you're offici-
> ating and not feeling confident is that you don't hesitate
> when making close or critical calls and never second guess
> yourself. You just go ahead and make your calls knowing
> you are doing your best.

Without question, self-confidence is a crucial factor in effective
sports officiating. When you are confident in your abilities, your
mind is free to focus exclusively on the action and is not cluttered
with irrelevant thoughts. The more confident you feel as an official,
the more likely you will maintain control in adverse situations, especially when dealing with irate athletes and coaches. From a
career standpoint, confident officials are more likely to set challenging goals and expend the time and effort required to achieve
those goals.

Now that you understand the benefits of self-confidence in sports
officiating, you need to assess your own level of confidence by examining your reactions to a variety of situations. To get started,
answer the following questions as they relate to sports officiating:

When are you overconfident?
How do you react to adversity?
Are you afraid of certain situations?
How do you recover after making a bad call?
Is your confidence consistent throughout the competition?
Do you look forward to, and enjoy, a tough assignment?
Are you tentative or indecisive in certain situations?

Your responses to these questions can serve as a starting point for
getting in touch with your current level of self-confidence. Self-
help Test 9.3: Confidence Inventory has been designed to provide
a more detailed assessment of your confidence as a sports official.

MOTIVATION

Becoming an effective sports official requires hard work, dedication, and practice, all of which require a high level of motivation. Top officials enjoy their jobs immensely, deriving a good deal of motivation from their love of the sport and the role that they fulfill in the competition. However, if an official's enjoyment for officiating diminishes, there will be a corresponding loss of motivation to practice and work hard at the job. Simply put, you can not give a 100 percent effort to your officiating if you have to struggle to get yourself up for each game.

A common theme among officials who have *burned out* is that they have, at least temporarily, lost their enjoyment for officiating. In many cases, this results from the intense pressures of the job or the lack of appreciation for their efforts that most officials feel from time to time. A former high school and college football official sums up the feeling this way:

> I used to look forward to getting up in the morning on the day of a game in which I was to officiate. I couldn't wait for the game to start as I enjoyed the experience of being involved in the action. But as time went on, it became more and more difficult for me to get motivated to officiate, even when it was a big game. I'm not sure if it was all the abuse I took over the years from players, coaches, and fans, or just the boredom of doing the same thing over and over again. Whatever the reason, I just lost my enthusiasm; when officiating was no longer fun, I knew it was time to get out.

Although most sports officials start off with a high level of motivation, maintaining it game in and game out over a long period often proves difficult. As a major league umpire once observed, "I think every umpire who works in the minor leagues thinks once or twice about quitting." Given the nature of the job, burn-out among sports officials is scarcely surprising, particularly in the initial stages of one's career. Officials typically receive little in the way of financial rewards, and it is unusual to receive praise or positive reinforcement from coaches, athletes, or fans. Consequently, it takes a strong sense of self-esteem and a high level of motivation to overcome these drawbacks. As a sports official, you simply cannot become overly concerned about how other people view your performance. Rather, you must focus on your self-perceptions of performance and progress as an official.

As long as you see steady improvement and advancement toward meaningful goals, chances are extremely good that you will continue to be motivated. Goal setting, in particular, can play a critical role in maintaining one's motivation to officiate. Goals help provide a sense of direction and help ensure an ongoing challenge for the future. As Keith Bell aptly noted in his book <u>Championship Thinking</u>:

> Floundering in the world of sports without setting goals is like shooting without aiming. You might enjoy the blast and kick of the gun, but you probably won't get the bird.

While establishing career goals can go a long way in helping officials develop and maintain motivation and commitment over the long haul, they are no substitute for intrinsic motivation. Most veteran officials are motivated by the desire to continue participating in a sport they love, or at least remain a part of a sporting environment after their own athletic careers have come to an end. In fact, a recent survey of sports officials revealed that most chose to get involved in the field because of their love of the sport and the challenges involved in officiating it. For these officials, the sport itself provides the strongest motivation of all.

However, it is easy to lose sight of your motivation due to the hassles and pressures that often arise in sports officiating. At such times, keep in mind that being part of competitive sports is an exciting and emotionally rewarding endeavor, and that you play a critical role in facilitating fair and equitable competition. Focus on the reasons that originally led you to choose a career officiating and the sense of challenge and accomplishment that officiating provides.

DEVELOPING MENTAL SKILLS

Thus far, I have attempted to demonstrate that being an effective sports official requires not only knowledge of the rules and mechanics, but specific personal qualities as well. Once you have achieved the correct *internal climate,* your skill as an official will more consistently approach your potential. The key, of course, is developing the optimal internal climate for your personality.

It would be great if all officials were born with the characteristics that have just been presented; unfortunately, this is not the case. However, most of these characteristics are nothing more than psychological skills which most veteran officials have learned to acquire. For example, establishing rapport with coaches and athletes requires the development of communication skills; learning to communicate effectively and being a good listener are aspects of communication which can be mastered through practice. Remaining poised and maintaining self-control are related to one's ability to relax; relaxation techniques such as controlled breathing and positive self-talk are just some of the steps used to develop this skill. Being decisive and making sound judgments require good concentration skills and attentional focus; these skills can be honed by recognizing attentional triggers, exercising eye control, and remaining focused on the present.

The point is, the qualities of top flight officials are all rooted in psychological skills which can be acquired and developed to a high degree through practice and an awareness of one's weaknesses. Unfortunately, as noted previously, the training most sports officials receive emphasizes rules interpretation and mechanics over the psychological aspects. While the development of these skills will take some effort on your part, you have already demonstrated your interest in officiating just by taking the time to read this book. Whether you are just embarking on a career as a sports official, or are a veteran looking to improve yourself, the development of these skills is essential in achieving your career goals as well as your potential. By all means, enjoy the journey!

Publisher's Note:
Portions of this chapter have been adapted from the <u>Psychology of Officiating</u>, co-authored by Robert S. Weinberg & Peggy A. Richardson.

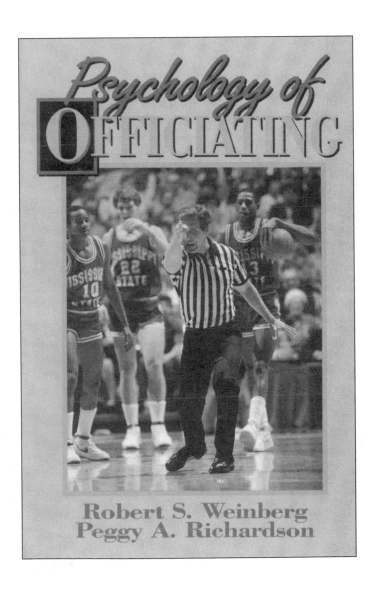

SECTION III:
OFFICIATING IN THE
MAJOR SPORTS

THE
BASEBALL
UMPIRE

BASEBALL OFFICIATING AT A GLANCE

Entry Level: Recreational and little leagues; junior high and high school

Minimum Age: 18 in most states

Certification: State (high school) athletic association certification required for junior high and high school officiating in most states (see Section V).

Average Pay: Baseball officials earn $5 to $10 per game in Little League. High school junior varsity pays $15 to $40 per game; high school varsity pays $35 to $60 per game. Major college baseball officials earn $75 to $110 per game. The pay for major league umps varies depending on experience, but sea-soned officials can gross well over $300,000 per season.

Schedule: The interscholastic and collegiate baseball regular seasons generally run from late March through early June. The major and minor league regular season begins in early April and runs through September. Post-season games are played in October.

Baseball continues to be one of the nation's most popular sports for players and spectators.

BASEBALL: GENERAL INFORMATION

The rules of baseball have changed little since 1900; the game is played by two opposing teams of nine players each. The game is played on a grass field known as a *diamond* with four bases set 90 feet apart. The diamond is surrounded by an outfield. The fielding team pitches to the batting team with the teams switching positions after each inning of play. From an offensive standpoint, the objective of the game is to outscore the opposing team by batting in more runs; defensively, the fielding team attempts to prevent the opponent from scoring by catching balls, or throwing runners out at home plate or the other three bases. The game consists of nine innings; extra innings are played in the event of a tied score.

Baseball long has been considered the national pastime, and the game is played by young and old alike in a variety of leagues across the country. Major league baseball, in particular, has a devoted following with millions of fans following the action of their favorite teams throughout the summer months. The culmination of professional baseball's regular season is the World Series championship that is held each fall.

OFFICIATING BASEBALL

Officiating a baseball game requires thorough familiarity with the complex set of rules and regulations which govern the game, as well as the ability to apply these rules in a multitude of situations that can arise during play. Although officiating baseball does not require the same level of stamina as basketball or soccer, umpires must possess sharp eyesight and quick reflexes in order to keep pace with the movement of the ball and properly position themselves to make calls. Due to the constant ebb and flow of the action that typifies the game of baseball, one of the umpire's biggest challenges is to remain focused on the game at all times so as not to miss a call. Perhaps to a greater degree than other sports, baseball umpires often are subject to spirited challenges of their rulings. Ridicule from baseball fans often comes with the territory.

BASEBALL OFFICIALS

Baseball officials are classified according to their position on the field. The primary umpire is the *home plate umpire* who works every game, regardless of the level of competition. His position on the field is either bending or kneeling behind the catcher, ready to judge the pitcher's throws. In general, the home plate umpire controls the tempo of the game by calling balls and strikes and ruling on fair and foul balls. The home plate umpire also has final say on any disputes that may arise during the game, including player conduct.

Unlike some sports which require officials to master a complex array of mechanical signals, the baseball umpire gets by with only six simple hand signals. The home plate umpire's hand signals include safe and out, fair and foul, strike, and time out. The baseball umpire uses his voice rather than hand signals to start play and will often use a simple finger signal to alert the pitcher as to the status of the count.

Depending on competition level, the home plate umpire is assisted by one or more base umpires. The *base umpire* is responsible for calling base runners *out* or *safe* and for ruling on fly balls. At the little league and interscholastic levels, base umpires are optional, although high school varsity baseball generally employs at least one base umpire. In minor league A and AA, only one base umpire is used; two base umpires are used in AAA. At the major league level, each base is covered by one base umpire.

In most league championship series, two extra umpires, known as *foul line umpires*, are assigned to work each foul line. Each foul line umpire monitors the outfielders to rule on catches and also assists in ruling on fair and foul balls. The presence of line umpires greatly enhances the performance of the base umpires by allowing them to more closely focus on their primary duties.

SEASONS OF PLAY

There is no universal starting date for little league baseball. In states with a warm climate year round, little league can be played throughout the year, but in most cases, play starts around May and continues until the end of June. Interscholastic and collegiate baseball starts around the end of March and runs through late May or early June. However, teams which advance to the state tournaments play even later. American Legion Baseball takes place in the summer, generally between high school terms from June through August. The major and minor league regular season begins in early April and runs through September. Post-season games typically are played in October.

Quick reflexes and sharp eyesight are essential skills for the baseball umpire.

UNIFORMS & EQUIPMENT

Umpires usually wear a light blue, short sleeve shirt with long, dark pants and a dark cap. At the professional level, umpires wear a navy blue shirt and cap. Home plate and base umpires carry an indicator or counter that helps them keep track of balls, strikes, and outs. Because of the constant threat of being hit with a foul ball or wild pitch, the use of special protective gear is a must for the home plate umpire. His face is covered by a catcher-like mask; he wears a chest protector under his shirt and shin guards under his pant legs. The home plate

umpire also has a bag of extra baseballs on his hip in case a ball is fouled off or damaged during the game.

COMPETITION LEVELS & CERTIFICATION REQUIREMENTS

Little league baseball, which encompasses players age 7 to 11, is normally sponsored by local community recreational leagues. Some communities hire only state-licensed officials while others do not. Contact your local recreation department for details; if state certification is required, refer to Chapter 2. Little league umpire salaries range from about $5 to $20 a game, depending on the community or league.

Interscholastic baseball includes middle school and varsity/junior varsity high school events. Competition and officiating at this level are regulated by the state high school athletic association in accordance with the guidelines and rules set forth by the National Federation of State High School Associations. In most states, certification by your state athletic association is required to umpire at this level. At the high school varsity level, teams average three to four games a week. In some states, umpire game fees are set by

Baseball: A Brief History

While Abner Doubleday is widely credited with the invention of baseball, historians believe the game originated from a 17th century English sport called rounders. Like modern-day baseball, rounders involved hitting a ball with a bat and advancing around a series of bases. Unlike baseball, however, rounders involved hitting base runners with the ball to achieve an out, a technique known as *plugging* a runner. By the middle of the 19th century, the rules were amended to tag the base runner with the ball instead of hitting him with it.

In 1845, Alexander Cartwright founded the Knickerbocker Base Ball Club of New York. Cartwright also established a new set of rules for the game, many of which are essentially the same as used in modern baseball. The first professional baseball team in the United States was the Cincinnati Red Stockings, which began compensating its players in 1869.

The popularity of baseball began to spread during the Civil War, when the game was often played as a form of recreation by Union soldiers. In 1876, eight professional teams were organized as the National League. The American League followed in 1901. National fervor for the game became widespread near the turn of the century and has continued almost unabated since.

American Association Kansas City Cowboys players, 1888

individual schools; in other states, the high school athletic association makes the determination. On average, junior varsity umpires make $15 to $40 a game, while varsity umpires earn between $35 and $60 a game.

The American Legion sponsors a popular youth baseball program which has yielded many top players and umpires over the years. American Legion Baseball is a summer league, which allows players and officials an opportunity to extend their game time well after the conclusion of interscholastic competition. The American Legion normally schedules between two and six games a week, including double-headers. The American Legion maintains offices in most states that hire umpires. Refer to the Resources section of this chapter for contact information. The American Legion uses a set pay rate for game officials – umpires are paid $30 per game plus travel expenses.

Collegiate baseball programs typically are governed by the National Collegiate Athletic Association. It is not possible to start a professional officiating career at this level. The major conferences typically obtain new officials through periodic umpire scoutings at high school varsity games. To increase your chances of being recruited to collegiate baseball, it is important to develop professional references and a history of steady employment as an official at the interscholastic level. College umpires' salaries vary depending on the conference but typically range from $75 to $110 a game. In some conferences, a weekend game will pay more than a weekday game.

Minor league baseball is a professional league that hosts younger players who are not yet ready for the major leagues. Minor league baseball consists of three divisions: A, AA, AAA. The triple-A division is the highest level of competition, and single-A the lowest. At the minor league level, a minimum of four umpires are employed, including the home plate umpire and three base umpires; a pair of line umpires are added in the playoffs. Minor League Baseball schedules four to six games a week, leaving open days for travel. To increase your chances of advancement to minor league officiating, the Baseball Umpire Development Program recommends your enrollment in a minor league umpire training school (see Directory of Sports Organizations Appendix). At the end of these five-week programs, top graduates are given an opportunity to participate in an Umpire Evaluation Course. If you are selected, you can begin working in either a Rookie, two-month class A, or full-season class A minor league. From here, you can progress to class AA, and then to class AAA, where you become eligible for major league officiating. Minor league umpire salaries range from $1,900 to $3,300 a month, not including travel expenses, lodging, or meal expenses.

The major leagues are the ultimate competitive level of professional baseball. Umpiring at this level generally requires a minimum of seven-plus years experience in officiating professional minor league games. Due to the low rate of turnover among major league umpires, coupled with the limited number of officiating berths, the big leagues need recruit only those umpires who exhibit consummate skill and ability. In addition to all the other skills required of a professional umpires, The Umpire Development Program recommends courses in speech, English grammar, management, and even Spanish to increase your chances for acceptance. Major league games are scheduled four to six times a week with days off for travel. Major league umpires earn from $75,000 to $300,000 per year with all travel expenses fully reimbursed and plenty of fringe benefits.

BASEBALL
LEVELS OF COMPETITION

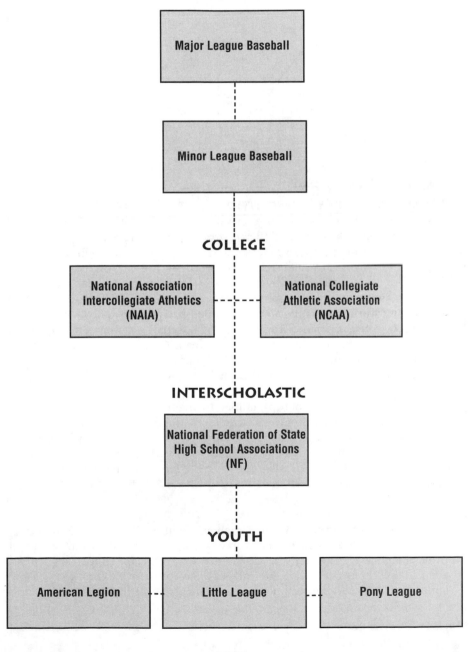

PROFESSIONAL

Major League Baseball

Minor League Baseball

COLLEGE

National Association Intercollegiate Athletics (NAIA)

National Collegiate Athletic Association (NCAA)

INTERSCHOLASTIC

National Federation of State High School Associations (NF)

YOUTH

American Legion

Little League

Pony League

COMPENSATION

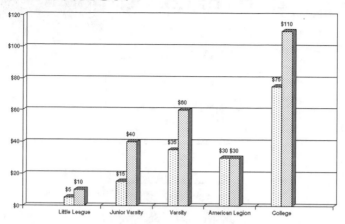

BASEBALL OFFICIATING
COMPENSATION BY COMPETITION LEVEL: EVENT FEES

The graph above reflects average event fee ranges for baseball officials at all levels of competition. Officials working one game per week can expect to earn amounts ranging somewhere between the high and low ranges for their level. At all levels of competition, it is not uncommon for officials to work more than one game per week, thereby increasing their earnings. For example, an interscholastic umpire can easily pull in $70 to $120 by working two high school games per week, which translates into $280 to $480 per month during the baseball season. Not bad for roughly six or seven hours of work per week. Compare this to a part-time job paying a minimum wage of $4.75 per hour, which would yield less than $400 over a month and 80 hours of work.

As you move up the officiating ladder to higher levels of competition, your pay goes up accordingly. College-level umpires earn substantially more than interscholastic officials but must also work their way up from smaller divisions to the more prestigious NCAA Division I. At nearly all levels of competition, officials receive a higher event fee for championship and playoff games than for games played during the regular season.

Minor league umpires bring in anywhere from $1,900 to $3,300 per month, plus travel expenses. The top earnings for officials occur at the professional level. The lucky ones who make it to Major League Baseball earn $75,000 per season in the initial phases of their careers; the seasonal pay for experienced major league officials can exceed $300,000.

OFFICIAL PROFILE:
JERRY MEALS
AAA UMPIRE

LR: Jerry, how did you get started in umpiring?

JM: I've always played baseball and I used to umpire little league games. I decided to go to umpire school when I was 21, although I had no intentions of becoming an umpire for a career. I ended up being very lucky, and I was chosen as a minor league umpire right away.

LR: How many years have you been an umpire?

JM: 14 years in the minors, with parts of seasons working the majors in the National League.

LR: What are the pros and cons of full-time sports officiating.

JM: It's not an easy road. In the minors, you have to be prepared to drive a lot, sleep in hotels, eat all your meals out, and be away from your family. Many guys spend 10 years in the minors without even working one day in the majors. Once you're out, that's it. Umpire Development reviews your skills and evaluates your abilities each season. You are either retained or let go. Once you are let go, that's it. You have to start a new life because there is no pension or anything like that. It's tough. Very few people ever make it to the majors.

For me, the best part of umpiring is being called up to work the major league games. I have been very fortunate and have been able to consistently work in the majors since 1992.

LR: Describe a typical day in the life of a professional umpire.

JM: In the minors, I work with the same two guys for an entire season. We are a three-man umpiring team, and so we end up doing practically everything together for five months, which is a difficult concept to imagine. It takes some adjustments. We usually get up around 9:00 or 10:00 a.m., perhaps play golf or read the paper, do errands, then grab a late lunch. We eat just one big meal a day, around 2:00, then take a nap or do other errands before the game.

Umpires are required to be at the ball park an hour before the game begins, usually around 6:00. Games are generally two and a half to three hours and fifteen minutes, each. We then have a bite to eat and sometimes have a beer somewhere. Our uniforms are washed by someone at the minors organization, and many times they provide food for us as well. This basic schedule goes on day after day for five months, with only about five days off the entire season.

LR: Describe some of your most memorable experiences.

JM: There have been many. One of the most memorable was the first time I was called up to the majors. It was very exciting. September 13, 1992 I worked a series in Chicago at Wrigley Field. As most first-time-up umpires want to do, I hoped to get the plate umpire experience out of the way first thing, but it didn't happen. First day I worked third base, next day second, next day first, then finally on the fourth day I worked the plate and did just fine!

Another experience that I am grateful for and will never forget is having my family watch me work a National League game. My father was able to watch me work a big game in 1994 before he passed away a few weeks later. This meant a lot to me.

LR: Finally, what advice would you give someone interested in becoming a baseball umpire?

JM: If you have the desire to do it, you must be very dedicated. You must work very hard and you have to be mentally tough. You have to realize that there is no such thing as seniority in this business. Umpires are evaluated each season and, if there's someone younger and better than you, that is who will move up, not necessarily the umpires with more experience.

RESOURCES

Regulatory Bodies
Children's/Interscholastic
American Legion
700 N. Pennsylvania
Indianapolis, IN 46204
Phone: (317) 630-1213 Fax: (317) 630-1369
e-mail: tal@iquest.com

Pony Baseball
P.O. Box 225
Washington, PA 15301
Phone: (724) 225-1060 Fax (724) 225-9852
e-mail: pony@pulsnet.com

Babe Ruth League, Inc.
P.O. Box 5000
1770 Brunswick Pike
Trenton, NJ 08638
Phone: (609) 695-1434 Fax: (609) 695-2505

National Federation of State High School
Associations (NFSHSA)
11724 NW Plaza Circle
P.O. Box 20626
Kansas City, MO 64195-0626
Phone: (816) 464-5400 Fax: (816) 464-5571
Internet: www.nfhs.org

Amateur
USA Baseball
Hi Corbett Field, 3400 E. Camino Campestre
Tucson, AZ 85716
Phone: (520) 327-9700 Fax: (520) 327-9221
e-mail: usabaseball@aol.com
Internet: www.usabaseball.com

National Amateur Baseball Federation, Inc.
P.O. Box 705
Bowie, MD 20718
Phone: (301) 262-5005 Fax (301) 262-5005

Professional
Major League Baseball (MLB)
245 Park Ave.
New York, NY 10167
Phone: (212) 931-7800
Internet: www.majorleague.com

National Baseball Congress
300 S. Sycamore
Wichita, KS 67213
Phone: (316) 267-3372 Fax (316) 267-3382
e-mail: wranglers@feist.com

National Association of Pro Baseball Leagues
P.O. Box A
201 Bayshore Dr. SE
St. Petersburg, FL 33731
Phone: (727) 822-6937 Fax (727) 821-5819
Internet: www.minorleaguebaseball.com

International
International Baseball Federation
Avenue de Mon-Repos 24
Case Postale 131
1000 Lausanne 5
Switzerland
Phone: (41-21) 311-1863 Fax: (41-21) 311-1864
e-mail: iba@dial.eunet.ch
Internet: www.alpcom.it/digesu

BASEBALL RULES BOOKS
Baseball rules books applicable to a variety of competition levels are available. Contact the organization governing the level of competition in which you are involved. The National Collegiate Athletic Association (NCAA) annually publishes a baseball rules book which is available each December. Cost of the 1999 NCAA rules book is $5. The interscholastic baseball rules book is available through the National Federation of State High School Associations. Cost is $5.

BASEBALL UMPIRING SELF-TEST

1. How many players play in the field at one time?

2. How many balls does it take to earn a walk?

3. How many umpires work in a Major League Baseball game?

4. True or false: The designated hitter must bat fourth.

5. What is the umpire's ruling if a fair ball bounces over the home run fence?

6. How long is a baseline in high school? In the Pros?

7. Who was nicknamed the *Bambino*?

8. Who holds the record for major league home runs in a career and how many?

9. Which city's Major League team is named *The Indians*?

10. True or false: A base runner can tag-up if a ball is caught in foul territory.

11. How many foul balls make an out?

12. True or false: Minor league professionals use wooden bats.

13. True or false: Pine tar is not allowed in the major leagues.

14. True or false: Pro umpires must be former college players.

15. True or false: A sacrifice bunt does not count as an official at-bat.

16. If a player has two strikes against him and tries to bunt but the ball goes foul, what is the ruling?

17. On the scoreboard, what do each of these three letters mean: *R, H, E*?

18. True or false: High school players are not required to use aluminum bats.

19. What happens if the catcher catches a foul tip with two strikes on the batter?

20. What is a player called if he can hit from both the left and right sides of the batter's box?

21. Name the area in which the relief pitchers warm up.

22. What term describes a home run that is hit when the bases are loaded?

23. What does *RBI* stand for?

24. How many innings are played in a high school game?

25. How many games are possible in the World Series?

BASEBALL UMPIRING SELF-TEST ANSWERS

1. Nine; 2. Four; 3. Four; 4. False; 5. Ground double rule; 6. 90 feet; 7. Babe Ruth; 8. Hank Aaron, 755; 9. Cleveland; 10. True; 11. None; a batter cannot *foul out* unless he bunts foul with a two-strike count; 12. True; 13. False; 14. False; 15. True; 16. He is out. 17. Runs, Hits, and Errors; 18. True; 19. The batter is out. 20. A switch hitter; 21. The bullpen; 22. Grand slam; 23. Runs Batted In; 24. Seven; 25. Seven

SCORING THE SELF-TEST

Incorrect Answers	Officiating Aptitude
0	Perfect: You have a solid knowledge of the game.
1-3	Average: You need to review the baseball rules book.
4-5	Below average: It's been some time since you've seen a baseball game.
6+	Far below average: You should consider officiating a different sport.

THE
BASKETBALL
REFEREE

BASKETBALL OFFICIATING AT A GLANCE

Entry Level: Youth and recreational leagues; interscholastic basketball programs

Minimum Age: 18 in most states

Certification: State (high school) athletic association certification required for junior high and high school officials in most states (see Section V).

Average Pay: Basketball officials earn $10 to $15 at the youth and recreational levels; in some areas such leagues also employ volunteer officials. Interscholastic basketball officials earn $15 to $40 a game at the junior varsity level and $35 to $65 at varsity games. Collegiate officials in major college conferences can earn up to $350 per game and much more in championship tournaments. NBA officials gross between $75,000 and $211,000 per year.

Schedule: Basketball is a winter sport. The interscholastic season generally runs from mid-November through March. Basketball also is played indoors and outdoors throughout the year in competitions sponsored by recreational leagues. Basketball officials literally can work almost year round.

Basketball is an increasingly popular women's sport, affording growing opportunities for female officials at the interscholastic, collegiate and professional levels.

BASKETBALL: GENERAL INFORMATION

Basketball is played on a rectangular court by two opposing teams, each consisting of five players. The basketball court is 50 feet in width, and 84 to 94 feet in length, depending on the level of competition. Teams alternate between offensive and defensive roles with each change of ball possession. The offensive team scores by shooting the ball into a raised basket, while the defensive team attempts to thwart their efforts. Two points are awarded for a field goal and one point for foul shots and free throws. Free throw opportunities are provided to players who are fouled by an opponent. Three points are scored for shots completed a specified distance from the basket. The three-point shot distance varies by competition level. Players advance the ball across the court and toward their goal by dribbling (bouncing the ball) or by passing it to a teammate while their opponents attempt to prevent them from scoring. A team wins by scoring more points than its opponent.

Although basketball has long been dominated by male athletes, significant growth and serious recognition of women's basketball in the United States began in the 1970s. State tournaments for high school girls are held in almost every state and at the collegiate level; basketball is the fastest growing women's sport. More recently, the summer Olympic Games and the organization of the Women's National Basketball Association have helped women's basketball gain additional prominence worldwide.

OFFICIATING BASKETBALL

Basketball is a difficult game to officiate. In no other sport are the demands of positioning, signaling, and teamwork more continuous or crucial. The chief officials in basketball are the floor officials who must constantly reposition themselves to keep pace with the action. This requires a great deal of physical conditioning and stamina. Action is nearly continuous during the game, and basketball officials are challenged to maintain focus and mental alertness throughout the game. The basketball official must also master a multitude of hand signals.

BASKETBALL OFFICIALS

Basketball is officiated by a referee who is assisted by one or two umpires. The use of a second umpire significantly increases officiating coverage and is common in collegiate and professional competition. The referee and umpire work the game as equals. Neither has the authority to set aside or question the decisions of the other.

The referee starts and stops play with his or her whistle, calls fouls and rules infractions, rules on all matters involving the scorers and timers, and is tasked with a variety of pre-game duties. The referee also approves the score at the end of each half and makes decisions on any matters not specifically outlined in the rules. The umpire backs up the referee by providing an extra set of eyes to monitor the action.

On the floor, the referee and umpire alternate between *lead* and *trail* positions with each change of ball possession or foul committed. During action near either basket, the lead official maintains a position out-of-bounds and adjacent to the endline. The trail official is positioned in-bounds, close to the sideline, at the midcourt area.

The official timer is responsible for starting and stopping the game clock and regulating the duration of time-outs and intermissions between periods. At higher levels of competition, a separate timer is responsible for maintaining the 30-second shot clock. The scorekeeper records successful and unsuccessful field goals and free throws and maintains a running tabulation of points scored. In addition, the scorekeeper tracks personal fouls, technical fouls, and time-outs, and in some cases, operates the scoreboard.

COMMON PENALTIES

Generally, violations penalize illegal player movement and ball handling; personal fouls penalize illegal player contact while technical fouls penalize unsportsmanlike conduct on the part of players, coaches, or fans. The penalties for technical fouls are more severe than those for personal fouls. Penalties imposed range from change of ball possession to the award of free throws. Players exceeding the allowed number of fouls are ejected from the game.

SEASONS OF PLAY

Basketball is played indoor and outdoors throughout the year in competition sponsored by recreational leagues. Interscholastic, collegiate, and professional basketball primarily is a winter sport. The interscholastic season runs from mid-November through the end of March. Men's and women's basketball is included as part of the summer Olympic Games.

UNIFORMS & EQUIPMENT

Basketball floor officials' uniforms generally are black and white: a black and white vertically striped, short-sleeved shirt, and black pants, belt, socks, shoes and shoelaces. A navy blue jacket is recommended attire for half-time and pre-game. Some college conferences require officials to wear a solid gray shirt. Each basketball official should have available two high quality whistles with cords. The timer should have a stop watch or clock available in the case of a faulty scoreboard clock.

COMPETITION LEVELS & CERTIFICATION REQUIREMENTS

At the local level, basketball teams for youths and adults are sponsored by community recreation departments, park districts, religious organizations, and youth centers, among others. Officials for recreational leagues typically are employed by, or volunteer for, the sponsoring organization. If state certification is required, applicants must take classes, participate in clinics, and successfully complete examinations to be registered. Recreational league officiating is considered an entry level for potential officials. Recreational league officials earn $10 to $15 per game.

Interscholastic competition is regulated at the state level by the high school athletic association which follows guidelines set forth by the National Federation of State High School Associations (NF). The NF, in turn, maintains active membership in USA Basketball. High school junior varsity officiating is considered an entry level position. Officials at this level must be state-certified in most states, attending classes and clinics and passing a written examination administered by their state high school athletic association prior to certification. High school varsity level officials typically are selected from among the ranks of experienced junior varsity referees and umpires. High school junior varsity officials earn $15 to $40 a game, and varsity officials are paid $35 to $65 a game, as determined by local school districts or state athletic associations.

At the amateur level, USA Basketball-affiliated organizations sponsoring regional amateur competition include Youth Basketball of America, Inc., the YWCA, the Jewish Community Center Association of North America, and the National Association for Girls and Women in Sport. USA Basketball-affiliated organizations sponsoring national amateur competition include the Amateur Athletic Union, the National Wheelchair Basketball Association, and the U.S. Armed Forces.

Collegiate-level programs affiliated with USA Basketball include National Collegiate Athletic Association, National Association of Intercollegiate Athletics, and National Junior College Athletic Association competition. Officials at this level typically are hired by

BASKETBALL: A BRIEF HISTORY

James Naismith is widely credited with the invention of basketball in 1891. Naismith, a physical education instructor at the International Young Men's Christian Association (YMCA) Training School in Springfield, Massachusetts, created the game as an alternative to men's gymnastics, at that time the only indoor winter sport.

Naismith's version of the game was played with a soccer ball. Peach baskets attached to gymnasium balconies served as goals. By 1893, metal hoops with attached net bags replaced the peach baskets. Although more durable, the closed end net bags necessitated the manual release of the ball after every successful goal. In 1894, the backboard was introduced, along with a larger ball to replace the soccer ball, and in 1913, bottomless nets replaced the early net bags.

In comparison to modern basketball, early games were low-scoring events. Players used only two basic shooting techniques: the lay-up and a two-handed set shot. Rules changes effected in the 1930s, including the 10-second rule which required the offensive team to advance the ball across the court division line within 10 seconds, and the introduction of the one-handed shot and the jump shot in the 1930s and 1940s, respectively, resulted in increased offensive movement and higher scores.

Naismith's game provided the foundation of rules later formally established by the YMCA and the Amateur Athletic Union. Today, the national governing body of men's and women's basketball is USA Basketball.

The Father of Modern Basketball, Dr. James Naismith

individual athletic conferences from the ranks of talented inter-scholastic officials. In many cases, there is no formal certification process for officials. However, a proven track record and attendance at annual training clinics or seminars is mandatory for consideration. In seeking basketball officials, college athletic conferences rely typically on recommendations from coaches and athletic directors. Earnings at the collegiate level vary by conference, some paying officials $300 to $350 per game plus expenses. In the larger NCAA Division I athletic conferences, basketball officials may earn up to $600 per game, plus a per diem fee and travel expenses.

The United States Basketball League (USBL) is a summer professional league. The USBL selects officials from among participants in USBL-sponsored training camps. Training camp participants are selected from among individuals submitting applications to the USBL. For some individuals, officiating for the USBL can provide a stepping stone to a career with the National Basketball Association. USBL officials typically earn $100 per game.

National Basketball Association (NBA) competition, considered the elite level for players and officials alike, employs officials selected from among the ranks of Continental Basketball Association (CBA), the USBL, and collegiate conference officials who have been invited to participate in NBA officials tryout camps. In fact, the CBA serves as a developmental program for potential NBA players and officials. Both the USBL and the CBA are affiliated with USA Basketball. According to *USA Today*, a contract approved in 1996 by the NBA and NBA officials provides salaries ranging from $75,000 annually for first-year officials to $211,000 a year for veteran officials, generally with more than 20 years experience.

COMPENSATION

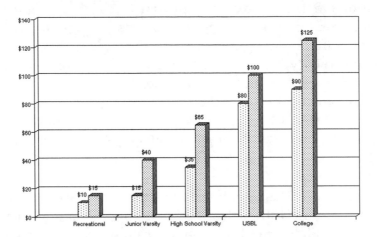

BASKETBALL OFFICIATING
COMPENSATION BY COMPETITION LEVEL: EVENT FEES

The graph above reflects average event fee ranges for basketball officials at various levels of competition. Officials working one game per week can expect to earn amounts ranging somewhere between the high and low range for their level. At all levels of competition, it is not uncommon for officials to work more than one game per week, thereby increasing their earnings. For example, an interscholastic basketball referee can easily pull in $30 to $80 by working two high school games per week, which translates into $120 to $320 per month during the basketball season. Not bad for roughly 10 hours of work per month. Compare this to a part time job paying a minimum wage of $4.75 per hour, which would yield less than $400 for 80 hours of work.

As you move up the officiating ladder to higher levels of competition, your pay goes up accordingly. College-level referees earn substantially more than interscholastic officials, but must also work their way up from smaller divisions to the more prestigious NCAA Division I. Event fees for college-level basketball officials range from $90 to $125, depending on the division and geographic area. In all divisions, event fees for championship and playoff games are higher than for games played during the regular season.

The top earnings for officials occur at the professional level. National Basketball Association referees earn anywhere from $75,000 to $200,000 and more annually, depending on tenure and experience.

BASKETBALL
LEVELS OF COMPETITION

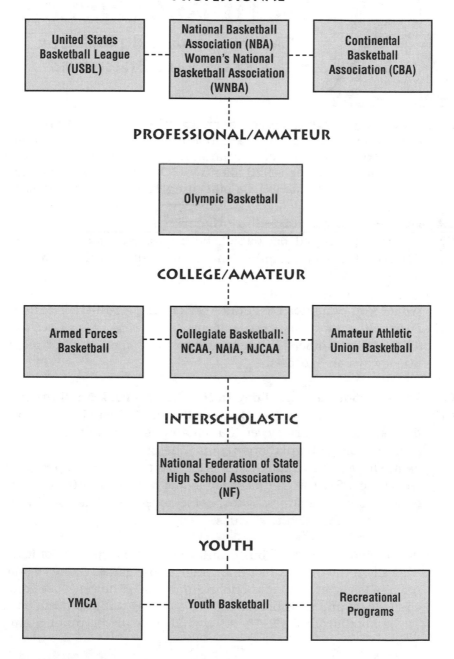

PROFESSIONAL

United States Basketball League (USBL)

National Basketball Association (NBA) Women's National Basketball Association (WNBA)

Continental Basketball Association (CBA)

PROFESSIONAL/AMATEUR

Olympic Basketball

COLLEGE/AMATEUR

Armed Forces Basketball

Collegiate Basketball: NCAA, NAIA, NJCAA

Amateur Athletic Union Basketball

INTERSCHOLASTIC

National Federation of State High School Associations (NF)

YOUTH

YMCA

Youth Basketball

Recreational Programs

OFFICIAL PROFILE:
DR. HENRY O. NICHOLS
NCAA NATIONAL COORDINATOR, MEN'S BASKETBALL OFFICIATING

LR: How many years have you been an official, Dr. Nichols?

HN: About 20 years. Right now, I'm in a director's position, but I officiated the game for many years. Highlights of my officiating career included the 1976 Montreal Olympics, the 1984 Los Angeles Olympics, as well as officiating 10 Final Four series.

LR: How did you get started in officiating?

HN: I've always enjoyed basketball, both as a player and a coach. Officiating was just another chance to dabble in the game and stay close to it.

LR: Would you consider basketball officiating a full-time career?

HN: Definitely not for most people. If you are an NBA official, yes, but all the college officials I know of have full-time jobs. For me, it was always an avocation.

LR: Tell me about a typical day in the life of a basketball official.

HN: Let's say I had a game at Duke University. I'd catch a 3 o'clock flight to Raleigh, drive over to the campus area, and check into a hotel. College regulations require the officials to arrive at the game site one and a half hours prior to start time for a pre-game conference. So, I would meet my fellow refs around 6 o'clock to go over floor mechanics, rules, game coverage issues, and anything else we needed to discuss.

We are generally pretty busy until the game starts. The officials then go on the court a half hour prior to the game. Games would usually begin at 7:30 and end around 9:30. Shower, post-game conference, and possibly having a bite to eat would put me back at the hotel around 11. Then, I would typically be up at 5 a.m.

to catch an early flight and make it to my full-time job the next day.

LR: What would you say is the best part of being an official?
HN: Being closely involved in the game.

LR: How about the worst?
HN: The idea that nobody likes you, except maybe your family.

LR: Dr. Nichols, could you share some of the most memorable experiences of your officiating career?
HN: On the positive side, when you finish a game and it went well, that is with few complaints about the calls made, it's always a satisfying feeling. It is exciting to be part of the game, especially when there are no problems. On the other hand, when it is perceived that you have made a bad call, you have to deal with the crowd booing as well as upset coaches. Also, the travel involved often takes time away from family and work commitments.

My most memorable experience occurred in Mexico City. I was officiating an international game between Mexico and Russia. I made what the Mexican team thought was a bad decision when I called a foul on their team captain. The captain spit on me and the crowd went into an uproar and threw debris onto the court. After the court was cleaned, the game proceeded and Russia won by a close margin. The crowd tried to attack me and another referee immediately following the game. Fortunately, we were encircled by the police and escorted out of the stadium and directly into the police paddy wagon. We were taken directly to our hotel, and the police had to collect our items and clothing from the locker room. It was quite an experience.

LR: What a story! Finally, what advice would you give to someone interested in becoming a basketball official?
HN: Have a love for the game and a love for making sure that it is played in such a way that both sides have a chance to win. Be fair and have the courage to keep your integrity.

RESOURCES

Regulatory Bodies

Children's/Interscholastic

National Federation of State High School
Associations (NFSHSA)
11724 NW Plaza Circle
P.O. Box 20626
Kansas City, MO 64195-0626
Phone: (816) 464-5400 Fax: (816) 464-5571
Internet: www.nfhs.org

Collegiate

National Association of Intercollegiate
Athletics (NAIA)
6120 S. Yale Ave., Ste. 1450
Tulsa, OK 74136-4223
Phone: (918) 494-8828 Fax: (918) 494-8841
Internet: www.naia.org

National Collegiate Athletic Association
(NCAA)
6201 College Blvd.
Overland Park, KS 66211-2422
Phone: (913) 339-1906 Fax: (913) 339-1950
Internet: www.ncaa.org

National Junior College Athletic Association
(NJCAA)
1825 Austin Bluffs Pkwy., Ste. 100
P.O. Box 7305
Colorado Springs, CO 80933-7305
Phone: (719) 590-9788 Fax: (719) 590-7324
e-mail: info@njcaa.org
Internet: www.njcaa.org

Professional/Minor League

National Basketball Association (NBA)
645 Fifth Ave.
New York, NY 10022
Phone: (212) 407-8000 Fax: (212) 832-3861

Continental Basketball Association (CBA)
400 N. 5th St., Ste. 1425
Phoenix, AZ 85004
Phone: (602) 254-6677 Fax: (602) 258-9985
Internet: cbahoops.com

United States Basketball League (USBL)
46 Quirk Rd.
P.O. Box 211
Milford, CT 06460-3745
Phone: (203) 877-9508 Fax: (203) 878-8109

National

USA Basketball
5465 Mark Dabling Blvd.
Colorado Springs, CO 80918-3842
Phone: (719) 590-4800 Fax: (719) 590-4811
Internet: www.usabasketball.com

International

Federation Internationale de Basketball (FIBA)
Boschetsrieder Str. 67
P.O. Box 700607
81306 Munich, Germany
Phone: (49-89) 74-81-5800
Fax: (49-89) 74-81-5833

BASKETBALL RULES BOOKS

Basketball rules books applicable to a variety of competition levels are available. Contact the organization governing the level of competition in which you are involved. For example, the National Collegiate Athletic Association (NCAA) annually publishes an illustrated men's and women's basketball rules book which is available each August. Cost is $5 a copy.

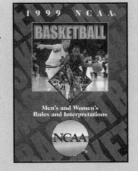

BASKETBALL OFFICIATING SELF-TEST

1. How many players are on the court at one time for each team?

2. True or false: At the high school level, boys and girls use the same size ball.

3. What is it called when the referee throws up the ball in the middle of two players to begin the game?

4. True or false: Girls' basketball rules make provisions for a three-point shot.

5. How many referees officiate an NBA game?
a. 2; b. 3; c. 4

6. True or false: A professional referee must be a former pro player.

7. How many fouls does it take for a high school player to foul out from the game?

8. True or false: The ball can be touched when it is still on the rim in international play.

9. What is the foul called when an offensive player runs into a defensive player who is standing still?

10. How high off the floor is a regulation basket?
a. 10 feet; b. 10.5 feet; c. 11.5 feet

11. True or false: A team can call a time out when they do not have possession of the ball.

12. What is a one-and-one?

13. What is the penalty for an intentional foul?

14. How many times can a player re-enter a game after being substituted for?

15. How many foul shots does a high school player get if he or she is fouled while shooting a three-pointer?

16. True or false: To keep games fair, there is a player height limit at the junior varsity level.

17. What is the violation called when a player takes too many steps without dribbling the ball?

18. How many technical fouls does it take for a player to be ejected from the game?

19. In high school, how many points must a team be winning by before the game is ended by a mercy rule?
    a. 35; b. 50; c. There is no mercy rule.

20. In college basketball, teams play two, ___ -minute halves?
    a. 20; b. 25; c. 30

BASKETBALL OFFICIATING SELF-TEST ANSWERS

1. Five; 2. False; 3. Jump ball; 4. True; 5. b; 6. False; 7. Five; 8. True; 9. Charging; 10. a; 11. False; 12. A type of foul shot. If the player makes the first shot, he or she gets a second. If he or she misses the first shot, the ball is live and can be rebounded by either team. 13. Two foul shots and possession of the ball; 14. There is no limit. 15. Three; 16. False; 17. Traveling; 18. Two; 19. c; 20. a

SCORING THE SELF-TEST

Incorrect Answers	Officiating Aptitude
0	Perfect: You have a solid knowledge of the game.
1-3	Average: You need to review the basketball rules book.
4-5	Below average: It's been some time since you've seen a basketball game.
6+	Far below average: You should consider officiating a different sport.

THE
FOOTBALL
REFEREE

FOOTBALL OFFICIATING AT A GLANCE

Entry Level: Pop Warner Leagues, Junior High School and High School Junior Varsity

Minimum Age: 18 in most states

Certification: State (high school) athletic association certification required for junior high and high school officials in most states (see Section V).

Average Pay: Football officials earn $10 per game in children's leagues and Pop Warner League. High school junior varsity pays $17 to $28 per game; high school varsity pays $35 to $65 per game. Major college football officials earn $500 to $700 per game, and NFL officials can earn as much as $4,000 per game.

Schedule: The football season runs from September through December and into January for post-season play in some leagues. Regular season games are scheduled once a week with 12 to 16 games played per season. At the junior high and high school levels, some officials work more than one level of competition, thereby increasing their number of games per week.

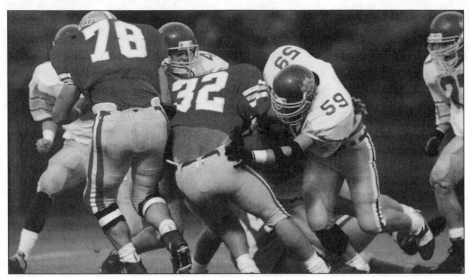

Football is an American sports tradition and widely played at all levels of competition.

FOOTBALL: GENERAL INFORMATION

Traditionally, the game of football is played by two opposing teams of 11 players each. Each team maintains offensive and defensive squads which rotate time on the field as possession of the ball changes. On the field, the quarterback controls the offensive squad and is responsible for passing the ball to receivers or handing it off on running plays. The defensive team attempts to prevent the offensive team from scoring by tackling receivers and ball carriers, blocking the offensive line, and generally trying to thwart the attempts of the quarterback to complete his passes. Football is an aggressive contact sport and players are equipped with protective helmets and padding to help minimize the chances of injury.

The football season begins in September and typically runs into November or December. Post-season play, depending on the level of competition, may continue into mid-January. Football has long been played outdoors on a grass field, although the game is often played indoors on artificial turf. Outdoors, football is one of the few sports that is played without regard to the weather; with few exceptions, only lightning can force postponement of a football game.

In the United States, football rivals baseball in terms of popularity, although far fewer football games are played in a typical season. National Football League and collegiate games are widely promoted, particularly those games that involve long-standing team, city, or college rivalries. The NFL Super Bowl, played each January at the conclusion of the regular season, consistently achieves the highest viewer ratings of any televised sport.

OFFICIATING FOOTBALL

By nature, football is an aggressive sport. As an official, your job is to ensure that the players follow the rules with a minimum of uncontrolled violence. Beyond mastery of a complex set of rules and situations, it takes an especially talented individual to fulfill the duties of football officiating. Effective football officials share several common qualities including a decisive attitude, the ability to communicate with and read the mood of others, the ability to remain calm and clear thinking in moments of stress, and, most of all, the ability to concentrate. Seasoned football officials have also learned to work with the flow of the game, signaling fouls only as necessary to maintain control while hustling to keep the game moving.

One of the most challenging aspects of football officiating is positioning yourself so as to see the plays without obstructing the players. This is part physical, part mental. Physically, you'll frequently have to run to keep up with the action; mentally, you'll need to anticipate how the action will unfold. This combination of mental and physical exertion can be exhausting. Stamina is understandably a must for the football official. Although designated playing time is one hour, three or more hours generally are required to complete an average game.

Just like players, officials need to keep their heads in the game. A lapse in focus at a key moment could prove embarrassing. In addition, you must constantly be on guard against potential personal injury; many a football official has been decked because he was unable to get out of the way in time. Even an errant cleat on a player's shoe can wreck your day. While the umpire works in the middle of the action and is subject to injury with virtually every play, even side line officials are at risk at some point. Always remember, while the players are amply protected, as an official, only your wits and agility stand between you and potentially serious injury.

To be effective on a field crew, you must have a *team player* mentality, as well as the ability to communicate well with others. Just like the sport, football officiating is definitely a group effort. On-field officials work in a tightly knit group known as the field crew. Although each crew member has an assigned job, officials are expected to work and act as a team. For example, officiating field crews typically enter and depart the field of play as a group and back up one another on close or contested plays. Top-notch officiating crews reinforce the team image by coordinating every detail of their uniforms, even down to the number of stripes on their socks.

As noted earlier, football is an all-weather sport, typically played in fall and early winter. Football games are not canceled because it's too cold or the field is too muddy. If the thought of working outside for several hours in a driving rain storm or howling blizzard does not excite you, you'd do well to forget about football and consider an indoor sport.

Football Officials

The football officiating crew varies in size from three to seven members, depending on the level of competition. Through the high school junior varsity level, only three-man crews consisting of a referee, linesman, and umpire are used. Four and five-man crews commonly are used at the high school varsity level. At high school varsity playoff games and competition between small college teams, an additional official, the back judge, rounds out the five-man crew. Many larger colleges also employ a side judge. Professional football employs a total of seven field officials: referee, linesman, umpire, line judge, back judge, side judge, and field judge. The following section profiles the individual officials who make up the field crew and the duties of each.

Michigan High School Athletic Association

An interscholastic football referee sizes up the action on a punt return.

THE REFEREE

The referee is the chief game official and is in charge of the officiating crew. The referee's pre-game duties include visiting team dressing rooms to provide a list of officials to the head coaches and to verify, in the presence of the umpire, that all players are legally equipped; conducting an officials conference to review special assignments; approving the clock operator and reviewing timing procedures; approving the game ball; and conducting the pre-game coin toss. Once the game is underway, the referee is responsible for maintaining the official score, interpreting game rules, and monitoring decisions made by the other officials on the field. The referee may also assist in counting offensive players before each play, discussing penalty decisions with team captains, and announcing penalties to players and spectators. Fouls committed by or against a passer and a punter are the responsibility of the referee, who also rules on illegal passes and watches for illegal blocks behind the line of scrimmage. At the start of scrimmage plays, the referee takes a position to one side and slightly behind the offensive team's backfield.

THE UMPIRE

The umpire works in the thick of the action, standing on the field just behind the defensive line. The umpire watches for player equipment violations and fouls committed by interior linesmen. The umpire also shares with the linesman responsibility for calling encroachment violations and false starts. On passing plays, the umpire watches for ineligible receivers and determines whether a forward pass goes beyond the line of scrimmage. On running plays, the umpire watches for potential fouls near the ball carrier. Generally, the umpire spots the ball after each play and determines possession after player pile-ups.

THE LINESMAN

The linesman, backed up by the referee, keeps track of the number of downs; oversees the placement of the line-to-gain markers; instructs the line-to-gain crew as to the correct positioning of the yard markers on the sideline; and shares with the umpire the responsibility for calling encroachment and false starts by the players. In addition, the linesman calls illegal use of the hands and improper direction by a man in motion toward the opposite sideline. On each down, the linesman checks the number of players on the scrimmage line and determines the eligibility of pass receivers. The starting position of the linesman on a play from scrimmage is outside the widest defensive and offensive players; in the neutral zone, the space between imaginary lines extending from the front and back tips of the ball to the sidelines; and on the side of the field opposite the press box. On passing plays, after the snap, the linesman moves downfield to observe contact between pass receivers and defensive backs. On running plays up the middle, the linesman determines the forward progress of the ball. In the sideline spot, the linesman stops the clock if the ball carrier steps out of bounds.

THE LINE JUDGE

Maintaining a position in the neutral zone at the opposite side of the field of the linesman, the line judge assumes the same general responsibilities and coverage as the linesman on plays from scrimmage. On punt or passing plays, however, the line judge assumes a position off the line of scrimmage. While the linesman retains responsibility for the line-to-gain crew in this situation, the line judge is charged with covering the goal and end lines.

THE BACK, SIDE, AND FIELD JUDGES

The back and side judges work on the same side as the line judge and are responsible for checking the number of defensive players before each snap and the number of eligible pass receivers. The field judge is responsible for kicks from scrimmage, forward passes along the defensive end line, and time on the field.

COMMON PENALTIES

Common football penalties and rules violations include: offsides, when a player crosses the line of scrimmage before the snap, a five-yard penalty; offensive holding, when an offensive player grabs a defensive player to prevent that player from executing a tackle, a five-yard penalty; defensive holding, when a defensive player illegally grabs an offensive blocker or a pass receiver, a 15-yard penalty; illegal motion or procedure, when an offensive player moves forward before the snap or when more or less than the required seven players line up at the line of scrimmage, a five-yard penalty; offensive pass interference, when a receiver is tackled or held before he has the opportunity to catch a passed ball, a 15-yard and loss-of-down penalty; and defensive pass interference, a 15-yard penalty in college football and, in professional ball, resulting in the spotting of the ball at the site of the foul.

UNIFORMS & EQUIPMENT

At most levels of competition, football officials wear black and white vertically striped shirts, black caps, socks, and shoes and white knickers. The referee, the head official, wears a white cap and uses a whistle to signal the start and end of play. Field officials use a white colored bean bag to mark the position where a kicked ball is first touched or a ball is fumbled; a light gold flag is thrown to the field to signal penalties. Both the referee and field judge carry a watch. The referee uses his watch as a cross-check on the play clock. The line judge cross-checks the official game clock.

Roger Perlmuter

FOOTBALL: A BRIEF HISTORY

The game Americans call football, a team sport deeply rooted in English rugby and soccer, made its debut at the intercollegiate level in 1869. The first game was played in New Brunswick, New Jersey by Rutgers and the College of New Jersey (Princeton), nine years after rugby was banned at Harvard due to the violent nature of the sport. The fledgling Intercollegiate Football Association was formed in 1876, although the game at that time had far more in common with rugby than with modern-day football. The rules of the game slowly evolved over the latter half of the 19th century, largely through the efforts of Walter Camp, a coach at Yale University. Camp is credited with the introduction of *downs*, the 11-man team, and the basis of the modern playing field. Camp's scoring system, however, reflected a heavy bias toward the kicking aspects of rugby, with five points awarded for a field goal and only two points for a touchdown.

Although modern football is considered an aggressive contact sport, 19th century football was far more brutal. Gang tackling and the infamous *flying wedge* offensive formation were commonplace in early football, and the effects of such practices were compounded by the rudimentary protective gear of the day. The violent nature of the game culminated in 1905 with 18 football-related deaths, and nearly 200 debilitating injuries reported in college games alone. In 1906, following a decree for football reform from President Theodore Roosevelt, the Intercollegiate Athletic Association of the United States (now the NCAA) was founded, and the rules of the game were modified to make the

game safer. Among the rules changes that emerged were the forward pass, the creation of the neutral zone, and the prohibition of gang tackling plays that had caused so many injuries in prior years.

Although professional players were introduced to the sport in 1895, the game did not achieve national prominence until many years later. In 1919, a group of players and football enthusiasts met in Canton, Ohio, to discuss the organization of football as a professional sport. Led by the legendary Jim Thorpe, the group went on to form the National Football League.

The great Jim Thorpe

SEASONS OF PLAY

Interscholastic football is a fall sport, typically beginning in early September and running through November. At the collegiate and professional levels, the game also is played through the fall; however, post-season play extends competition into January.

COMPETITION LEVELS & CERTIFICATION REQUIREMENTS

Pee Wee football leagues, including the Pop Warner Football League, are available for nine- and 10-year-olds. Players at this level typically are classified by weight to ensure safe and fair competition. Pop Warner officials are certified by the state upon successful completion of classes, clinics, and tests. Salaries of youth league officials typically start at $10 per game.

Both junior high and high school competition are regulated by individual state high school athletic associations, which adhere to the guidelines and rules put forth by the National Federation of State High School Associations. Certification requirements for football officials at this level include classwork, clinic attendance, written examinations, and field testing. Some schools, however, employ officials certified by independent contractors.

Junior high (7th and 8th grades) and high school junior varsity is the level at which most football officials attain their initial experience. Varsity football does not offer entry-level officiating positions; officials at this level normally are promoted, based on job performance, from the junior varsity level. High school junior varsity level officials earn approximately $17 to $28, and varsity football officials earn from $35 to $65, depending on the school boards through which officials are contracted.

The standards for collegiate competition are determined by college conferences and intercollegiate athletic associations, including the National Collegiate Athletic Association (NCAA), the College Football Association (CFA), and the National Association of Intercollegiate Athletics (NAIA). College officials are promoted from the ranks of high school varsity officials based on personal references and past performance. Scrimmage officiating and an extensive interview process are also prerequisites for advancement into collegiate-level officiating. Most college officials begin their careers at smaller division schools, earning berths with larger and more prestigious divisions as needed and if selected. Football officials employed by the major college conferences are paid from $500 to $700 per game.

Professional competition, including Arena, Canadian, and National Football League games are regulated by their affiliated organizations. In the United States, college-level officials typically officiate Arena football competition. They frequently are selected by league scouts, but candidates can apply directly to the Arena Football League. Similarly, the Canadian Football League selects officials from the ranks of officials affiliated with Canadian colleges. The National Football League is the most popular and prestigious level of competition for both players and officials. NFL officials typically are scouted and selected from the ranks of large college conference officials. If deemed qualified, prospective officials are then assigned to scrimmage competition; and, if an opening becomes available, they may earn a position. Salaries at the professional level range from approximately $300 and higher for Arena Football officials, between $300 and $625 in the Canadian Football League, to salaries of $600 to $4,000 per game for officials employed by the National Football League.

COMPENSATION

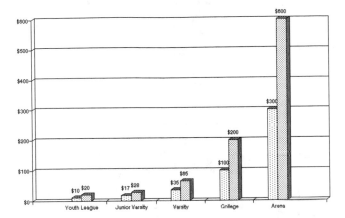

FOOTBALL OFFICIATING
COMPENSATION BY COMPETITION LEVEL: EVENT FEES

The graph above reflects average event fee ranges for football officials at all levels of competition. Officials working one game per week can expect to earn amounts ranging somewhere between the high and low ranges for their level. At the lower levels of competition, it is not uncommon for officials to work more than one game per week, thereby increasing their earnings. For example, an interscholastic official can easily pull in $130+ by working two high school games per week, which translates into over $500 per month during the football season. Not bad for roughly seven or eight hours of work. Compare this to a part-time job paying minimum wage of $4.75 per hour, which would yield less than $400 for 80 hours of work.

As you move up the officiating ladder to higher levels of competition, your pay goes up accordingly. College-level officials earn substantially more than interscholastic officials, but also must work their way up from smaller divisions to the more prestigious NCAA Division I. At nearly all levels of competition, officials receive a higher event fee for championship and playoff games than for regular season games.

The top earnings for officials occur at the professional level. The lucky few who make it into the National Football League command upwards of $4,000 per game after they have gained the requisite experience. Officials working the Super Bowl can earn as much as $11,000. To put this in perspective, NFL officials earn more in a 16-game season than most people make at a full-time job in an entire year.

FOOTBALL
LEVELS OF COMPETITION

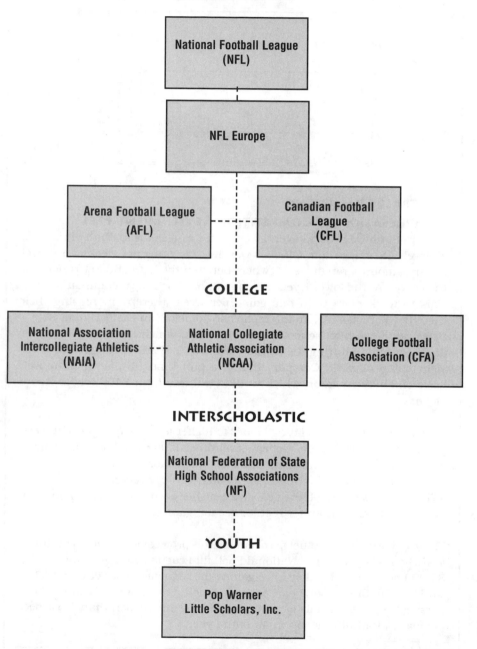

PROFESSIONAL

National Football League (NFL)

NFL Europe

Arena Football League (AFL)

Canadian Football League (CFL)

COLLEGE

National Association Intercollegiate Athletics (NAIA)

National Collegiate Athletic Association (NCAA)

College Football Association (CFA)

INTERSCHOLASTIC

National Federation of State High School Associations (NF)

YOUTH

Pop Warner Little Scholars, Inc.

OFFICIAL PROFILE:

DAVID PARRY

SUPERVISOR OF FOOTBALL OFFICIALS,
BIG TEN CONFERENCE

LR: How did you get involved in football and football officiating?

DP: I played football in junior high school and college. As I loved sports, especially football and basketball, I stayed close to the game by becoming an official.

LR: How long have you been a referee?

DP: My tenure as a referee is as follows: Football, Big Ten Supervisor for seven years, NFL side judge and back judge for 15 years, Mid-American Conference back judge for six years, and high school referee for 15 years; basketball, Mid-American Conference for 20 years, Big Ten for six years, and high school for 15 years.

LR: Describe the qualities of a successful football referee.

DP: Knowledge of the rules, passion for the game, courage and integrity, athletic appearance and fitness, mobility and agility, common sense and good judgment, poise and calmness, firmness and fairness and people-handling skills under stressful and emotional circumstances.

LR: What have been some highlights of your career?

DP: Officiating Super Bowl XVII involving the Washington Redskins and Miami Dolphins, 20 post-season basketball tournaments, 11 NFL playoff assignments, and being named Supervisor of the Big Ten Conference.

LR: What advice can you give to an individual starting out in football officiating?

DP: Study the rules, attend football clinics, maintain excellent fitness and appearance, seek the advice and counsel of veteran officials, study the qualities of successful and well known officials, maintain humility, develop a sense of humor, accept and learn from criticism, have patience, and commit to a long-term dedication.

RESOURCES

Regulatory Bodies:

Children's/Interscholastic

Pop Warner Little Scholars, Inc.
586 Middletown Blvd., Ste. C 100
Langhorne, PA 19047
Phone: (215) 752-2691 Fax: (215) 752-2879

National Federation of State High School
Associations (NFSHSA)
11724 NW Plaza Circle
P.O. Box 20626
Kansas City, MO 64195-0626
Phone: (816) 464-5400 Fax: (816) 464-5571
Internet: www.nfhs.org

Collegiate

National Association of Intercollegiate
Athletics (NAIA)
6120 S. Yale Ave., Ste. 1450
Tulsa, OK 74136-4223
Phone: (918) 494-8828 Fax: (918) 494-8841
Internet: www.naia.org

National Collegiate Athletic Association
(NCAA)
6201 College Blvd.
Overland Park, KS 66211-2422
Phone: (913) 339-1906 Fax: (913) 339-1950
Internet: www.ncaa.org

Professional

National Football League (NFL)
280 Park Ave.
New York, NY 10017
Phone: (212) 450-2000 Fax: (212) 681-7599

Arena Football League (AFL)
75 E. Wacker Dr., Ste. 400
Chicago, IL 60601
Phone: (312) 332-5510 Fax: (312) 332-5540

Canadian Football League (CFL)
110 Eglinton Ave. W., 5th Fl.
Toronto, Ontario M4R-1A3
Canada
Phone: (416) 322-9650 Fax: (416) 322-9651

NFL Europe
280 Park Ave.
New York, NY 10017
Phone: (212) 450-2107 Fax: (212) 681-7577

Officials Associations:

Professional Football Referees Association
9739 Keystone Ave.
Skokie, IL 60076
Phone: (847) 677-9739 Fax: (847) 475-5226

National Federation Interscholastic Officials
Association (NFIOA)
P.O. Box 20626
Kansas City, MO 64195
Phone (816) 464-5400 Fax: (816) 464-5571

FOOTBALL RULES BOOKS

The official rules book for Pop Warner youth football is available directly through Pop Warner Little Scholars. Interscholastic football rules are published by the National Federation of State High School Associations and updated annually. Copies of the current edition may be obtained through the NF. Cost is $5. The National Collegiate Athletic Association (NCAA) annually publishes a guide to collegiate football rules and interpretations. Copies of the current edition are $5.

FOOTBALL OFFICIATING SELF-TEST

1. What is the length of a football field?

2. How many players from one team are permitted on the field at one time?

3. What term is used to describe the areas in which touchdowns are scored?

4. How do referees indicate a foul has been committed?

5. What is the name used to describe the player who hikes the ball to the quarterback?

6. What is the penalty, in yards, for a false start?

7. What term is used to describe a player running parallel to the line of scrimmage before the snap?

8. What term is used to describe the area that, before the snap, extends from each tip of the football to the sidelines?

9. How many officials work a college football game?

10. True or false: In the NFL, a pass interference call is penalized 15 yards from the line of scrimmage.

11. True or false: There is a two-point conversion in high school football.

12. How long is a quarter in an NFL game?

13. True or false: In college competition, a receiver is required to touch one foot inbounds to complete a catch.

14. What is the call signaled by a referee who extends both arms sideways, parallel to the ground?

15. How many receivers can participate in one play?

16. True or false: A coach cannot call a time out when his team does not have possession of the ball.

17. True or false: The punter, at any level of competition, can not play another position.

18. True or false: In the NFL, a team plays twice a week for 16 weeks.

19. True or false: College football teams play teams both in and out of their conferences.

20. True or false: The quarterback has to throw the ball at least three times per game.

FOOTBALL OFFICIATING SELF-TEST ANSWERS

1. 100 yards; 2. 11; 3. End zone; 4. They throw a yellow *flag.* 5. Center; 6. Five yards; 7. Man in motion; 8. Neutral zone; 9. Seven; 10. False; 11. True; 12. 15 minutes; 13. True; 14. Unsportsmanlike conduct; 15. Five; 16. False; 17. False; 18. False; 19. True; 20. False

SCORING THE SELF-TEST

Incorrect Answers	Officiating Aptitude
0	Perfect: You have a solid knowledge of the game.
1-3	Average: You need to review the football rules book.
4-5	Below average: It's been some time since you've seen a football game.
6+	Far below average: You should consider officiating a different sport.

THE
GYMNASTICS
JUDGE

GYMNASTICS JUDGING AT A GLANCE

Entry Level: USA Gymnastics (USAG) Level 5

Minimum Age: 16 years old

Certification: Applicants must score 70% or better on a USAG written examination.

Average Pay: Level 5 judges earn $10 per hour. Pay goes up by level to $21 per hour at Level 10 and $25 per hour for Brevet judges.

Schedule: The majority of gymnastics competition is scheduled between January and April. Gymnastics meets generally run a minimum of three hours and, in some cases, can last all day.

Although male gymnasts compete at many levels, men's gymnastics programs have not attained the level of popularity of female competition.

GYMNASTICS: GENERAL INFORMATION

The most common form of gymnastics competition for women is known as *artistic gymnastics*. Female gymnasts perform on four apparatus: the vaulting horse, the uneven parallel bars, the balance beam, and the floor. A gymnast performs a routine which is a continuous series of movements, while being evaluated by a judge. The judge awards points on the basis of how well the gymnast executes the movements, or elements, in his or her routine. These moves, or elements, are categorized according to difficulty. Despite the obvious physical demands of gymnastics, the objective is to make the movements look as effortless as possible.

Although the majority of public interest lies in the performance of women's gymnastics, men also compete in the sport. The men's gymnastics program differs significantly from the women's program. Men compete on six apparatus: the vaulting horse, the rings, the floor, the pommel horse, the parallel bars, and the horizontal bar. The differences between men's and women's gymnastics are significant enough to require separate judging certifications. For information on becoming a judge for men's gymnastics, refer to the Reference section of this chapter.

Rhythmic gymnastics, a competition restricted to women, requires athletes to skillfully manipulate various apparatus while performing a routine on the floor mat. There are five types of apparatus: hoop, clubs, ribbon, rope, and ball. Rhythmic gymnasts are not allowed to perform flips or other acrobatic elements. The gymnasts concentrate on expressing their choreography, demonstrating mastery of the apparatus, and performing leaps, spins, and rolls.

JUDGING GYMNASTICS

A judge is responsible for scoring and evaluating individual routines based on four criteria:

3.0	Difficulty
.4	Bonus Points
2.0	Combination/Composition
4.6	Execution
(10.0	Total points possible)

According to the Gymnastics Code of Points, there are certain requirements for each routine. Difficulty points are earned by meeting the requirements with skills of high risk. Bonus points are earned through originality, special combinations, or extraordinary difficulty. Combination/composition refers to the rhythm and flow of the routine. Execution refers to the *cleanness* of a gymnast's performance. For example, bent arms and legs will result in deductions.

There is a wide variety of deductions that can be taken from a routine depending on the event, and each apparatus has specific deductions. For example, an *extra swing* on the uneven bars results in a 0.3 penalty from the gymnast's final score. On the floor exercise, if a gymnast steps out of bounds at any time during his or her routine, the judge raises a hand to note the mistake and deducts 0.1 from the routine. A standard deduction for all of the events is when a gymnast falls from the apparatus; a loss of 0.5 will be reflected in the gymnast's final score. A gymnastics judge must report to the Meet Director and is bound by the USA Gymnastics Code of Ethics.

SEASONS OF PLAY

Most gymnasts train year-round to maintain physical strength, awareness of technique, and overall conditioning. Although gymnastics is a year-round sport in terms of training, the vast majority of gymnastic competitions occur between January and April. Outside of Olympic competition, there are only limited opportunities for judging gymnastic events in the pre-season, which runs from August through December, and the off-season, between May and July.

UNIFORMS & EQUIPMENT

The attire and equipment used in gymnastics officiating are basic. Judges wear a standard navy blue blazer for identification. The majority of judges in the USA wear the official NAWGJ navy uniform (navy blazer with logo and navy skirt.) First-year judges can wear a white blouse and navy skirt. A judge generally sits at a table, facing the apparatus at an angle that will provide an adequate view of the gymnast's performance. The judge uses a notebook and pencil to write down the elements and deductions that the gymnast executes. USA Gymnastics requires that judges evaluate routines with a unique shorthand specially established for gymnastics judging. A green flag or the raising of a judge's hand signals the gymnast that he or she may begin a routine. Once a routine is completed, the gymnast salutes (raises his or her arm) and the judge's marks are tabulated. A final score is then posted by an assistant, and the judges prepare for the next competitor.

Roger Perlmuter

COMPETITION LEVELS & CERTIFICATION REQUIREMENTS

As in other sports, gymnasts compete at many levels, ranging from the most basic exercises to Olympic-level competition. USA Gymnastics Federation programs are divided into 10 levels. Gymnasts begin at

GYMNASTICS: A BRIEF HISTORY

The origin of gymnastics can be traced to ancient Greece, where physical fitness and development of the human form were considered ultimate virtues. Gymnastics at this time was more of an exercise routine than a performance and did not utilize the apparatus that has become standard today. Gymnastics subsequently was adopted by the Romans, who discovered the sport during their conquest of Greece around 146 B.C. Interest in gymnastics greatly diminished after the fall of ancient Rome between the years 400 and 900 A.D., and was not revitalized for some 1,000 years. Friedreich Hahn of Germany is widely credited with the introduction of modern artistic gymnastics apparatus, including the pommel horse, parallel bars, rings, and balance beam in the early 19th century. Hahn opened the first modern gymnastics clubs in Berlin around 1810. The sport soon spread to other parts of Europe and then to the United States after the Civil War.

Men's artistic gymnastics events were included in the first modern Olympic games, which were held in 1896. Women's artistic gymnastics events were introduced to Olympic competition in 1928 and have become one of the most closely followed events of the Summer games. Gymnastics gained tremendous international prominence through the emergence of several talented, high-profile female competitors. Rhythmic gymnastics was not included in the Olympic games until 1984 and has yet to develop the stature of the artistic version.

According to USA Gymnastics, the governing body of the sport, an estimated 62,000 athletes are registered in competitive gymnastics programs today. Over 5,000 sanctioned competitions and events are scheduled each year.

Larissa Latynina of the URS, pictured at the 1964 Tokyo Olympics, is considered the most successful Olympic gymnast. She won 18 medals.

Level 1, the most basic level, and advance to Level 10 based on their skills. Levels 1 to 4 are for training and are the more basic levels. Levels 5 to 7 are based on what is known as *compulsory competition*. Compulsories are routines that are the same for Level 5 to 7 gymnasts. At the more advanced levels (8 to 10), a gymnast completes *optional routines* during which he or she can perform elements that best suit his or her abilities. It is also at these more advanced levels that gymnasts can join high school programs and compete for college scholarships. The highest level a gymnast can reach is known as the *elite* status. It is from this group of athletes that the United States Olympic team is chosen. While gymnastics judging opportunities exist at every level, officials generally start at the lower levels.

Listed below are the general qualifications for becoming a gymnastics official. Once an applicant becomes certified at any of the various levels, he or she is then certified to judge at that level in any state. The certification process begins at the first competition level (Level 5). The highest level of gymnastics official is the *Brevet judge*. USA Gymnastics selects Olympic judges from Brevet status judges.

LEVEL 5: This is an entry level position.
- The minimum age is 16
- Applicant must pass a written exam with a score of 70% or higher
- Once certified, an official must judge at least two competitions before he or she is eligible to test into Level 6/7

LEVEL 6/7: This is not an entry level position.
- The age minimum is 16
- Must be certified at Level 5
- Must pass a written exam with a score of 75% or higher

LEVEL 8: This is not an entry level position.
- Minimum age is 16
- Applicant must take a written exam and a practical exam in which a minimum score of 70% must be achieved on both
- Must maintain *active status* for one competition year (January 1 through December 31) before testing into Level 9 (active status requires an official judge at least two competitions over a one-year period)
- A Level 8 judge must pass the level 6/7 test before eligible to test into Level 9

LEVEL 9: This is not an entry level position.
- Minimum age is 18
- Required to have been a judge at both the Level 5 and 8 positions for at least one year
- Must pass a written and practical exam with a score of 75% or higher on each
- Must maintain active status for at least one year before he or she is eligible to test into Level 10

LEVEL 10: This is not an entry level position.
- A minimum age of 20 is required
- Must have been a Level 9 judge for one year
- Must pass a written exam and a practical exam with scores above 80%
- After being certified at Level 10, an official can judge at Level 8, 9, and 10 (All NCAA college gymnastic officials have reached Level 10 status).

ELITE: This level of judging is achieved by invitation only of USA Gymnastics.
- After being selected into this group of judges, a USA Gymnastics course must be taken and appropriate exams passed.
- A Level 10 judge must work at Level 10 for a minimum of eight years before he or she is eligible to take the elite certification course

Although the majority of these qualifications apply to anyone interested in becoming a gymnastics official, there are special circumstances that apply to former gymnasts and coaches. A gymnast who has reached the Elite Level, past or present, is immediately eligible to test into Level 10 status. Similarly, a coach who has trained an athlete qualified for *Classic* competitions at the Elite Level is also eligible to begin testing at Level 10.

GYMNASTICS
LEVELS OF COMPETITION*

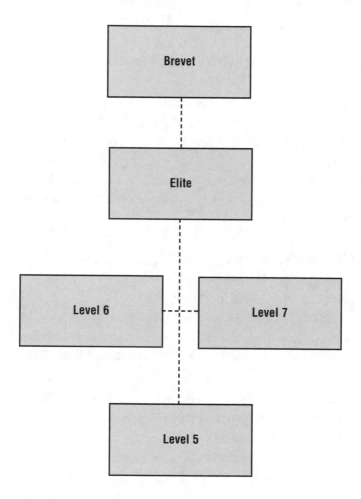

*As recognized by USA Gymnastics

COMPENSATION

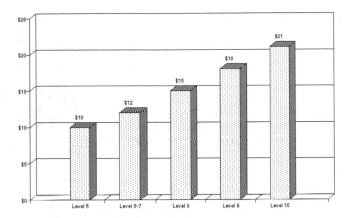

GYMNASTICS OFFICIATING
COMPENSATION BY COMPETITION LEVEL: HOURLY RATES

The graph above provides a comparison of hourly rates for USA Gymnastics judges at all levels.

A gymnastics judge can easily pull in $150 to $200 by working two meets per week, which translates into over $650 per month during the prime gymnastics season which runs from January through April. Not bad for roughly 40 hours of work per month. Compare this to a part time job paying a minimum wage of $4.75 per hour, which would yield less than $400 over a month for 80 hours of work.

As you advance to higher levels, your pay goes up accordingly. Level 10 judges work at more than double the rate of Level 5 judges. In addition, Level 10 judges may officiate at seven different levels, Levels 5 through 10 and college meets, thus allowing more opportunities to earn money. The top earnings in gymnastics judging go to Brevet judges who earn $25 per hour. In addition to hourly fees, gymnastics judges at all levels are also compensated for travel expenses. For competition more than 30 miles from the judge's residence, a standard fee of $.30 per mile is paid by the Meet Director. If an overnight stay is required, the judge's lodging is also paid by the meet director, plus an allowance of $10 per meal.

**Hourly compensation information courtesy USA Gymnastics
and current through July 31, 1997.**

OFFICIAL PROFILE:
BETTY SROUFE

NATIONAL ASSOCIATION OF WOMEN'S GYMNASTICS JUDGING (NAWGJ)

LR: Describe a day in the life of a judge.

BS: A day . . . it usually starts days prior with preparation and review of the level of competition you have been assigned to. This is most important to every judge.

The day begins with travel to the site, either in a car with a car-pool of other judges or by air travel. Arrive at the site and then dress in official NAWGJ uniform. There is always a judges meeting prior to every meet. Usually half an hour to one hour in length. It is also a judge's obligation to arrive a minimum of one half hour prior to march-out time. Many times, we are asked to arrive earlier, depending on the level of the meet. The purpose of the judges meeting is to go over rules, equipment, and the actual way the meet it set up, as well as chief judge and acting judges going over the event they will be judging. All of this preparation helps toward a smooth running meet, as well as minimizing the stress factor.

Most meets have a minimum of two sessions, usually two and one-half to three hours in length, and a lunch break of 45 minutes to an hour. Some meets run three sessions per day with two one-hour breaks worked into the schedule. A judge is expected to be focused and to be as perfect as possible in his or her decision-making, no matter the length of time spent sitting in the judges chair and judging. It is easy to understand why a judge needs to be dedicated and love the sport of gymnastics – this is just one day of many.

LR: What is the best part about being a gymnastics judge?

BS: The challenge and the opportunity to see the best gymnasts up close. The judging friends that you've made from all over the country and the opportunity to travel are also exciting, though tiresome at times. Actually, the camaraderie, the laughing, the fun are parts that make it all worth every stressful moment.

Every meet is a challenge and every meet is a favorite memory – each special and different. There is always a memory from every meet you judge.

LR: What is your most memorable experience as a judge?

BS: I have been lucky enough over these 20 plus years of judging to have many, but if I were to pick one it would be the 1984 Olympics in Los Angeles: having the opportunity to work with judges from all over the world and being there when our own gymnast, Mary Lou Retton, took the gold medal and seeing her score her 10.0 in vaulting. What a thrill that was for all of us!

LR: How did you get started?

BS: Well, my husband, Bud, was a gymnast in school, so he knew the sport. I was in the dance field, owner of dance studios, as well as a high school physical education teacher. This combination worked, I guess, along with hard work and study, because we became rated gymnastics judges in 1968. We both actually started coaching high school gymnastics in 1966. I believe that might have been the trigger for us to become judges as well.

LR: How many years have you been judging?

BS: Actually, I've been judging since 1968 and received my national rating in 1972. I have held an elite and national elite rating since 1976.

LR: Do you have any advice for someone interested in becoming a gymnastics official?

BS: The best advice I have for anyone starting out in judging is do it mostly because you love the sport, you love kids, you can handle stress, and you have the stamina to last through thick and thin. Be willing to put a lot of time into studying and observing and attending workshops, clinics, symposia, congresses. You can never stop studying and learning. This sport is ever changing, and we do have rules changes and re-certification every four years. It takes a lot, but the rewards are great (at least I think so). I must because I've been doing it for over 20 years.

LR: Do you consider gymnastics officiating a potential career for someone interested in judging?

BS: No, the sport of gymnastics is very seasonal, not a full-time job so to speak, especially for a judge. I think most judges consider it a good supplemental income, but mostly it is a hobby. Others may feel differently about this, this is only my opinion.

LR: What duties do you perform and/or other titles do you hold?

BS: I am presently executive national secretary/treasurer for the National Association of Women's Gymnastics Judging (NAWGJ). We service approximately 1,800 judges in the USA. I have had this elected executive board position since 1974. I am vice president of education/evaluation with Judges Certification, Inc. This organization certifies all judges in the USA. I've held this appointed position since 1980. I am one of the Ohio women who helped in the formation of the High School Gymnastics Programs in Ohio in 1968; I served on the OHSAA board for Women's Gymnastics from 1968-76, was elected OHSAA board chairman for Women's Gymnastics for 1974-75; I was appointed state USGF technical director for Ohio in 1972 and remained so until 1976; and I designed and developed the NAWGJ Judges Uniform in 1976 and was in charge of its distribution until 1992. I judge all levels of meets: local, statewide, regional, and national. I do not judge international competitions. My love for this sport has no bounds. One of my biggest ambitions has always been to help develop and train and certify as many judges as possible so that the young gymnasts can be judged as fairly as is humanly possible.

RESOURCES

Regulatory Bodies

USA Gymnastics
Pan American Plaza, Ste. 300
201 S. Capital Ave.
Indianapolis, IN 46225
Phone: (317) 237-5050 Fax: (317) 237-5069
Internet: www.usa~gymnastics.org

Federation Internationale de Gymnastique
(FIG)
Rue des Oeuches 10
Case Postale 359
2740 Moutier 1
Switzerland
Phone: (41-32) 494-6410
Fax: (41-32) 494-6419
Internet: www.worldsport.com/sports/
gymnastics/home.html

Officials Associations

National Association of Women's Gymnastics
Judging (NAWGJ)
Betty Sroufe, National Secretary/Treasurer
2096 Rolling Hills Blvd.
Fairfield, OH 45014
Phone: (513) 829-5671 Fax: (513) 829-4959

National Association of Sports Officials
(NASO)
2017 Lanthrop Ave.
Racine, WI 53405
Phone: (414) 632-5448

Networking Contacts

Carolyn Bowers
Brevet Judge
1996 Olympic Official
1315 Bourgogne Ave.
Bowling Green, OH 43402
Phone: (419) 352-6179

Judy Dobransky
Brevet Judge
Certification Test Administrator
3446 Gordon Dr.
Sterling Heights, MI 48077

Amy Rager
Brevet Judge
Certification Test Administrator
Judging Director, Region 7
Fax: (301) 384-5566
e-mail: arager@ids2.idsonline.com

GYMNASTICS RULES BOOKS

The *Code of Points* is the official scoring manual of gymnastics competition. The Code sets forth the standards by which a gymnast's routine is evaluated and features illustrations and explanations of each move. The Code is an excellent source of information on job functions and standards of conduct.

The *Code of Points* is revised every four years. The current edition, published in 1997, can be purchased through USA Gymnastics for $39.95. To order, call (800) 487-2496.

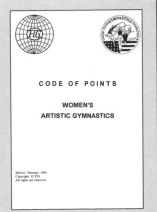

CODE OF POINTS

WOMEN'S
ARTISTIC GYMNASTICS

Edition: February 1994
Copyright © FIG
All rights are reserved.

GYMNASTICS JUDGING SELF-TEST

1. Name the four apparatus on which women gymnasts perform.

2. True or false: Women have one chance to perform their vault.

3. Who was the first female gymnast to score a perfect 10.0?

4. What is the minimum age required to become an entry-level gymnastics judge?

5. True or false: The balance beam is four inches wide.

6. Name the coach who defected from Romania in the 1970s and coached Nadia Commenici, Mary Lou Retton, and Kim Zmeskal.

7. True or false: The standard deduction for a fall from an apparatus is one point.

8. Who won the all-around title in the 1984 Olympic Games?

9. How many gymnasts make up the U.S. Olympic team?

10. Is it possible to receive a college scholarship in gymnastics?

11. True or false: The tumbling portion of the floor exercise counts more than the dance elements.

12. How old must a gymnast be to compete in the Olympics?

13. True or false: Gymnasts are required to use floor music that includes lyrics.

14. Name the official rules book for gymnastics.

15. Once a gymnast has fallen from an apparatus, how much time does he or she have to remount?

16. True or false: To become an Olympic Level Judge, an official must have been a gymnast at the Elite level.

17. If a gymnast steps out of bounds on his or her floor routine, how much of a deduction is taken from the score?

18. How many levels of competition are there in the USA Gymnastics program?

19. At the college level, how many gymnasts compete in each event? How many of those scores count towards the team score?

20. In what season do most gymnastic competitions take place?

GYMNASTICS JUDGING SELF-TEST ANSWERS:

1. Vault, uneven parallel bars, balance beam, and floor exercise; 2. False; 3. Nadia Commenici; 4. 16; 5. True; 6. Bela Karoli; 7. False; 8. Mary Lou Retton; 9. Six; 10. Yes; 11. False; 12. 16 years old; 13. False; 14. The Code of Points; 15. 30 seconds; 16. False; 17. One tenth of a point; 18. 10 plus the Elite Level; 19. Six girls compete, Five scores count; 20. Winter/spring

SCORING THE SELF-TEST

Incorrect Answers	Officiating Aptitude
0	Perfect: You have a solid knowledge of the sport.
1-3	Average: You need to review the Code of Points.
4-5	Below average: It's been some time since you've seen a gymnastics meet.
6+	Far below average: You should consider officiating a different sport.

THE
ICE HOCKEY
REFEREE

ICE HOCKEY OFFICIATING AT A GLANCE

Entry Level: Recreational and youth leagues; junior high and high school

Minimum Age: 16 in most states

Certification: State (high school) athletic association certification required for junior high and high school officiating in most states (see Section V). USA Hockey certification required for Levels 1-4.

Average Pay: Ice hockey officials earn $8 to $40 per game in youth leagues. Interscholastic officials earn $35 to $70 per game. Major college ice hockey officials earn $150 to $200 per game. The pay for professional level officials varies depending on experience, but seasoned officials can gross well over $200,000 per season.

Schedule: The interscholastic and collegiate ice hockey regular seasons generally run from mid-November through late March.

Ice hockey is a fast-moving sport that challenges the referee's skating ability as much as it does his officiating skills.

ICE HOCKEY: GENERAL INFORMATION

Ice hockey is one of the fastest moving of sports, challenging for players and officials alike. The game is played on an ice rink by two teams of five skaters who score points by moving a rubber disk or puck with a wooden stick into a netted goal defended by the opposing team's goal tender or goalie. The goalie is responsible for blocking the puck, using any part of the body, and preventing the offensive team from scoring. The puck remains in continuous motion. Play of the puck off the rink walls prevents stopping or slowing of competition for out-of-bounds play. Unlike any other major sport, substitution players move on and off the ice while the game is in progress. Games typically are played over the course of three 20-minute periods with 10- to 15-minute intermissions after the first and second.

OFFICIATING ICE HOCKEY

In addition to a thorough knowledge of the game rules, hockey officials must possess exceptional skating skills in order to maintain a position within sight of play action. Like soccer, the hockey official requires a great deal of stamina as the players are in almost continuous motion during the match. And, as in any sport in which players wear heavy protective equipment, hockey officials are in constant danger of sustaining serious injury if they collide with a player. The puck itself can become a deadly weapon, reaching speeds near 100 mph or higher. To minimize the risk of injury, hockey officials must be constantly alert and focused on the action. Beyond the competitive and mechanical aspects of hockey officiating, the sport is notorious for flagrant and outrageous conduct (including fights and brawls) on the part of the players. The old adage, "I went to see a fight and a hockey game broke out," rings true for many a hockey official. Consequently, hockey officials face a more difficult task than other sports officials in maintaining both the respect of the players and control of the game.

ICE HOCKEY OFFICIALS

Ice hockey requires a variety of officials to keep track of the game. On the rink, the referee (on skates) is the chief official and has final say in the case of any disputed call. The referee controls the game, supervises play, and calls all penalties. The referee uses a wide variety of hand signals, most of which are used to call out fouls and illegal conduct. The referee is assisted by two linesmen (also on skates) who watch for off-sides infractions, icing violations, and other rules violations.

Depending on the level of competition, up to five additional non-skating officials are employed in ice hockey. Off the ice, the timekeeper keeps the official game time, starting and stopping the clock as instructed by the referee and linesmen, and signaling the beginning and end of each period. The penalty timekeeper is responsible for tracking the time players are forced off the ice as a result of fouls; the official scorer records goals scored and player assists on scores. Two goal judges, one positioned behind each goal in a screened cage, are responsible for determining whether the puck crosses the goal line, between the goal posts and under the crossbar.

COMMON PENALTIES

Most rules violations result from excessive body contact between players and improper player position on the rink. For some rules infractions, including tripping, holding, and fighting, the offending players are forced off the ice for periods ranging from two to 10 minutes, and the penalized team must play shorthanded. Play begins with the face-off at the center of the rink. The puck is faced-off by the referee or a linesman who drops the puck on the ice between the sticks of the two players (one from each team) facing off.

SEASONS OF PLAY

Hockey primarily is a winter sport and is included in the games of the Winter Olympics. However, USA Hockey-sponsored hockey is an event of the National Sports Festival, a competition conducted during the summer in non-Olympic years. Interscholastic ice hockey generally is played from mid-November through March.

UNIFORMS & EQUIPMENT

On-ice officials wear black and white, vertically striped shirts and black pants. The referee is distinguished from the linesmen by orange stripes worn on both shirt sleeves. On-ice officials' ice skates are black, conform to a design approved by the rules committee, and are equipped with approved safety heel tips. The referee and the linesmen should wear black hockey helmets.

The referee uses a whistle to signal the start and stop of play. Timekeepers use a stop watch to track official game and penalty times.

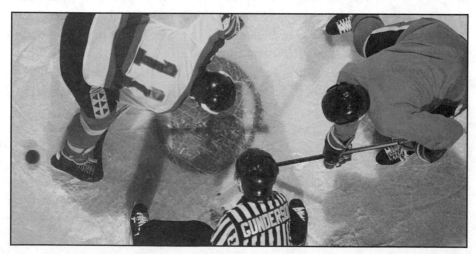

COMPETITION LEVELS & CERTIFICATION REQUIREMENTS

Initiation programs sponsored by USA Hockey are available for children four years old and younger. Youth programs have been established for several age groups: eight years old and under, 10 and under, 12 and under, 14 and under, and 17 years old and younger. Junior hockey competition includes three divisions for players 20 years old and under. Junior A and Junior B programs require paid spectator admission. Junior A referees earn $90 to $200 per game, while the pay for Junior B officials ranges from $50 to $100 per game. Junior C competition is considered recreational, and referees at this level earn from $40 to $70 a game.

The Amateur Hockey Association of the United States conducts National Championships in 12 age classifications: Mites for boys nine and under; Squirts for boys 10 and 11, girls eight to 12; PeeWees, boys 12 and 13, girls 13 to 15; Bantams, boys 14 and 15; Midgets for men 16 and 17, and women 11 to 19; Juniors for men aged 17 to 19; and Seniors for men and women older than 20.

USA Hockey and the Canadian Hockey Association have established four levels of certification for officials. Certification levels are determined by an applicant's score on an open book, written examination. Level 1 certification requires a score of 70% to 84%. Level 1 officials are authorized to work at games for youth age 12 and younger. Level 2 certification is earned by applicants scoring 85% to 89% who are then qualified to officiate games for players age 14 and younger. Level 3 officials score 90% or above on the open-book exam and are qualified to officiate play for youth age 17 and under. For certification at Level 4, applicants must score 90% or above on the open-book test, 40 out of 50 on a closed book exam, and pass an ice skating evaluation. Level 4 officials are certified for participation at all USA Hockey levels. Forty-four percent of the 16,500 officials currently registered by USA Hockey are under age 18. Event fees for USA Hockey referees vary widely depending on geographic location and the level of competition. Fees paid to ice hockey referees in USA Hockey youth programs range from $8 to $40 per game.

ICE HOCKEY: A BRIEF HISTORY

The origins of modern ice hockey can be traced to mid-19th century Canada where the first organized hockey match took place between Canadian soldiers around 1855. During the 1870s, students from McGill University altered the original rules for field hockey, replacing the rubber ball with a puck, decreasing the team size from nine to six players, and, most notably, adapting the game for play on ice. The first official game to be played under the new rules took place in 1875 and led to the organization of the first amateur hockey league in 1885. Hockey's prestigious Stanley Cup was created around 1893 by Lord Stanley of Preston, Governor General of Canada, as a reward to Canada's best hockey team.

The first United States game was played in 1895 and in 1909 a professional league of four teams, the National Hockey Association (NHA), was formed. The National Hockey League (NHL) was created in 1917 to represent the interests of Canadian hockey teams; the first American hockey team to join the NHL was the Boston Bruins in 1924. The NHL exists to this day as the primary regulatory body of professional ice hockey. Lord Stanley's famous cup is now presented each year to the winner of the NHL championship game.

The Amateur Hockey Association of the United States (AHAUS) was established in 1937 and is the national organizing body for amateur hockey. AHAUS is the exclusive United States representative of the International Ice Hockey Federation (IIHF) and is responsible for organizing teams for annual competition during the World Championships.

A member of the Japanese Olympic ice hockey team, 1936

Interscholastic ice hockey is regulated by state athletic associations. To work as an official at this level, most states require certification by the state athletic association in accordance with National Federation of State High School Associations rules tests, clinic attendance, and association membership. Interscholastic ice hockey referees earn $35 to $70 per game.

At the collegiate level, ice hockey is governed by the National Collegiate Athletic Association. Officials at the collegiate level generally are selected by individual college conferences from among high school and USA Junior hockey officials. Collegiate level officials often are scouted for minor league work. College level ice hockey officials earn $150 to $200 per game, plus expenses, during the regular season. NCAA post-season championship competition pays even more.

Minor league hockey programs have been established by the American Hockey League, the International Hockey League, the East Coast Hockey League, and the Central Hockey League. The East Coast Hockey League is a minor league professional hockey organization which employs Level 4 officials certified by USA Hockey. The league conducts camps and clinics for prospective officials. American Hockey League linesmen are chosen from among those at the collegiate level or from other professional leagues. AHL referees are supplied by the National Hockey League as part of an officials development program. International Hockey League officials typically are referred by USA Hockey, college conferences, or the Canadian Hockey Association.

At the professional level, ice hockey is governed by the National Hockey League. National Hockey League referees and linesmen are selected primarily from certified officials participating in development programs sponsored by the AHL, IHL, USAH, and CHA. Officiating at this professional level of competition requires full-time commitment. However, professional hockey referees are well compensated. Starting salaries for NHL apprentice officials average $50,000 per year; the NHL starts experienced referees at $80,000 per year.

COMPENSATION

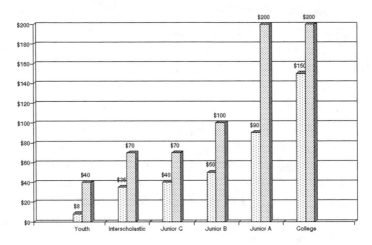

ICE HOCKEY OFFICIATING
COMPENSATION BY COMPETITION LEVEL: EVENT FEES

The graph above reflects average event fee ranges for ice hockey officials at various levels of competition. Officials working one game per week can expect to earn amounts ranging between the high and low ranges for their level. At the lower levels of competition, it is not uncommon for officials to work more than one game per week, thereby increasing their earnings. For example, an interscholastic official easily can pull in $70 to $140 by working two high school games per week, which translates into over $280 to $560 per month during the ice hockey season. Not bad for roughly seven or eight hours of work per week. Compare this to a part-time job paying a minimum wage of $4.75 per hour, which would yield less than $400 over a month for 80 hours of work.

As you move up the officiating ladder to higher levels of competition, your pay goes up accordingly. College level officials earn substantially more than interscholastic officials, but also must work their way up from smaller divisions to the more prestigious NCAA Division I. At nearly all levels of competition, officials receive a higher event fee for championship and playoff games than for the regular season.

The top earnings for ice hockey officials occur at the professional level. Those who advance to the National Hockey League start at $80,000 per year ($50,000 in the NHL's apprentice program). As they build tenure and experience, NHL officials can easily pull in $220,000 or more per year.

ICE HOCKEY
LEVELS OF COMPETITION

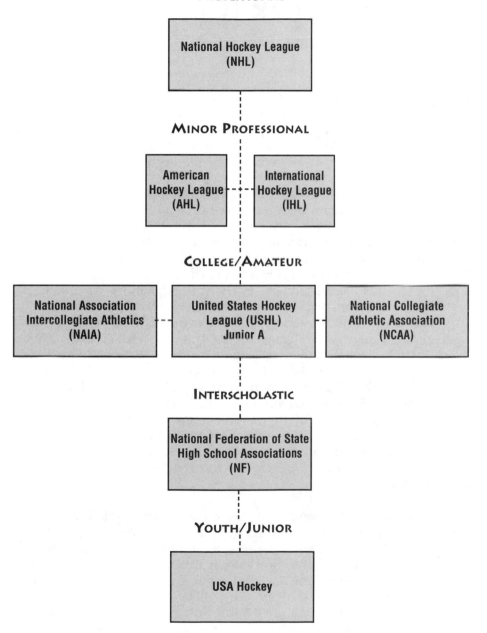

PROFESSIONAL

National Hockey League
(NHL)

MINOR PROFESSIONAL

American Hockey League (AHL)

International Hockey League (IHL)

COLLEGE/AMATEUR

National Association Intercollegiate Athletics (NAIA)

United States Hockey League (USHL) Junior A

National Collegiate Athletic Association (NCAA)

INTERSCHOLASTIC

National Federation of State High School Associations (NF)

YOUTH/JUNIOR

USA Hockey

OFFICIAL PROFILE:
MARK RILEY
REFEREE, EAST COAST HOCKEY LEAGUE

LR: How did you get started in officiating?

MR: I've played ice hockey all my life and I love it. In fact, I played Division III hockey for Curry College outside of Boston, but then I realized I would never make the pros as an athlete. My brother had been officiating for years at the high school and college level, and he is the person who encouraged me to get involved. During my senior year in college, I began officiating youth hockey. I did this for three years on a part-time basis.

LR: Mark, tell me about your career path so far.

MR: After my three years in youth hockey, I attended the Eastern Regional Camp in Lake Placid, NY. The following year, I officiated high school level games. After this season, I attended the National Camp, also held in Lake Placid. I was very fortunate at this point in my career, because after the camp, I went from officiating junior varsity games to the United States Hockey League (USHL), the top junior A league in the country. (There are 3 junior A leagues in the United States.) I worked full time as a referee for this league. I then went to Select Camp in Colorado Springs. This was an intense camp, with only 12 guys, ages ranging from 22 to 30. It was a great learning experience. Beginning in fall, 1996 I will be working full time for the East Coast Hockey League. I will need to relocate to Raleigh, NC in order to be centrally located so that I can drive to all my assignments.

LR: What will be the next rung on your officiating ladder?

MR: The next level, which is what I am aiming towards, will be to get signed as a trainee with the National Hockey League. After a trainee is signed, they work East Coast and IHL games, then move up to American Hockey League games; and finally, if they are very talented and lucky, they will be called up to the National Hockey League. There are 15 full time refs in the NHL, and you have to wait until someone retires or gets fired in order to move up.

LR: What is your favorite part about being a referee?

MR: Being able to stay in close contact with the sport I've loved all my life. I love to be on the ice and right in the action, too. I worked at a bank for three years after college, while I officiated part time. It is a great feeling to be able to earn a living as a referee! I look forward to every game.

LR: What is the worst part of being a referee?

MR: Definitely the travel. I got married this summer and it is difficult to have to travel all the time, as well as to relocate. Luckily, I have a supportive wife who understands the demands of this career.

LR: Describe your most memorable experience as an official.

MR: Actually, two stand out. Last season, I officiated my first professional game for the Central League. This was the highlight of my career so far, as the hockey is played at an extremely high level.

Another memorable experience was game four of the U. S. Hockcy League (USHL) finals, between Green Bay and Rochester. There were 18 penalties in the first period, and the crowd was going wild. As I walked past the Green Bay locker room during half-time, the Green Bay coach started yelling at me and had to be restrained by the linesmen. Then, the coach had to be calmed down by the sheriff and was thrown out of the game! By the end of the game, which had a total of 42 penalties, the crowd was throwing cigarette lighters, coins, and other items at me and chanting,"Riley Sucks!" It was an incredible experience.

LR: Tell me about a typical day as an official.

MR: During the season, I get up and have a good breakfast because officiating is so physically demanding. I then watch TV, relax, or do errands. I have lunch and then begin planning my work day, which usually involves extensive travel and driving. Many of my games are at least a two or three hour drive. I drive to the ice rink where the game will be held, where I do a stretching routine and look over my rule books. After driving for a few hours, it is important to stretch and get warmed up before going onto the ice. The games usually last about two hours, 15 minutes.

Last season, I would drive home after games, which would be another two to three hours in the car, late at night. This year will be better, since the league has apartments set up in several cities as well as compensation for hotel expenses.

RESOURCES

Regulatory Bodies

Interscholastic/Children's

National Federation of State High School
Associations (NFSHSA)
11724 NW Plaza Circle
P.O. Box 20626
Kansas City, MO 64195-0626
Phone: (816) 464-5400 Fax: (816) 464-5571
Internet: www.nfhs.org

National

USA Hockey, Inc.
1775 Bob Johnson Dr.
Colorado Springs, CO 80906
Phone: (719) 576-8724 Fax: (719) 538-1160
e-mail: usah@usahockey.org
Internet: www.usahockey.org

International

International Ice Hockey Federation (IIHF)
Parkring 11
8002 Zurich
Switzerland
Phone: (41-1) 289-8600 Fax: (41-1) 289-8622
Internet: www.iihf.com

Professional/Minor Professional

American Hockey League (AHL)
425 Union St.
West Springfield, MA 01089
Phone: (413) 781-2030 Fax: (413) 733-4767

Hockey North America
11501 Sunset Hill Rd., 4th Fl.
Reston, VA 22190-4704
Phone: (703) 471-0400 Fax: (703) 904-7160
Internet: www.hna.com

International Hockey League (IHL)
1395 E. 12 Mile Rd.
Madison Hts., MI 48071
Phone: (248) 546-3230 Fax: (248) 546-1811
Internet: www.theihl.com

National Hockey League (NHL)
1251 Avenue of the Americas, 47th Fl.
New York, NY 10020
Phone: (212) 789-2000 Fax: (212) 789-2020

Amateur

United States Hockey League
P.O. Box 1187
Hayward, WI 54843
Phone: (715) 634-6226 Fax: (715) 634-5755

ICE HOCKEY RULES BOOKS

Rules books are available through the regulatory bodies
listed in the Resources section. Revisions and modifications are made frequently, so it is best to order the most
current rules book available for the level of competition
in which you are involved. For example, the National
Federation of State High School Associations publishes
a rules book pertinent to interscholastic competition.
Cost of the 1999 edition is $5. The cost of the NCAA
men's ice hockey rules book is $5.

ICE HOCKEY OFFICIATING SELF-TEST

1. True or false: It is against the rules to take a goalie out of the game and replace him or her with another forward.

2. How long is a full size hockey rink?
   a. 150 feet; b. 175 feet; c. 200 feet

3. How many players play on each team at one time?

4. What is it called when the referee drops the puck between two players to begin the game?

5. True or false: A player can knock the puck down with his or her hand.

6. Does a team have to wait for a stop in the game to substitute a player?

7. True or false: In the NHL, fighting is penalized by an automatic ejection.

8. Where is the neutral zone on the rink?
   a. At the visitors end; b. On the sides of the ice; c. In the middle of the ice

9. Which of the following is not a penalty in ice hockey?
   a. Off sides; b. Charging; c. Tripping; d. Checking

10. How long is a player penalized for a minor penalty?

11. How long is a period in the NHL?

12. How many face-off circles are on the ice?

13. Can a goalie score a goal?

14. Can a player deliberately kick the puck into the goal?

15. If a player has a broken stick, he or she must:
a. Play without a stick until a new one is made available; b. Leave the ice; c. Be penalized two minutes for lack of proper equipment

16. If the puck goes out of the rink, what happens?

17. True or false: A team can call time out whenever it feels the need.

18. Can a player throw a hockey stick to stop the puck?

19. How long does a team have to rest between periods?

20. What is the term for when a player scores three goals in one game?

ICE HOCKEY OFFICIATING SELF-TEST ANSWERS

1. False; 2. c; 3. Six; 4. Face off; 5. True; 6. No; 7. False; 8. c; 9. d; 10. Two minutes; 11. 20 minutes; 12. Five; 13. Yes; 14. No; 15. a; 16. The teams have a face-off; 17. False; 18. No; 19. 15 minutes; 20. Hat trick

SCORING THE SELF-TEST

Incorrect Answers	Officiating Aptitude
0	Perfect: You have a solid knowledge of the game.
1-3	Average: You need to review the hockey rules book.
4-5	Below average: It's been some time since you've seen a hockey game.
6+	Far below average: You should consider officiating a different sport.

THE
SOCCER
REFEREE

SOCCER OFFICIATING AT A GLANCE

Entry Level: Interscholastic high school and junior high, recreational and youth soccer

Minimum Age: No minimum age for USSF Associate Referee certification

Certification: State (high school) athletic association certification required for interscholastic officiating in most states or certification through USSF as Associate or Referee Class 2 (see Section V for state certification requirements in your area).

Average Pay: Varies widely by area; at the high school varsity level, soccer referees typically earn $35 to $55 per game. Amateur and collegiate soccer pay ranges from $40 to $70.

Schedule: Interscholastic soccer is a fall sport, beginning in early September and running through November 30. Indoor soccer is becoming a popular winter sport. Olympic soccer is included in the summer games.

Michigan State High School Association
Soccer truly is an international sport and is becoming increasingly popular at the youth and interscholastic levels throughout the United States.

SOCCER: GENERAL INFORMATION

The game of soccer (once referred to as *association football*) is played by two teams of 11 players each. The objective of the game is to score points by maneuvering a round leather ball into the opposing team's goal. A goalkeeper for each team is assigned to protect the goal, and he or she alone is allowed to play the ball with his or her hands. The remaining players on each team are designated as defenders, midfielders, and forwards. These players may kick the ball or play it off their bodies but may not touch it with their hands or arms.

In soccer, play is continuous, stopping only when a goal is scored, the ball goes out of bounds, or a foul is called. The game involves considerable movement as players criss-cross the field many times during the course of the game. A typical soccer game consists of two 45-minute halves with a short half-time break. Outdoor soccer is played on a field measuring approximately 100 yards in length by 80 yards in width with a netted goal located at each end. Indoor soccer generally is played on more compact fields.

OFFICIATING SOCCER

Officiating a soccer match requires a high degree of physical conditioning and stamina in order to keep pace with the action as the players are in nearly constant motion during the match. The referee has no fixed position on the field and must move with the flow of the action. This requires stamina, focus, and the ability to anticipate events before they happen. It is estimated that a soccer official may run eight miles or more during the course of a 90-minute match.

In addition to the physical demands of positioning, the soccer referee must master the basic hand signals which he or she must give during the game. The referee must also work with the linesmen and be fully conversant with their flag signals.

Unlike American football, soccer players wear only minimal protective gear which greatly lessens the chance of injuries to officials who collide with players. However, the high level of emotion that comes with international soccer competition is well documented. In such cases, soccer officials face a much higher threat of bodily injury off the field than on, particularly when an unpopular ruling is made against the home team. Fortunately, spectator rowdyism by American soccer fans has not yet reached the fervor that it has in other countries.

SOCCER OFFICIALS

In the game of soccer, the referee exercises general control of the competition as well as the other officials. The referee is responsible for starting and stopping the action, ruling on fouls and infractions of the rules, keeping track of game time, and terminating play in the event of bad weather or an unruly crowd. Before the game, the referee checks field markings, the goal nets, and the game ball; the referee also meets with the team coaches and players to discuss the rules, checks player equipment, and conducts the coin toss to determine first possession.

The soccer referee uses a whistle to start and stop the game and carries colored cards to signal fouls and penalties. The referee holds a yellow card aloft to signal fouls. Penalty kicks are the normal remedy for minor infractions of the rules. Indirect free kicks (in which the ball must touch a player before entering the goal) are awarded for such offenses as obstruction and off-side violations. Direct free kicks (which count as goals regardless of whether the ball touches a player before entering the goal) are meted out for more serious and safety-related violations such as tripping, kicking, pushing, or charging an opponent. Flagrant disregard for safety and failure to heed first warnings are among the most common reasons for player ejection. In the case of an ejection, the referee holds a red card aloft; this is referred to as *sending off* the player.

At most levels of competition, a pair of linesmen assist the referee by spotting the point where the ball goes out of bounds and keeping an eye out for offside violations, all from the vantage point of the side boundaries. The linesmen use flags to convey signals to the referee. Linesmen may point out rules violations to the referee if they spot something the ref missed. However, as head official, the referee has sole discretion on whether or not to act on calls by the linesmen. During the game, the linesmen normally are positioned on opposite sides of the field and stand just outside the field of play.

The Whistle Stop

UNIFORMS & EQUIPMENT

Soccer officials wear solid black shirts with white cuffs and a white collar, black shorts, and black shoes. The referee uses a whistle, attached to the forefinger, to signal the start and stop of play and carries a watch to keep time on the field. A second watch is carried as a backup. Yellow and red cards are used to signal warnings and player disqualifications. The linesmen also wear black uniforms and use flags to signal calls and off-side infractions.

SEASONS OF PLAY

High school and collegiate level competition typically is scheduled in the fall season, which begins in early September and runs through November. Soccer is included in the games of the Summer Olympics. Indoor soccer is gaining popularity as a winter sport.

COMPETITION LEVELS & CERTIFICATION REQUIREMENTS

According to the United States Soccer Federation (USSF), community and youth groups, which sponsor teams for boys and girls as young as six, are the foundation of organized soccer in the United States. Soccer programs generally are sponsored by USSF-affiliated members, including the United States Youth Soccer Organization, the Intercollegiate Soccer Football Association, the National Collegiate Athletic Association, the National Association of Intercollegiate Athletics, the Amateur Athletic Union, the United States Olympic Committee, and various local and regional soccer leagues.

Interscholastic competition is regulated by state athletic associations in accordance with rules established by the National Federation of State High School Associations (NF). The NF, in turn, works with the USSF.

Soccer referees and linesmen at all levels of competition are certified through the USSF. The National Referee Committee of the USSF has established nine grades of certification: Associate Referee, Referee Class 2, Referee Class 1, State Referee Class 2, State Referee Class 1, National Referee, National International Panel (IPC) Referee, International Linesman, and International Referee.

Determination of an official's grade is based on age, experience and training requirements, written examinations, field evaluations, and physical fitness standards issued by the USSF. Regardless of grade, annual re-certification of soccer officials is required. Following initial certification, officials generally must accrue at least 12 months experience before becoming eligible to apply for certification at the next higher grade.

SOCCER
LEVELS OF COMPETITION

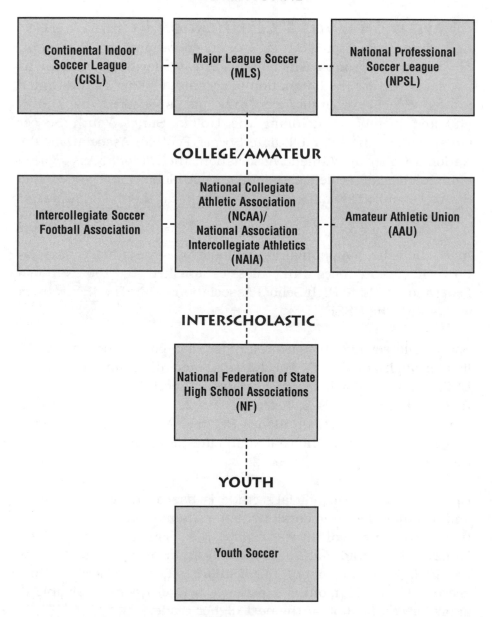

PROFESSIONAL

Continental Indoor Soccer League (CISL)	Major League Soccer (MLS)	National Professional Soccer League (NPSL)

COLLEGE/AMATEUR

Intercollegiate Soccer Football Association	National Collegiate Athletic Association (NCAA)/ National Association Intercollegiate Athletics (NAIA)	Amateur Athletic Union (AAU)

INTERSCHOLASTIC

National Federation of State High School Associations (NF)

YOUTH

Youth Soccer

The USSF assigns Associate Referee and Referee Class 2 grades to entry-level soccer officials. There are no minimum age or experience requirements for applicants at this level; however, applicants must successfully complete an associate level or entry-level training course, respectively, and score at least 75% on an entry-level test. Neither field evaluation nor physical examination is required. Officials at these levels are beginners, authorized to work youth games for boys and girls through age 11. USSF-certified Associate Referees are prohibited from accepting any compensation, fees, or reimbursement for expenses.

USSF Referee Class 1 certification is available to men and women, 17 years of age and older with at least 12 months experience prior to application, who have earned a minimum score of 85% on the entry-level test. A field evaluation is required at this level. Referee

Class 1 certification authorizes an individual to work as a referee for all youth games and mixed leagues or as a linesman in amateur games, including some collegiate matches at levels below the top division.

State Referee Class 2 applicants must be at least 18 years old; State Referee Class 1 applicants must be at least 19. State Class 2 officials are assigned as referees in youth games and amateur games through second division and as linesmen in the top amateur division and amateur cup games. State Class 1 certification enables an official to work as a referee in first division amateur competition and as a linesman in professional matches and international cup games.

National Referee certification is available to experienced applicants 25 years and older who successfully complete a National Referee examination and certification training session. Officials at this level work as referees in all games except formal FIFA international matches and as linesmen in international matches. Three years experience at this level is required before application to the next level is permitted.

The minimum age requirement for officials at the three highest levels of certification is 26. These grades are National International Panel Candidate (IPC) Referee, International Linesman, and International Referee. National IPC grade referees are certified to officiate all games except formal FIFA international matches; International Linesman and International Referee designations, which require United States citizenship, authorize assignment to all games as a linesman or referee, respectively.

COMPENSATION

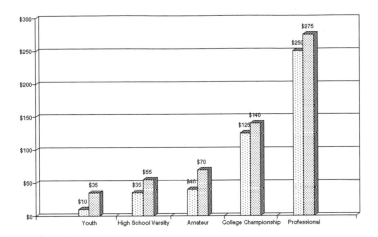

SOCCER OFFICIATING
COMPENSATION BY COMPETITION LEVEL: EVENT FEES

The graph above reflects average event fee ranges for soccer referees at various levels of competition. Keep in mind that fees vary widely by geographic location, and soccer officials in many areas work on a volunteer basis in the early stages of their careers.

At the lower levels of competition, it is not uncommon for officials to work more than one game per week. An interscholastic soccer referee can easily pull in $75 to $100 by working two high school games per week, which translates into over $300 per month during the season. Not bad for roughly 16 to 20 hours of work per month. Compare this to a part-time job paying a minimum wage of $4.75 per hour, which would yield less than $400 over a month for 80 hours of work. At all levels of competition, officials receive a higher event fee for championship and playoff games than for games played during the regular season.

As you move up the officiating ladder to higher levels of competition, your pay goes up accordingly. Amateur and collegiate level officials earn only slightly more than those at the high school varsity level. Those who pursue the college route do so more for the love of the sport than for the money. The top earnings for officials occur at the professional level. Major league soccer referees earn $275 per game.

OFFICIAL PROFILE:
FRED DUBIN
NATIONAL FEDERATION OF INTERSCHOLASTIC OFFICIALS ASSOCIATION

LR: How many years have you been an official?
FD: Ten years.

LR: What is the best part of being an official?
FD: Knowing that you are doing a small job that helps the community is a good thing. I have two kids myself, and it's clear that young people are important.

LR: And the worst?
FD: The most difficult times are the early years. Many things can only be learned through experience. Hang in there.

LR: What advice would you offer to someone interested in becoming an official?
FD: Watch soccer matches in person, or better, watch matches on TV where you'll see more varsity and more matches of high quality. Watch what the refs do. Try to figure out what's happening from the ref's point of view. Find someone who is experienced and have that person as your mentor.

Years ago I saw an experienced referee make a whole series of mistakes and I realized that all of us, no matter how experienced, are capable of making mistakes. Don't let anyone put you down. We are all more equal than you might think. Work hard for the kids and for yourself. Remember that the field is an extension of the classroom.

LR: Does soccer officiating have career potential?
FD: It could be a career if you have the time and interest. Most people officiate part-time.

LR: What is your most memorable experience as an official?

FD: Meeting and becoming friends with Mario Donnangelo has been memorable. He really embodies what a high school soccer ref should be. Most refs never get a chance to meet him. Donnangelo is a very high quality ref. [Editor's note: Mario Donnangelo is the associate director of the National Intercollegiate Soccer Officials' Association and former chairman of the National Federation Soccer Rules Committee.] In June of 1996 the National Federation had its 10th annual meeting. Looking around at all the different types of people from all over the country who were sports officials was very memorable. It is the Olympics for high school officials except, instead of competing, we exchange ideas.

LR: Describe a day in the life of a soccer official.

FD: High school soccer in Delaware starts after 3:00 p.m. weekdays and at random times on weekends. About an hour before the match, I get in uniform and start getting psyched up for the match. Who is playing and where? Earlier in the day I have called the school to make sure the match is being played and to find out if there are any last minute changes. Then I go to the match at least one-half hour before it is set to begin and go through the officiating procedures outlined in the rules.

LR: How did you get involved in officiating?

FD: My dad was a ref. No one grows up saying, "When I grow up I'm going to be a ref." I was always more interested in sports than most people. Playing in sports helps. Many different types of people ref.

SOCCER: A BRIEF HISTORY

The game of soccer is believed to have originated in ancient Rome, although several other countries are thought to have played the game in one form or another. The modern game was developed in 19th century England, where the sport was called football. The London Football Association, formed in 1863, developed the first set of official rules for the game. The first known international soccer match occurred in 1872 when England competed against Scotland. The popularity of soccer quickly spread across Europe and other continents as sailors of the Royal Navy played the game wherever they were stationed.

In 1904, the Federation Internationale de Football Association (FIFA) was organized as the international regulatory body of soccer and remains so to this day. In 1930, soccer's first World Cup international championship match was held; this competition has since become the sporting event of the year for much of the world, particularly in Europe, South America, and Africa.

Although the game of soccer was introduced in America even before the turn of the century, it was not nearly as popular as American football. Soccer finally began to attain national prominence in this country in 1959 when the National Collegiate Athletic Association (NCAA) sanctioned soccer as a college sport. The United States Soccer Federation (USSF), originally the United States Soccer Football Association, was founded in 1913 and is the governing body for soccer at all levels of competition in the United States. Traditionally played outdoors, an

indoor version of the game was created in 1939 as a means of playing the game during the winter months. Indoor soccer is played by teams of five players each, on a smaller field with smaller goals than the outdoor game.

Depiction of an early American soccer match, 1890

RESOURCES

Regulatory Bodies

Interscholastic
National Federation of State High School Associations (NF)
11724 Plaza Circle
P.O. Box 20626
Kansas City, MO 64195
Phone: (816) 464-5400
Fax: (816) 464-5571
Internet: www.nfhs.org

Amateur
Amateur Athletic Union (AAU)
The Walt Disney Resort
P.O. Box 10000
Lake Buena Vista, FL 32830-1000
Phone: (407) 934-7200
Fax: (407) 934-7242
Internet: www.aausports.org

Collegiate
National Association of Intercollegiate Athletics (NAIA)
6120 S. Yale Ave., Ste. 1450
Tulsa, OK 74136-4223
Phone: (918) 494-8828
Fax: (918) 494-8841
Internet: www.naia.org

National Collegiate Athletic Association (NCAA)
6201 College Blvd.
Overland Park, KS 66211-2422
Phone: (913) 339-1906
Fax: (913) 339-1950
Internet: www.ncaa.org

Professional
Major League Soccer (MLS)
110 E. 42nd St., Ste. 1502
New York, NY 10017

Continental Indoor Soccer League (CISL)
16027 Ventura Blvd., Ste. 605
Encino, CA 91436
Phone: (818) 906-7627

National Professional Soccer League (NPSL)
115 Dewalt Ave., NW
Canton, OH 44702
Phone: (330) 455-4625

National
U.S. Soccer Federation (USSF)
U.S. Soccer House
1801-1811 S. Prairie Ave.
Chicago, IL 60616
Phone: (312) 808-1300
Fax: (312) 808-9566
e-mail: socfed@aol.com
Internet: www.us~soccer.com

International
Federation Internationale de Football Association (FIFA)
Case Postale 85 (Hitzigweg 11)
8030 Zurich
Switzerland
Phone: (41-1) 384-9595
Fax: (41-1) 384-9696
Internet: www.fifa.com

SOCCER RULES BOOKS

The *Laws of the Game*, the official rules publication of the FIFA, is available through the United States Soccer Federation. Cost of the 1998-99 edition is $3. A soccer rules book is also available through the National Federation of State High School Associations for $5. Collegiate level rules books are available through the National Collegiate Athletic Association for $5.

SOCCER OFFICIATING SELF-TEST

1. How many players from one team can play in a game at the same time?

2. When do teams change ends of the field?

3. How long is a soccer field?
    a. 90 to 110 yards; b. 90 to 120 yards; c. 100 to 120 yards; d. 100 to 130 yards

4. What part of the foot should contact the ball on the punt?
    a. the toe; b. the inside; c. the outside; d. the top

5. What is the status of soccer in the United States in terms of popularity?
    a. remaining the same; b. decreasing rapidly; c. decreasing slowly; d. increasing rapidly

6. The team trying to gain possession of the ball is called:

7. What is it called when a player stops the ball?
    a. dribbling; b. trapping ; c. tackling; d. catching

8. What does the term *stalemate* mean?
    a. a tie game; b. two opposing players waiting for each other to make a move; c. successfully stopping an offensive play

9. Which of the following equipment is legal?
    a. casts; b. face and/or glasses guards; c. helmets; d. soft knee pads

10. Which team kicks off in the second period?
    a. the same as the first period; b. the opposite team as the first period; c. the team ahead in scoring; d. the team behind in scoring

11. How many points does a goal count?

12. If a ball rolls on the touchline, is the ball considered in bounds?

13. Which statement describes the standard for soccer cleats?
a. Plastic cleats are illegal; b. Detachable cleats or studs are illegal; c. Metal cleats are legal; d. Rubber cleats are legal.

14. What is the regulation time for a high school soccer game?
a. two 45-minute halves; b. four 20-minute quarters

15. How is the game begun?
a. a drop ball; b. a kick-off; c. a face-off; d. a goal kick

16. How many points does a penalty kick count?

17. Name the governing body of soccer.

18. True or false: Soccer referees are required to pass a physical fitness test.

19 True or false: Soccer officials must work for one year at each certification level before advancing to the next class.

20. True or false: High school soccer matches are longer than those played at the intercollegiate level.

SOCCER OFFICIATING SELF-TEST ANSWERS

1. Eleven players; 2. At halftime; 3. c; 4. d; 5. d; 6. The defensive team; 7. b; 8. c; 9. d; 10. b; 11. One point; 12. Yes; 13. d; 14. a; 15. b; 16. One point; 17. United States Soccer Federation; 18. True; 19. True; 20. False

SCORING THE SELF-TEST

Incorrect Answers	Officiating Aptitude
0	Perfect: You have a solid knowledge of the game.
1-3	Average: You need to review the soccer rules book.
4-5	Below average: It's been some time since you've seen a soccer match.
6+	Far below average: You should consider officiating a different sport.

THE
SOFTBALL
UMPIRE

SOFTBALL OFFICIATING AT A GLANCE

Entry Level: Interscholastic high school and junior high, recreational and youth softball

Minimum Age: 18 in most states

Certification: State (high school) athletic association certification required for interscholastic softball umpires in most states (see Section V).

Average Pay: Varies widely by geographic location; at the high school junior varsity level, softball referees typically earn $25 to $35 a game. Varsity softball umpires earn $30 to $45 a game. Collegiate championship softball umpires can earn as much as $750 a game in NCAA Division I.

Schedule: Interscholastic softball is a spring sport, beginning in early March and extending into June. In many areas, the game is also played in the fall. Indoor softball leagues allow the game to be played throughout the year.

Roger Perlmuter
Umpiring boys and girls softball games at the local level is one of the most common starting points for new officials.

SOFTBALL: GENERAL INFORMATION

Softball exists in two forms: fast-pitch and slow-pitch. The rules of softball are similar to those of baseball, although equipment requirements, playing field dimensions, pitching regulations, and base running restrictions are different. In addition, the distance between baselines, the pitching distance, and the distance to the outfield fence from the home plate are different in fast-pitch, slow-pitch, men's, women's, and co-ed competitions.

Fast-pitch softball typically is played in interscholastic competition. The softball, approximately 12 inches in circumference, is pitched underhand at speeds that can reach 100 mph. As in baseball, bunting and base stealing are allowed. Nine players comprise a team.

Slow-pitch softball, the form most commonly practiced in recreational leagues, utilizes a ball that is 12 inches, 14 inches, or 16 inches in circumference. Pitchers are required to throw the ball underhand with a prescribed arch. Ten players comprise a team.

UMPIRING SOFTBALL

Umpiring softball is analogous to umpiring baseball in many respects. The duties are similar, as are the emotions of players and spectators. In order to be effective, the softball umpire must possess a thorough knowledge of the applicable rules and be able to interpret them in the multitude of situations that can arise during a typical game. In many leagues, only one umpire is employed. Umpires working solo are further challenged with the demands of positioning as they are responsible for observing action in the infield and outfield, as well as at the plate.

The softball umpire must also be able to keep a level head in the face of criticism. By nature, softball umpires tend to have a *people person* mentality as their job tends to bring them in contact with a wide range of individuals. As with all officials, a positive demeanor and clear communication skills go a long way toward effective officiating.

SOFTBALL UMPIRES

One or two umpires are employed for softball games. The number of umpires required varies by competition level. In two-umpire games, the home plate umpire judges balls and strikes. Decisions involving fielding and base runners are the responsibility of the base umpire. If only one umpire is assigned to a game, he or she assumes all officiating duties.

In two-umpire games, the home plate umpire maintains a position behind the catcher. The base umpire takes different positions on the infield, moving to maintain the best possible position to observe plays as they develop. If only one umpire is assigned to a game, he or she assumes a starting position behind home plate for each pitch and then quickly moves to the infield to observe plays at the bases.

In two-umpire games, the home plate umpire has final say on pitching and hitting calls and plays at the plate. However, the base umpire has equal authority to call runners out for leaving a base too soon, call time for suspension of play, eject players, coaches, managers, or other team members for rules violations or misconduct, call illegal pitches, and, in extreme cases, declare forfeitures. In single umpire games, all of these responsibilities fall on the shoulders of the home plate umpire.

Most decisions by softball umpires are final. However, in two-umpire games, team managers may appeal a ruling by one umpire if they believe the other umpire was in a better position to make the call. In such cases, the umpires may confer and, if agreed, reverse the initial call.

In addition to the game duties outlined above, the softball umpire is responsible for inspecting the ball diamond, field boundaries, and equipment before the game begins. Softball umpires must be particularly observant for softballs of an incorrect diameter for the league they are working. Softball umpires generally hold brief pre-game *plate* meetings with representatives of each team to clarify the ground rules. This is an opportunity for the umpire to ask about any adaptations of league rules that might apply to his or her calls during the game.

Ron DeCarlo

UNIFORMS & EQUIPMENT

The uniform requirements for softball umpires vary by league or organization. USSSA umpires typically wear red broadcloth short-sleeved shirts, black pants, shoes, socks, and belts, and caps bearing the USSA logo. ASA umpires wear powder blue short-sleeve shirts, navy blue slacks and socks, black shoes, and white and blue caps with the ASA logo. In most leagues, umpires do not wear protective gear. However, ASA fast-pitch plate umpires are required to wear black masks, black padding, and black throat protectors or extended wire protectors attached to their masks. Softball plate umpires also carry black ball bags and use ball-strike counters. Base umpires also may use their own ball-strike counters as a backup.

SEASONS OF PLAY

The outdoor softball season extends from early spring through fall. Some indoor recreational softball leagues, however, schedule games all year. The interscholastic season typically begins in early March and runs into June.

COMPETITION LEVELS & CERTIFICATION REQUIREMENTS

Interscholastic high school, collegiate, and Olympic softball competition is available only to women. Recreational play is open to males and females of all ages, ranging from youth leagues for children 6 years old and younger to seniors competition for seniors aged 70 and older. At every competitive level, softball umpires are selected from the rosters of one of several softball associations.

The three major softball organizations in the United States are the United States Slo-Pitch Softball Association (USSSA), the National Softball Association (NSA) and the Amateur Softball Association (ASA). The ASA is recognized as the national governing body of softball and is a member of the United States Olympic Committee. In addition, the ASA sponsors national softball umpire training schools to encourage umpire development. The USSSA maintains professional softball umpire associations in each state and in many local districts. Umpires can also receive additional training through classes sponsored by USSSA.

General certification requirements for softball umpires include umpiring school attendance and successful completion of written examinations and field tests. International Softball Federation (ISF) certification, available through ASA, allows an umpire to represent the United States as an umpire in ISF-sanctioned world championships, the Pan American Games, and the Olympics. Softball umpires typically earn between $8 and $45 per game, depending on the level or the league. In some cases, softball umpiring is performed on a voluntary basis.

SOFTBALL
LEVELS OF COMPETITION

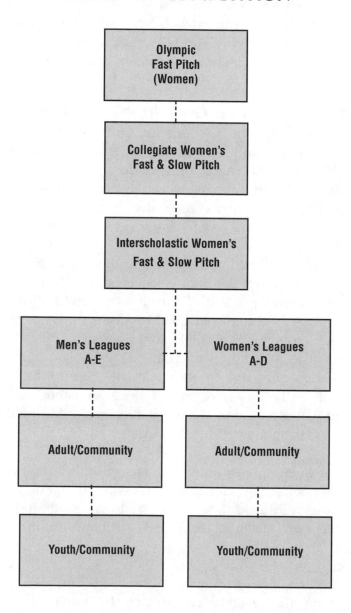

COMPENSATION

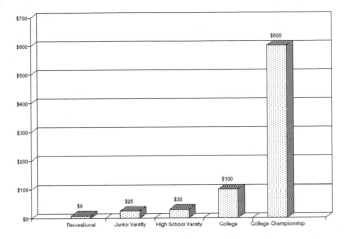

SOFTBALL OFFICIATING
COMPENSATION BY COMPETITION LEVEL: EVENT FEES

The graph above provides a comparison of event fee ranges for softball umpires at various levels of competition. Keep in mind that fees vary widely by geographic area and that umpires frequently work on a volunteer basis during the early stages of their careers.

At the lower levels of competition, it is not uncommon for softball umpires to work more than one game per week. An interscholastic softball umpire can easily pull in $60 to $90 by working two high school games per week, which translates into over $240 a month during the season. Not bad for roughly 20 hours of work per month. Compare this to a part-time job paying a minimum wage of $4.75 per hour, which would yield less than $400 over a month for 80 hours of work. Add to this the potential of working championship and playoff games which pay substantially more than regular season games.

As you move up the officiating ladder to higher levels of competition, your pay goes up accordingly. During the regular season, collegiate level softball umpires earn only slightly more than high school varsity umpires. However, at the championship level, NCAA umpires earn top dollar.

OFFICIAL PROFILE:

DALE F. DAVIDSON

USSSA OHIO STATE
UMPIRE-IN-CHIEF

LR: How did you start your officiating career and how long have you been umpiring?

DD: I started officiating one day at my son's high school baseball game. One of the umpires was sick, so the coach asked me to fill in. I had never called a game before. After the game, the coach said that I had done a better job than a lot of the usual umpires and that I should think about going to umpire school, so I pursued it! I've been umpiring now for 30 years.

LR: In your opinion, what are the best aspects of officiating?

DD: I really enjoy traveling, and I also enjoy the opportunity to work at various levels of competition.

LR: What is your least favorite part?

DD: I would have to say the long hours. I once worked a tournament game for high school baseball that lasted 21 innings. It was unbelievable. In fact, it set a record. The game began at 10:00 in the morning and lasted until 5:00 p.m. The games which were scheduled for 1:30 and 4:00 had to be called off.

Another problem is rain. When it rains, you often have to sit around and wait for the rain to stop and the field to be prepared for playing which is very time-consuming.

LR: What is your typical schedule on a game day?

DD: In the morning, I like to take it easy and relax. I make sure and have a good meal and drink plenty of fluids. When I get to the ball field, my body sort of shuts down. I don't eat or drink while I'm calling a game, even if it lasts eight hours. I do very little talking as well unless it has to do with calling the game. My goal is to be 100% focused on the game. Whether it's 40 degrees outside or 90 degrees, I adhere to this plan.

When I arrive at the field, the first thing I do is let the tournament director or person in charge know I'm there. It is a big relief for that person to know the officials are there. I then go over how to call the game and how to handle various plays with my officiating partner. After the game, I leave the game site and general area. I don't want to run into disgruntled players or fans after the game!

LR: What are some of your most outstanding experiences?
DD: There are many. In 1979, when the major league umpires went on strike, I was called to work for two months. I worked a lot of games, and they wanted to sign me as a replacement umpire beginning June 1st. The strike ended May 31st. Then, in 1982 when the umpires went on strike again, I was called to work second base at the All-Star game. The strike ended just before the big game.

Another unique experience was being among the four umpires chosen by USSSA to travel to the Soviet Union in 1990 for the first ever softball instructional tour. We took with us 60 of the top U.S. female players and helped the Russians learn how to play softball. At one point, the Soviet men's baseball team was making fun of the American women. So, the women challenged the men to a game of softball and won! The entire trip was a terrific experience.

LR: Any words of wisdom for new umpires?
DD: Work a lot of games and learn from the veteran umpires. Go to all the clinics you can. You may hear a number of things repeated, but you will always come away with something new. Be careful how you say things to players and coaches. If you think about it, there is usually a way to say things that puts pressure on someone other than the officials. For example, if a pitcher has tape on her hand, I might say to the pitcher between innings that I don't care if she keeps the tape on her hand and if the other team doesn't say anything, it's o.k. Then, if the other team makes a fuss and I need to confront the pitcher, she understands and she is mad at the other team, not me!

You see, a ball game is like a tea kettle on the fire. You don't want it to boil over, so you have to let the steam off once in awhile. If a player is really upset, listen to the comments and even check the call with your officiating partner. This will often make the player feel better, even if no decision is changed.

Keep in mind that the official controls the game and is able to set the pace. When I umpire, I hustle and make sure the players are up to bat as soon as possible. I try to keep the game moving along by doing all the little things I can to keep it going. I don't call every tiny detail or the games would never get finished. It's similar to basketball. You could either call every single technical foul you see, or you could decide to call only the major fouls. As an official, it's your decision.

Softball: A Brief History

Softball was developed as an indoor version of baseball in the mid-1880s by George W. Hancock. Lewis Rober adapted the game to the outdoors and, in the early 1930s, the Amateur Softball Association of America (ASA) established the rules of the game. As in baseball, softball players score runs by completing a circuit of the bases, and the team scoring the most runs at the completion of the game wins. Unlike baseball, a softball game is played in seven innings, and a coin toss determines the order of play.

RESOURCES

Regulatory Bodies

Children's/Interscholastic
National Federation of State High School
Associations (NFSHSA)
11724 NW Plaza Circle
P.O. Box 20626
Kansas City, MO 64195-0626
Phone: (816) 464-5400 Fax: (816) 464-5571
Internet: www.nfhs.org

National
Amateur Softball Association (ASA)/
USA Softball
2801 N.E. 50th St.
Oklahoma City, OK 73111-7203
Phone: (405) 424-5266 Fax: (405) 424-3855
e-mail: info@softball.org
Internet: www.softball.org

United States Slo-Pitch Softball Association
(USSSA)
3935 S. Crater Rd.
Petersburg, VA 23805
Phone: (804) 732-4099 Fax: (804) 732-1704

National Softball Association (NSA)
P.O. Box 7 .
Nicholasville, KY 40340
Phone: (606) 887-4114 Fax: (606) 887-4874

Pony Softball
P.O. Box 225
Washington, PA 15301
Phone: (724) 225-1060 Fax: (724) 225-9852

International
Federation Internationale de Softball (ISF)
4141 NW Expressway
Oklahoma City, OK 73116
Phone: (405) 879-2004 Fax: (405) 879-9801
e-mail: isfsoftball@accessacg.net

International Softball Congress (ISC)
6007 E. Hillcrest Circle
Anaheim Hills, CA 92807-3921
Phone: (714) 998-5694 Fax: (714) 282-7902

SOFTBALL RULES BOOKS
Each softball association annually publishes a rules
book. ASA rules, with modifications, generally are
used in NCAA, NAIA, and NJCAA competition. Rules
books typically are available at sporting goods stores
and also can be ordered directly through each regulatory organization. Cost of the NF softball rules book is
$5; cost of the NSA rules book is $2.

Softball Umpiring Self-test

1. True or false: Softball fields must have a home run fence.

2. In most leagues, how many players can be in the field at one time?

3. How long are the baselines of a regulation softball field?

4. How far is the men's pitchers rubber from home plate?

5. True or false: Home plate is wider in softball than in baseball due to the bigger ball.

6. True or false: Players in fast-pitch softball are allowed to steal after the ball leaves the pitcher's hand.

7. Is a softball catcher required to wear a protective mask?

8. True or false: A batter does not get to go to first base if he or she is hit by a pitch.

9. Is there an infield-fly rule in softball?

10. True or false: Slow-pitch softballs must be pitched with a certain amount of arch on the ball.

11. A regulation softball bat can not be longer than ___ inches. a. 34; b. 38; c. 40

12. Can softball pitchers put spin on the ball to purposely make the hitters miss?

13. How many innings does a softball game last, assuming there is not a tie at the end?

14. True or false: All softball fields must have dirt rather than grass infields.

15. True or false: A team can field 5 outfielders and 3 infielders during a game.

16. True or false: A softball pitcher cannot pitch both games of a double header.

17. Can a batter in softball begin batting from the right side of the plate and then switch to the left side?

18. True or false: It is illegal to use a hardball bat in a softball game.

19. True or false: Metal spikes are not allowed to be worn in a softball game.

20. True or false: The designated hitter in softball must hit for the pitcher.

SOFTBALL UMPIRING SELF-TEST ANSWERS

1. False; 2. 10; 3. 65 feet; 4. 50 feet; 5. False; 6. True; 7. Fast-pitch, yes; slow-pitch, no; 8. Fast-pitch, true; slow-pitch, false; 9. Yes; 10. True; 11. a; 12. Yes; 13. Seven innings; 14. False; 15. True; 16. False; 17. Yes, if the batter first requests a time out and the pitcher has not yet begun his or her pitching motion; 18. True; 19. True; 20. False

SCORING THE SELF-TEST

Incorrect Answers	Umpiring Aptitude
0	Perfect: You have a solid knowledge of the game.
1-3	Average: You need to review the softball rules book.
4-5	Below average: It's been some time since you have seen a softball game.
6+	Far below average: You should consider officiating a different sport.

SWIMMING & DIVING
OFFICIALS

SWIMMING & DIVING OFFICIATING AT A GLANCE

Entry Level: United States Swimming (USS) Local Swimming Committee (LSC). Opportunities for officiating swimming events at the interscholastic level exist in many areas.

Minimum Age: No minimum age for entry level LSC, although most swim officials are at least 18.

Certification: Criteria and training established by LSC Official Chairman

Average Pay: Swimming and diving officials work on a volunteer basis at most levels. However, at national swimming championship meets, the travel expenses of the Meet Referee, Administrative Referee, Head Starter, and Chief Judge are paid by USS. Diving officials sometimes receive reimbursement for room and board at large meets. In NCAA championship competition, officials fees range from $200 to $300 per meet. During the regular season, NCAA officials typically earn $50 to $100 per meet.

Schedule: USS conducts swimming competition year round; likewise, diving competition takes place throughout the year. Interscholastic swimming takes place in the winter season, typically mid-November through March. Collegiate competition takes place in the spring.

Swimming and diving competition is widely available to participants of all ages.

SWIMMING & DIVING: GENERAL INFORMATION

Swimming is an individual and a team water sport. Swimmers compete in individual and relay races during the course of a meet. The standard pool size used in long course competition is eight lanes wide and 50 meters long. Short course competition, widely used in the United States, requires a pool 25 meters in length. The first individual or team to cover a pre-determined distance, utilizing a pre-determined stroke or combination of strokes, wins. The four swimming strokes used in competition are: freestyle, breast stroke, butterfly, and back stroke. Individual medley, medley relay, and freestyle relay events comprise a meet program. United States Swimming, Inc. (USS) is responsible for the conduct and administration of swimming programs and competition throughout the nation.

Diving competition is comprised of men's and women's springboard and platform diving events. Competitors perform a specified number of dives, each of which is marked or scored by a judging panel. If more than 12 divers are participating, competition generally is divided into preliminary and final rounds. The diver earning the most marks in the final round wins. United States Diving, Inc. (USD) is the national governing body of the sport in the United

States. Swimming and diving competitions are regulated in zones and regions by Local Swimming Committees and Local Diving Committees which are affiliated with the USS and USD, respectively. Both USS and USD are members of the Federation Internationale de Natation Amateur (FINA), the international governing body of aquatics.

SWIMMING OFFICIALS

Swimming officials primarily rule on the physical technique of the competitors. Swimming officials ensure that swimming stroke mechanics are performed within the standards issued by FINA. Officiating crews at FINA-sanctioned swimming competitions generally include a referee; a starter; a clerk of course to assemble the swimmers prior to each event; a chief inspector of turns; one turning inspector for each lane at each end of the pool responsible for ensuring proper turn and relay takeover mechanics; and two stroke judges, one assigned to each side of the pool, walking abreast of the swimmers to ensure their stroke techniques conform to designated standards. The penalty for improper stroke is the disqualification of the offending swimmer. Additional swim meet officials generally include a chief timekeeper (also known as the head timer) who assigns other timekeepers: three for each lane and two additional to replace a timekeeper who, for any reason, including mechanical, is unable to record the time; a chief finish or placing judge; and finish or placing judges positioned in elevated stands at the finish line to determine the order in which the swimmers finish. Electronic timing equipment is required in Olympic competition. A chief recorder is responsible for checking the times and placing order of the swimmers.

The referee controls the meet and all other swimming officials, inspecting the course, assigning officiating duties, ensuring no rules are violated by the competitors, and adjudicating disagreements among officials or competitors. After receiving a signal from the referee, the starter directs the swimmers to *take your mark* and then actuates the starting signal. The starter is responsible for ensuring that each swimmer maintains the correct starting position and, subject to the decision of the referee, determines whether the start is valid. In USS competition, penalty for a false start is disqualification from the event. In FINA competition, the first false start is charged *to the field*. The next person who false starts is disqualified at the end of the race.

DIVING OFFICIALS

Diving competitions are judged by a panel comprised of a referee and, typically, five to seven judges who award points based on each competitor's execution of a dive. The referee controls the competition and supervises the scoring of the judges.

Judges award points for each dive, ranging from 0 to 10, generally based on the following rating system: very good, 8 1/2 to 10; good, 6 1/2 to 8; satisfactory, 5 to 6; deficient, 2 1/2 to 4 1/2; unsatisfactory, 1/2 to 2; and completely failed, 0. Diving judges consider the diver's approach, takeoff, technique and grace through the air, and entry into the water in determining final scores.

Roger Perlmuter

UNIFORMS & EQUIPMENT

Either all-white clothing, or navy blue pants (or skirts) and white shirts (as determined by the LSC) are worn by swimming officials. Key officials, including the referee, starter, and chief judges at national and regional meets typically wear white clothing topped with a blue blazer.

Lap counters for distance events, starting guns and shells (in the absence of electronic starting equipment), disqualification slips, and relay confirmation slips are included among the equipment required for swimming officials. In many cases, the starter wears a small holster on his or her belt to carry the starting gun. In addition, head sets or walkie-talkies may be required if communication among officials is deemed necessary.

SEASONS OF PLAY

Swimming and diving events are held virtually year round. Interscholastic swimming meets are scheduled during the winter months, typically mid-November through March. Collegiate level competition is held in the spring. Many local swimming leagues sponsor meets through the summer months. USS conducts swimming competitions year round. Diving competition also is conducted throughout the year. The USD outdoor season extends from June 1 through September 30. The indoor season includes all other months of the year.

COMPETITION LEVELS & CERTIFICATION REQUIREMENTS

United States Swimming, Inc. (USS) recognizes four competitive classifications: Senior, Junior, Age Group, and Open Water. Age Group competition is broken down into age brackets such as 10 and under, 11-12, 13-14, 15-16, 17-18, or other combinations. The Junior classification includes swimmers age 19 and under. Masters Swimming, for those 19 and over, is conducted by U.S. Masters Swimming (USMS). The Amateur Athletic Union (AAU) also sponsors competitive youth swimming events at the local, Association, Regional, and National levels. The AAU follows the competitive rules promulgated by USS.

Competition levels recognized by United States Diving, Inc. include Senior, Junior Olympics, and Masters. Senior competition, for divers of all ages, includes dual meets, invitational meets, association championships, preliminary meets, and national and international championships. Junior Olympics competition, for divers age 17 (sometimes 18) and under, includes novice meets, dual meets, invitational meets, association championships, regional championships, zone championships, the U.S. Junior Olympics championships, and international competition. The Masters program, for divers 21 and older, includes invitational meets, association meets, regional meets, and national championships.

Three certification levels for swimming officials are recognized by United States Swimming: LSC, National (Regional), and National Championship. Certification as a Local Swimming Committee (LSC) official is obtained through the LSC Officials Chairman. Each LSC establishes its own criteria for training and certification of officials but operates in accordance with regulations established by USS. In 1995, USS established minimum guidelines for the training and certification of swimming officials in order to obtain more consistency in officiating throughout the country. After acquiring one year's experience as an LSC-certified official, a swimming official is eligible for national (regional) certification by working with certified officials at local or regional championship meets approved by the USS Officials Committee. Applicants for National certification must maintain active membership in USS and attend an officials briefing session prior to each session of the meet. Candidates must work at least three preliminary and/or finals sessions prior to earning certification.

Certification requirements for National Championship officials include membership in USS and prior national (regional) certification. Certification at this level is earned by working with certified officials at a USS National Championship, i.e., the Junior or Senior Nationals, or the U.S. Open. An individual is eligible for certification after working a minimum of four sessions and attending an officials meeting prior to each session of the meet.

COMPENSATION
SWIMMING & DIVING OFFICIATING

Swimming and diving officials in many areas work on a volunteer basis, particularly during the regular season. Interscholastic officials, in particular, tend to volunteer their time. At the college level, swim officials do receive compensation. During the regular season, swimming and diving officials earn an average of $50 to $100 per meet. In NCAA championship competition, the Starter, Head Judge, and Referee (or Diving Referee) earn $200 per meet. The Meet Coordinator earns $300 per meet in NCAA Division I.

Swimming officials generally work as volunteers. At National Championship meets, the travel expenses of the Meet Referee, Administrative Referee, Head Starter, and Chief Judge are paid by United States Swimming. Diving judges also work as volunteers and most pay their own expenses, although at large meets, room and board expenses sometimes are paid by the sponsoring organization.

SWIMMING
LEVELS OF COMPETITION*

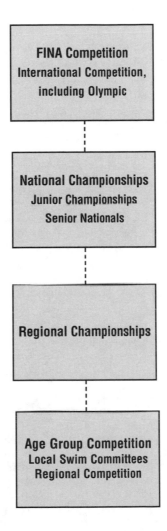

*As recognized by U.S. Swimming
Other levels of competition include high school, college, and U.S. Masters. U.S. Masters (for ages 19 and older) is governed by U.S. Aquatics, which is not affiliated with U.S. Swimming.

DIVING
LEVELS OF COMPETITION*

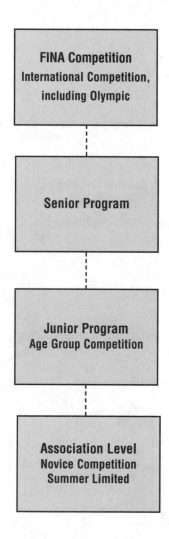

FINA Competition
International Competition,
including Olympic

Senior Program

Junior Program
Age Group Competition

Association Level
Novice Competition
Summer Limited

*As recognized by U.S. Diving
Other levels of competition include high school, college, and a Masters program (for ages 21
and older).

SWIMMING & DIVING: A BRIEF HISTORY

Although the practice of swimming dates back to at least ancient Egypt, it did not emerge as a competitive sport until the 19th century. Modern competitive swimming gained widespread popularity in England, where the first organized swimming events were held in the 1830s. The Amateur Swimming Association of Great Britain, established in 1880, became the major governing body of organized swimming in England. Competitive swimming achieved international recognition when it was included as an Olympic sport for men when the modern games were instituted in 1896. Female swimming competition was included on the Olympic roster in 1912. Recognition in the United States followed two years later when the Amateur Athletic Union was established. The Federation Internationale de Natation Amateur (FINA) was established in 1909 and remains today as the governing body for all international swimming and diving events.

Early swimming technique was characterized by the breast stroke, which eventually evolved into an overhand stroke that increased the speed of the swimmer. By the turn of the century, a crawl-like stroke was introduced which improved the efficiency of the swimmer even further and has since become the basis of the modern freestyle stroke. The butterfly stroke (a variation of the breast stroke) emerged in competitive swimming in the 1930s but was not recognized as a separate event in the Olympic Games until 1953.

Olympic swimming competition, 1908

Competitive diving is also rooted in 19th century England, where the first organized competition took place in the 1880s. Diving was first included in the Olympic Games in 1904 when it was featured as part of the men's swimming competition. Female diving was added to the games in 1912.

Official Profile:
Anneliese Eggert
Retired National Officials Chairman, USS; Secretary, USS Rules Committee

LR: How long have you been involved with officiating swimming events?

AE: Thirty-two years. I never swam competitively, but I have a husband and three children who are all swimmers, and I got tired of sitting in the bleachers. So, I decided to get involved.

LR: And you became more and more involved over the years?

AE: Yes. The swimming experience was always a family activity, since my children were all swimmers. Then, when my children were grown, I continued to travel to meets all over the country with my husband, who is also a swimming official. It has been wonderful to share all of the traveling.

LR: I understand you officiated at the Atlanta Olympics, too. How was that?

AE: It was incredible. Being selected to officiate at the Olympics is definitely the culmination of a swim official's career. Not many people ever get to experience this, and I really enjoyed it. I worked every day, at a variety of different events.

LR: What is the time commitment involved with your level of officiating?

AE: It gets busy! Last year, I took 52 days off work so I could travel to meets all over the country. National meets generally last five days, and local meets are usually held over the weekend. International events, like the Olympic Trials or the Pan Am Championships, which I worked in Argentina, last seven days.

LR: Is it true that most swim officials work as volunteers?

AE: Yes, and I am glad to see it this way. Over 10,000 people work as volunteer swim officials, and most of them travel to meets at their own expense. At large meets, the starter, head referee, and chief judge are compensated for their airfare and hotel expenses, but none of the other officials. The lack of compensation is due in large part to the great number of officials needed to run meets.

LR: What are some of the jobs performed by all these volunteers?

AE: That's the beauty of swimming. The variety of jobs is so vast, anyone who wants to get involved can find an area they like. For example, duties range from paperwork and administrative functions to running timing equipment and computers to acting as stroke and turn judges.

LR: Can you share some of your memorable experiences?

AE: The Olympics was of course incredible and very exciting. As were the Pan Am games and other international competitions. But, I'd have to say another very memorable experience I had recently was officiating at the Paralympic Trials held in Indiana. The competitive spirit was inspiring and uplifting. The first day, you noticed disabilities, but after that, you really only noticed the athletes' abilities.

LR: What are your most and least favorite aspects of officiating?

AE: My favorites are to be around young people who have learned to set a goal and keep it, the friendships you make, and the feeling you get when you know you've done a good job. The worst are that it sometimes gets tiring at long meets, and the travel can get expensive.

LR: Any advice for prospective swim officials?

AE: Get involved! Call U.S. Swimming for a list of the possible job duties. They have a brief list which basically describes all of the areas you can get involved in. You may also contact your local swim chapter. Learn the job well, through a training program which is available in most areas of the country. Most people really enjoy the work once they get started. It is so rewarding to work with young people and to know what they go through with training and competing. And, even though you don't get paid, the friendships you develop are quite rewarding and tend to last a long time.

RESOURCES

Regulatory Bodies

Interscholastic

National Federation of State High School
Associations (NFSHSA)
11724 NW Plaza Circle
P.O. Box 20626
Kansas City, MO 64195-0626
Phone: (816) 464-5400 Fax: (816) 464-5571
Internet: www.nfhs.org

Amateur

USA Swimming, Inc. (USS)
One Olympic Plaza
Colorado Springs, CO 80909-5770
Phone (719) 578-4578 Fax (719) 578-4669
Internet: www.usa~swimming.org

United States Diving, Inc. (USD)
Pan American Plaza, Ste. 430
201 S. Capitol Ave.
Indianapolis, IN 46225
Phone (317) 237-5252 Fax (317) 237-5257
e-mail: usdiving@aol.com
Internet: www.usdiving.org

Amateur Athletic Union (AAU)
The Walt Disney Resort
P.O. Box 10000
Lake Buena Vista, FL 32830-1000
Phone: (407) 934-7200 Fax: (407) 934-7242
Internet: www.aausports.org

Collegiate

National Collegiate Athletic Association
(NCAA)
6201 College Blvd.
Overland Park, KS 66211-2422
Phone: (913) 339-1906 Fax: (913) 339-1950
Internet: www.ncaa.org

International

Federation Internationale de Natation
Amateur (FINA)
Ave. de Beaumont 9
Rez-de-Chaussee
1012 Lausanne
Switzerland
Phone: (41-21) 312-6602
Fax: (41-21) 312-6610
Internet: www.fina.org

SWIMMING & DIVING RULES BOOKS

United States Swimming Rules and Regulations can be purchased directly through United States Swimming (USS). Cost is $6. The 1998-99 Rule Book of Diving can be purchased through United States Diving (USD). Cost is $10. A swimming and diving rules book pertinent to interscholastic competition is published by the National Federation of State High School Associations (NF). The National Collegiate Athletic Association (NCAA) also publishes a swimming and diving rules book annually, available each August. Cost of the current edition is $5.

SWIMMING & DIVING OFFICIATING SELF-TEST

1. True or false: Swimming is only a summer sport.

2. How many swimmers make up a relay team?

3. True or false: In Olympic competition, automatic officiating equipment is the primary timing source.

4. What is the governing body of swimming in the United States?

5. Name the four major swim strokes.

6. What is the length of an Olympic size swimming lane?
   a. 100 meters
   b. 50 yards
   c. 75 meters
   d. 50 meters

7. The ____ has overall control of the competition, ensuring the rules are obeyed during the meet.
   a. marshal
   b. starter
   c. referee
   d. clerk of course

8. In an international competition, how many false starts are allowed before a swimmer is disqualified?

9. Swimmers start at a point known as the:
   a. platform
   b. starting plank
   c. starting block
   d. board

10. Name the two types of diving boards.

11. How many diving judges are required at a major competition?
    a. 3 to 5
    b. 4 to 6
    c. 5 to 7

12. True or false: Diving is a sport for only women.

13. True or false: The diving judges at a competition know which dives the athletes will perform before the competition begins.

14. In diving competition, what term is used to describe a diver's near perfect entry into the water?
    a. *stuck*
    b. *ripped*
    c. *clean*

SWIMMING & DIVING OFFICIATING SELF-TEST ANSWERS

1. False; 2. Four swimmers; 3. True; 4. United States Swimming, Inc.; 5. Freestyle, breast stroke, butterfly, back stroke; 6. d; 7. c; 8. Two; 9. c; 10. Spring board, platform; 11. c; 12. False; 13. True; 14. b

SCORING THE SELF-TEST

Incorrect Answers	Officiating Aptitude
0	Perfect: You have a solid knowledge of the sport.
1-3	Average: You need to review the swimming and diving rules book.
4-5	Below average: It's been some time since you've seen a swimming and/or diving meet.
6+	Far below average: You should consider officiating a different sport.

THE
TENNIS
OFFICIAL

TENNIS OFFICIATING AT A GLANCE

Entry Level: United States Tennis Association (USTA) Provisional Official

Minimum Age: None

Certification: USTA certification required at all levels of competition; basic certification requires a written test and may involve attendance at a USTA-approved training school. Also requires active USTA membership.

Average Pay: Tennis officials work on a volunteer basis at many levels. Where offered, compensation ranges from $20 to $50 per match at the interscholastic level. At the collegiate level, officials may earn more or less, depending on the conference. Officials working NCAA Division II and III championship tournaments receive $500 and up to $1,000 in Division I. U.S. Open competition yields an average $130 per day plus expenses.

Schedule: Tennis is played year round in many areas. Interscholastic boys tennis primarily is a spring sport, running from early March until the beginning of June. Interscholastic girls competition is held in the fall. College tennis is played in either spring or fall, varying by school or division.

Today, tennis is played worldwide by young and old, amateurs and professionals alike.

TENNIS: GENERAL INFORMATION

Tennis is played by singles or doubles on a rectangular court separated by a short net. The ball, which is made of rubber with fabric covering, is played with the tennis racquet. The objective of the game is to propel the ball across the net into the opposing player's side of the court in such a way that he or she cannot return it. One point is scored for every ball that goes unreturned. Points may be awarded to either the serving or receiving side. However, the serving side may lose points if it fails to return the ball or commits a *fault* (failure to properly serve the ball in two attemps) in the process.

Technically, the game may be won as early as the fourth score, but only if the leader has a two-point lead. However, as long as the score remains tied, or within one point, the game continues until a victor emerges. In scoring tennis, the term *advantage* is applied to the first player or team to score a point after a tie; the advantage lies in the fact that the next score wins the match. *Love* is a quaint reference to a score of zero. Competitive tennis consists of individual games which comprise a set. A match typically consists of three to five sets.

OFFICIATING TENNIS

Tennis was once a game of the aristocracy, and perhaps for this reason, competitive tennis remains an extremely genteel sport. Tennis players are expected to act with decorum at all times and refrain from the kind of aggressive, antagonistic behavior that occupies officials in many other sports. Even the fans at a tennis match are expected to sit quietly.

For the tennis official, this courteous atmosphere makes the job much easier. Without the distractions that plague officials in other sports, tennis officials are free to focus on the action at hand. And focus they must; major tournaments run 14 days. Chair umpires, in particular, spend the majority of their time watching the ball move back and forth across the net.

Viewed from the on-court official's perspective, officiating tennis may be termed repetitive and fast paced. Unlike many sports which require extensive positioning on the part of the official, the physical demands on the tennis official are minimal. Nonetheless, tennis officials must stand (or sit, in the case of the chair umpire) nearly stationary throughout the event, and for many people, this can be even more difficult than officiating a sport that allows you some freedom of movement. Those who feel restless after sitting in class for an hour or possess a *can't sit still* mentality probably are better suited to officiating another sport.

TENNIS OFFICIALS

Indivdual matches are officiated by a team of on-court officials, the number of which depends on the level of competition. Typically, a chair umpire exercises overall control of the match. The chair umpire is positioned on a tall chair or platform located at one end of the net. From this vantage point, the umpire is able to follow the action on both sides of the court, as well as the progress of the ball. A net cord judge may also be employed at some levels. The net cord judge is positioned at the end of the net, directly beneath the chair umpire. During serves, the net cord judge rests his or her hand on the top of the net. Should the ball strike the net, even

247

slightly, during the serve, the vibration on the net will be detected, and the net cord judge will call a *let* to nullify the serve.

Line umpires are often positioned at the ends of the court and along the sideline opposite the chair umpire. The primary duty of the line judges is to watch the sidelines to verify that the ball hits in-bounds. Line judges may also monitor the server's feet for *foot faults*. Depending on the level of competition, up to 10 line judges may be employed for each game.

Seasons of Play

Tennis is played throughout the year in many areas. Interscholastic boys tennis primarily is a spring sport, beginning in early March and played through early June. Interscholastic girls competition takes place in the fall. College tennis is played in both the spring and fall, depending on the school or division. The Grand Slam, a professional-level competition, is played during the summer months, except for the Australian tournament, which is played in January.

Uniforms & Equipment

The basic uniform requirements of USTA-certified on-court officials include an umpire's shirt, khaki pants or shorts, a navy blue belt, and white socks and sneakers. Two uniform shirts have been approved by the National Official's Committee. Officials generally wear khaki and blue-striped shirts at non-professional competitions; blue shirts with khaki collars are reserved for wear at professional tennis events. However, the blue shirt has been adopted by some USTA Sections for all events.

TENNIS: A BRIEF HISTORY

Tennis is believed to have originated in 13th century France. As originally conceived, the game was played without rackets. Instead, early players used their hands to propel the ball. In fact, the game was initially known as *jeu de paume* (French for *game of the palm*). By the 14th century, *game of the palm* was replaced with a rather cumbersome indoor racquet game that was similar in some respects to badminton. The game was popular with the upper class but was not widely played elsewhere.

Some 400 years later, the game began to take on its present form through the involvement of an Englishman by the name of Major W.C. Wingfield. In the early 1870s, Wingfield introduced an updated version of the game known as lawn tennis which was played with a ball and rackets, a center dividing net, and a set of rules that were easy to comprehend. Wingfield marketed his game in the form of a portable tennis set that included everything necessary to play the game except the lawn. Public response to the game was overwhelmingly favorable. Competitive matches sprang up almost overnight and were widely followed. The first Wimbledon tournament, the premier international tennis event, was held a mere four years after Wingfield was granted a patent on his tennis set.

Tennis began to develop a following in the United States after Mary Ewing Outerbridge, a well-to-do New Yorker, saw the game being played while traveling abroad. In 1881, the first national championship tournament in the United States was held in Newport, Rhode Island. The tournament, which went on to become the U.S. Open, was later moved to Forest Hills, New York. The Davis Cup, awarded annually to the year's outstanding tennis team, was introduced in 1900.

While tennis steadily grew in popularity over the years, it was long regarded as a sport for the affluent. In 1968, the game was transformed by the introduction of the open tournament system which, for the first time, allowed professionals to compete against amateurs. Increased spectator interest, coupled with the emergence of many talented players, elevated the stature of the game. Tennis received official recognition as an Olympic sport in 1988.

Women's tennis exhibition, 1924 Olympic Games, Paris

COMPETITION LEVELS & CERTIFICATION REQUIREMENTS

The United States Tennis Association (USTA) is the primary governing body for tennis in this country and a member of the International Tennis Federation (ITF). The USTA consists of 17 sections, each of which represents one or more states. The USTA sections are further divided into specific districts. A Chairman of Officials is assigned to each USTA Section, as well as many individual districts.

In order to obtain certification as a USTA on-court official, a written test and attendance at a USTA-approved training school is required. Prospective officials must also maintain active membership in USTA. The entry level for USTA officiating is Provisional Official. This applies to inexperienced umpires who have passed a written examination, and in most districts, attended the training school. USTA certification is subject to annual renewal. In even years, applications for on-court officials (other than the entry level)

COMPENSATION
TENNIS OFFICIATING

Tennis officials, to a greater extent than officials in other sports, tend to work on a volunteer basis. The USTA has no set fee arrangement for certified tennis officials; pay varies by locale and is determined by the organization sponsoring the event. At the interscholastic level, officials either volunteer or receive nominal compensation. Compensation at this level typically ranges from $20 to $50 per match. Tennis officials at the collegiate level may earn more or less, depending on the conference. As with all sports, officiating in post season offers much higher pay than for the regular season. Tennis officials in NCAA Division II and III championship tournaments receive $500; in Division I, officials earn $1,000. Officials working at U.S. Open competition earn an average of $130 per day plus expenses.

must be accompanied by a statement from a qualified medical authority indicating that the applicant's vision is 20/20, either corrected or uncorrected.

Most USTA-certified officials initially work at the local level, either in tournaments or in interscholastic and collegiate competition. The USTA maintains an active roster of approximately 3,500 certified officials nationwide. According to the USTA, there is an ongoing need for talented officials at sanctioned events at the Section and District levels, particularly in the area of collegiate officiating.

USTA officials may advance to higher levels as they gain the requisite experience. The USTA maintains the following classifications for tennis officials:

On-Court Officials
Provisional Official
Sectional Official
USTA Official
National Official
Professional Official

Administrative Officials
Sectional Referee
USTA Referee
USTA Chief Umpire
National Referee
Professional Referee
Professional Chief Umpire

Trainer-Evaluator
Sectional Trainer-Evaluator
National Trainer-Evaluator

In addition to on-court officiating, the USTA also certifies various off-court officials, including those who work in administrative capacities and those involved with the training and/or evaluation of other tennis officials.

Prospective tennis officials are encouraged to contact the appropriate USTA Sectional Office (see Resources section of this chapter) for additional information on becoming certified as a tennis official.

TENNIS
LEVELS OF COMPETITION

INTERNATIONAL

Grand Slam of Tennis

PROFESSIONAL

Men's and Women's Events

SEMI-PROFESSIONAL

Satellite Level
Challenger Level

COLLEGE

United States Tennis
Association (USTA)

INTERSCHOLASTIC

USTA Junior Circuit

YOUTH

USTA Junior and Club
Level matches

OFFICIAL PROFILE:
MISSY MALOOL
TOUR DIRECTOR AND
TENNIS UMPIRE, USTA

LR: Tell us how you became involved in officiating.

MM: I've played tennis all my life, as well as taught and coached tennis. While I was teaching tennis at Sea Pines Resort in Hilton Head, South Carolina, my coach encouraged me to take an umpiring clinic. At the time, I had no desire or interest in officiating. In fact, I never ever thought I would be an official. That was back in 1990. In 1996, I served as the chair umpire for the U.S. Open Women's Tennis Finals between Monica Seles and Steffi Graf!

LR: Tell us about this experience.

MM: It was great, but I was pretty nervous climbing into the umpire's chair. I looked over the players as they were getting settled and ready to play. Monica looked fine. I looked over at Steffi and her hands were shaking so much she was spilling water everywhere. This helped calm me down! As it turned out, everything went smooth as silk, and I couldn't have asked for any better turnout.

LR: Tell us about your officiating career since 1990.

MM: In tennis, everyone starts as a line judge. I worked the line for two years, then advanced to chair umpire. I'm now in my sixth year, and I work approximately 150 matches per year. Some officials work as many as 300 matches a year, but with my full time job as tour director for the USTA, my time is limited.

LR: What is the best part of officiating tennis?

MM: The number one thing is that I have the best seat in the house! I love the game, and enjoy being on the court with some of the world's best players. I also enjoy the challenge of being an official. I get an enormous sense of satisfaction after a match where I know I have done well.

LR: What is the most difficult aspect of tennis officiating?

MM: The most difficult part of the job is maintaining your concentration. You have to focus on each point, often for several consecutive hours, sometimes in temperatures exceeding 110 degrees. The pressure on the chair umpire is intense at times.

LR: What about your compensation and other perks?

MM: The money isn't great, and most of the time, tennis officials are lucky to break even on expenses. Per diem expenses normally are picked up, typically at the rate of $50 to $80 per day. However, air travel and lodging are not always covered. As for perks, you can't beat the travel opportunities and the chance to meet the big stars, and all for a sport that I already love.

RESOURCES

Regulatory Bodies

International
International Tennis Federation (ITF)
Palliser Rd., Barons Court
London W14 9EN
Great Britain
Phone: (44-171) 381-8060
Fax: (44-171) 381-5257
Internet: www.itftennis.com

Collegiate
Intercollegiate Tennis Association (ITA)
Lenz Tennis Center
P.O. Box 71
Princeton, NJ 08544

National
U.S. Tennis Association (USTA)
70 W. Red Oak Lane
White Plains, NY 10604-3602
Phone: (914) 696-7000 Fax: (914) 696-7167
Internet: www.usta.com

USTA Regional Sections
USTA Caribbean Section
P.O. Box 40439
Santruce
Puerto Rico 00940-0439
Phone: (809) 724-7425
Includes Puerto Rico, U.S. Virgin Islands

USTA Eastern Section
550 Mamaroneck Ave.
Harrison, NY 10528
Phone: (914) 698-0414
Includes NY, northern NJ, parts of CT (within 35 miles of NYC)

USTA Florida Section
1280 S. South 36th Ave.
Pompano Beach, FL 33069
Phone: (305) 968-3434
Includes FL

USTA Hawaii-Pacific Section
2615 South King St.
Honolulu, HI 96826
Phone: (808) 955-6696
Includes HI, American Samoa, Guam

USTA Intermountain Section
1201 South Parker Rd.
Denver, CO 80231
Phone: (303) 695-4117
Includes CO, UT, WY, MT, southern ID, parts of NV (except Carson City, Washoe County)

USTA Mid-Atlantic Section
2230 George Marshall Dr.
Falls Church, VA 22043
Phone: (703) 560-9480
Includes MD, VA, DC, parts of WV

TENNIS RULES BOOKS

The United States Tennis Association (USTA) publishes a rules book which is available through its publications department. The USTA rules book covers all levels of competition, including interscholastic and collegiate. The USTA also publishes *Friend At Court* which is an excellent reference for tennis officials. The 1999 edition covers both USTA and ITA rules and includes officiating techniques and procedures. Copies are available through the USTA for $3.75, plus $2 shipping.

RESOURCES

USTA Middle States Section
460 Glennie Circle
King of Prussia, PA 19406
Phone: (610) 277-4040
Includes DE, PA, southern NJ

USTA Missouri Valley Section
801 Walnut St.
Kansas City, MO 64106
Phone: (816) 472-6882
Includes IA, KS, MO, NE, OK, parts of IL
(within 30 miles of St. Louis)

USTA New England Section
181 Wells Ave.
Newton Centre, MA 02159
Phone: (617) 964-2030
Includes ME, MA, RI, NH, VT, parts of CT
(except areas included in Eastern Section)

USTA Northern California Section
1350 South Loop Rd.
Alameda, CA 94502-7081
Phone: (510) 748-7373
Includes parts of CA (except Imperial, Kern,
Los Angeles, Orange, Riverside, San
Bernardino, San Diego, San Luis Obispo,
Santa Barbara, Ventura counties)

USTA Northwestern Section
5525 Cedar Lake Rd.
St. Louis Park, MN 55461
Phone: (612) 546-0709
Includes MN, ND, SD, parts of WI (Barron,
Bayfield, Buffalo, Burnett, Chippewa,
Douglas, Dunn, Eau Claire, Pepin, Pierce,
Polk, Rusk, St. Croix, Sawyer, Trempealeau,
Washburn counties)

USTA Pacific-Northwest Section
4840 S.W. Western Ave.
Beaverton, OR 97005
Phone: (503) 520-1877
Includes AK, OR, WA, parts of ID (north of
the 45th parallel), British Columbia

USTA Southern Section
Spalding Woods Office Park
3850 Holcomb Bridge Rd.
Norcross, GA 30092
Phone: (404) 368-8200
Includes AL, AR, GA, LA, MS, NC, SC, TN,
parts of KY (except Boone, Campbell, Kenton
counties)

USTA Southern California Section
P.O. Box 240015
Los Angeles, CA 90024-9115
Phone: (310) 208-3838
Includes all CA counties not included in
Northern California Section

USTA Southwest Section
6330-2 E. Thomas Rd.
Scottsdale, AZ 85251-7056
Phone: (602) 947-9293
Includes AZ, NM, El Paso County, TX

USTA Texas Section
2111 Dickson
Austin, TX 78704
Phone: (512) 443-1334
Includes parts of TX (except El Paso County)

USTA Western Section
8720 Castle Creek Pkwy.
Indianapolis, IN 46250
Phone: (317) 577-5130
Includes IN, MI, OH, parts of IL (except areas
included in Missouri Valley Section), western
WV, parts of KY not included in Southern
Section

TENNIS OFFICIATING SELF-TEST

1. What is the highest possible score in a tennis game?

2. True or false: Love refers to a score of zero in tennis.

3. What does the term *triple set point* mean?

4. True or False: When serving the ball, the server must stand behind the back line on the court.

5. A *let* is called during which of the following situations: a. A ball from another court rolls onto your court during a point; b. You get something in your eye; c. You have neglected to move one of your own balls off the court and now it is in your way

6. True or false: Tennis clothes must be white; no other colors are acceptable.

7. Where is the U.S. Open played?

8. During a twelve-point tie-breaker, the first opponent to _____ wins the game.

9. True or false: Fifteen all and Five all mean the same thing.

10. How many players compete in Canadian doubles?

11. When playing doubles, is it proper etiquette to yell "SWITCH!" to tell one's partner to cover the other side of the court?

12. If there is no line judge, which player has the final say on whether a ball is in or out?

13. When do players switch sides during an outdoor match?

14. True or false: The term *deuce court* describes the left-hand side of the court.

15. If a ball lands on the base line, is it in or out of play?

TENNIS OFFICIATING SELF-TEST ANSWERS

1. Infinite number of points. Game can go back and forth to deuce an unlimited amount of times. 2. True; 3. Score is 40-love and the player with 40 now has three chances in a row to win the set. 4. True; 5. A only; 6. False; 7. Flushing Meadows, NY; 8. Seven, but the game must be won by at least two points. 9. True; 10. Three; 11. Yes; 12. The player in the receiving court, not the player who hit the ball; 13. When the game total is an odd number, such as 1-0, 2-1, 5-2; 14. False. The term *deuce court* refers to the right-hand side of the court. 15. A ball that touches any part of the base line is considered in.

SCORING THE SELF-TEST

Incorrect Answers	Officiating Aptitude
0	Perfect: You have a solid knowledge of the game.
1-3	Average: You need to review the tennis rules book.
4-5	Below average: It's been some time since you've seen a tennis match.
6+	Far below average: You should consider officiating a different sport.

THE
TRACK & FIELD
OFFICIAL

TRACK & FIELD OFFICIATING AT A GLANCE

Entry Level: Interscholastic high school and junior high, recreational and youth meets, often as a statistician or scorekeeper

Minimum Age: 18 for starters/referees in most states; high school students may participate as statisticians and scorekeepers

Certification: State (high school) athletic association certification required for interscholastic officiating in most states. Secondary officials often require no certification (see Section V).

Average Pay: Varies widely by area; many track and field officials are employed on a volunteer basis. The only paid official at most track and field events is the starter/referee who can earn anywhere from $50 to $100 for a dual meet. At the college level, the starter earns $100 in NCAA division championship competition, while the referee and clerk can earn as much as $75 per day.

Schedule: Interscholastic outdoor track is a spring sport, beginning in early March and extending into June. Indoor track is a winter sport which runs from mid-November into late March. The interscholastic cross country season starts in early September.

Hurdling is one of many events included in track and field competition.

TRACK & FIELD: GENERAL INFORMATION

Track and field competition consists of several running, jumping, and throwing events. Collectively, the running events are encompassed in the term *track*; jumping and throwing events fall in the domain of *field* competition. Major track events include sprint, endurance, relay, and hurdle races. In sprint races, typically ranging from 100 to 400 meters, races run flat out from start to finish. Endurance races, which cover distances from 800 to 10,000 meters, force athletes to pace themselves in order to complete the course. Relay races involve teams of four runners. Each runs a leg of the race equal to one-quarter of the overall distance (except in medley races in which each competitor runs a different distance). The first runner on each team carries a baton that he or she passes (*relays*) to the next runner at the start of the next leg. Hurdle races are a variation of sprint races in which competitors jump over a series of 10 barriers spaced along the length of the course. The height of the hurdle depends on the length of the race. In men's competition, hurdles range from 36 to 42 inches in height; women's hurdles range between 30 and 33 inches high.

Field competition includes throwing events such as the discus, hammer, javelin, and shot put; and jumping events such as the long jump, triple jump, high jump, and pole vault. Throwing events are judged on the basis of distance. Jumping events are judged on distance or overall height.

Outdoor track meets are held on a standard oval track measuring 400 meters in circumference. Indoor meets typically are held on a 200 meter track. Field competition generally takes place in an area adjacent to the running track.

Track and field competition is considered both an individual and team sport. Scoring generally is conducted on a team basis with the results of individual events added to determine a team total. The specific events included, as well as the number of participants, are determined by meet organizers.

TRACK & FIELD OFFICIALS

Track and field events require a wide array of officials to monitor the many facets of competition. The referee is the chief official in track and field events and is responsible for ensuring the meet is conducted in accordance with the rules. Prior to competition, the referee verifies the proper marking of the track and field and the placement and condition of the equipment. At smaller meets, the referee may also be responsible for assigning other officials to specific events and reviewing their duties. The referee also handles disqualifications of contestants for unsportsmanlike conduct and/or unacceptable behavior. Depending on the competition level, separate referees may be assigned to the track and to the field events. At larger meets, the meet director is responsible for assigning officials and procuring the track.

At most levels, the referee works in conjunction with a Clerk of the Course, a starter, and a Head Umpire. The Clerk of the Course ensures the orderly progression of the meet (both track and field events), making sure the competitors are in the right place and ready to race at the scheduled time. The starter is responsible for starting races, ensuring the start is legal, and recalling the competitors for a restart if it is not. Traditionally, the Head Finish Judge watched the runners cross the finish line to determine the the finishing order of the other competitors, while the Head Timer recorded the winning time in each race. However, in Olympic and most other major competition today, electronic timing equipment has eliminated the need for these officials. The Head Umpire is responsible for ensuring races are run without lane violations; that is, the runners neither change direction nor impede the progress of their opponents. During relay races, the umpire ensures proper relay of the baton.

In field events, the Clerk of Course works with a variety of officials, including the Field Referee, Head Field Judge, and Event Judges. The Head Field Judge supervises the overall progress of the field events and the work of the Event Judges assigned to them.

Other officials required for track and field competition typically include a Scorer, who keeps a running tally of team scores and a record of individual winners and their performances; the Marshal, who is responsible for keeping spectators and non-competing athletes away from the areas of events in progress; and the Meet Announcer, who introduces each event, the competitors, and the results of each event. At the close of the meet, the announcer introduces meet winners, recaps final scores, and provides team standings. The Wind Gauge Operator uses an anemometer to determine wind direction and velocity during the long jump, triple jump, and races up to 200 meters. These readings are included as part of the permanent meet record and are factored into the validation of athletic performance during these events.

SEASONS OF PLAY

Track and field events are scheduled throughout the year. Interscholastic cross country competition begins at the start of the school year in the fall. Indoor track is a winter sport which typically runs from December through February; the outdoor season runs from early March into June, depending on climate. The summer season, which includes the Junior Olympics and Youth National meets, begins in May.

UNIFORMS & EQUIPMENT

The summer uniform for track and field officials consists of a white golf shirt, khaki slacks and belt, white socks and shoes, and a white golf-style hat. The winter uniform includes a navy blue blazer; gray slacks; a white shirt; a red, white, and blue tie; and black shoes and socks.

Track and field officials use red flags to signal fouls and white flags to indicate legal or successful attempts. The need for stopwatches generally has been eliminated by the use of automatic timing devices. Standard and metric steel measuring tapes (10, 25, 100, 150 and 300 feet) are required to check track lanes and jump distances.

Tom Lowry

COMPETITION LEVELS & CERTIFICATION REQUIREMENTS

Certification of track and field officials in the United States is regulated by USA Track & Field, which maintains a database of all certified officials and their specialties. However, not all track and field competitions require the participation of certified officials. Track and field officials typically work as volunteers because the number of officials required at a single meet makes their compensation cost-prohibitive for most schools and/or athletic organizations and associations.

Three levels of certification for track and field officials have been established by USA Track & Field: Association (training level), National, and Master. Certification is valid for four years, expiring at the end of each summer Olympic year. Cost of certification is $10. Upon certification, track and field officials are qualified to

COMPENSATION

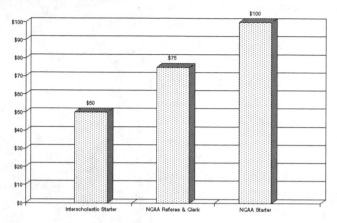

TRACK & FIELD OFFICIATING
COMPENSATION BY COMPETITION LEVEL: EVENT FEES

The graph above provides a comparison of meet fees for track and field officials at various levels. Keep in mind that fees vary widely by area, and track and field officials in many areas work on a volunteer basis.

Due to the large number of major and minor officials who typically work at an interscholastic track meet, compensation of officials can be cost-prohibitive in most districts. In some cases, the starter (the chief official) is compensated, typically earning $50 to $100 per meet. At the college level, the starter, referee, and clerk are paid for individual meets. Travel and lodging expenses, however, are not reimbursed.

officiate in any state in the United States. Officials advance from level to level by meeting USATF qualification standards. Candidates for Association level certification should contact USATF for more information.

Successful completion of an open-book written examination and attendance at a track and field clinic are required before a candidate is certified at the Association level. Once certified, an Association-level official is eligible to serve as an apprentice at all levels of track and field competition.

Officials at the National level are elected by their certified chairpersons and typically have three to five years' experience at the Association level. Similarly, Master officials are selected by a committee of Master level officials within each Association. Olympic officials are selected from this group.

Track and field competition involving junior high and high school students is regulated by state high school athletic associations, which adhere to the rules promulgated by the National Federation of State High School Associations. Officials at this level generally are certified upon successful completion of a National Federation examination. The only paid official at most interscholastic dual track meets is the starter/referee, who can earn from $50 to $100 per meet.

At the collegiate level, the National Collegiate Athletic Association (NCAA) sponsors both cross country and track and field competition. Officials are employed by individual college conferences. Collegiate-level officials pay their own food and lodging expenses. Olympic and major international track and field officials generally are compensated for travel, food, and lodging expenses.

Tom Lowry

TRACK & FIELD
LEVELS OF COMPETITION*

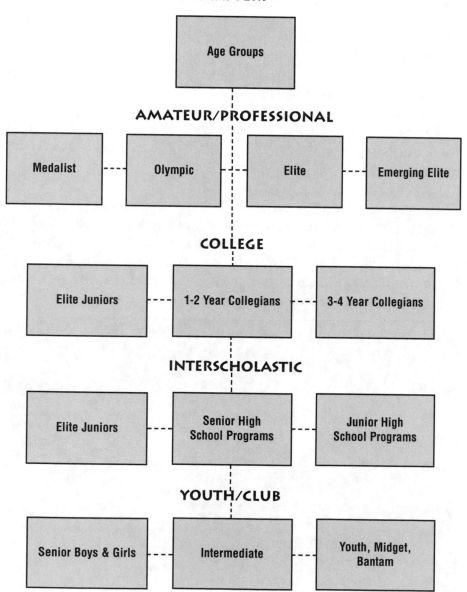

MASTERS

Age Groups

AMATEUR/PROFESSIONAL

Medalist — Olympic — Elite — Emerging Elite

COLLEGE

Elite Juniors — 1-2 Year Collegians — 3-4 Year Collegians

INTERSCHOLASTIC

Elite Juniors — Senior High School Programs — Junior High School Programs

YOUTH/CLUB

Senior Boys & Girls — Intermediate — Youth, Midget, Bantam

*As recognized by USA Track & Field

OFFICIAL PROFILE:
JEROME PERRY

NATIONAL OFFICIALS COMMITTEE CHAIR, USA TRACK & FIELD

LR: How many years have you been an official?

JP: I have been a track and field official for over 35 years, working meets at the high school, college, Junior Olympics, open competition, and Master athlete levels. My specialty has been as a starter or in field events, such as the shot put and discus.

LR: What is the best part of officiating?

JP: The best part of being an official is the opportunity to work with athletes at all levels – Youth to Master athlete – youth being age eight or under and Master from 40 years of age to over 90. Much of officiating is with athletes who will never compete in major competition but are involved for the love of the sport. Officiating can be a challenge. For example, as a starter there is much satisfaction in getting all runners to respond simultaneously. The camaraderie with fellow officials, coaches, and athletes is a plus.

LR: And the worst?

JP: Probably weather is the great improbable in track and field officiating. Outdoor meets are generally held as scheduled, regardless of weather conditions. Lightning, for example, is one factor that will stop a competition. As a meet may last six to eight hours, inclement weather can be a concern. Generally, officials at track and field meets are unpaid, and officiating can be a financial burden for those who travel to major competitions.

LR: What advice can you offer to prospective officials?

JP: My advice to someone interested in being an official would be to contact the coach at a local high school, college, or university and offer one's services. One can also contact the association officials certifier for USA Track & Field and get involved through this route. A potential official should go to a meet, observe, and work in all events before deciding on a specialty. In track, one can be a starter, clerk, umpire, etc. In field events, there are throwing competitions (shot put, javelin, discus, hammer), horizontal jumps (long and triple jump), and vertical jumps (high jump and pole vault). Try them all. Decide where your interests lie. Many enter officiating believing that timing races with a stopwatch is a major specialty, but automatic timing devices have eliminated hand timers, except in high school or local competitions.

LR: Would you consider track and field officiating to be a potential career?

JP: Track and field officiating would not be a potential career for the foreseeable future. Generally, there is little or no remuneration, even at the Olympic level.

LR: Describe your most memorable officiating experience.

JP: My most memorable experience in officiating was in being selected to officiate the Olympic Games in Los Angeles in 1984. Being selected as Chief Starter for the Atlanta Olympics (1996) was equally memorable. Starting Michael Johnson in the 400 meters indoor (1995) and 200 meters outdoor (1996) when he set world records for these events was most memorable as well.

LR: Describe a day in the life of a track and field official.

JP: A day in the life of an official can be quite varied, depending on the event one officiates and the caliber of the meet. In a major competition, there is an officials meeting prior to the start of events. A shirt and hat would be issued, otherwise the official uniform designated by the USATF Officials Committee would be worn. Officials involved in each event/assignment would get together, and the Chief Official would make individual assignments. The officials would then take their positions on the field before the arrival of the athletes in the event. The officials would supervise the warm-ups and competition. At the conclusion of the event, the Chief Official would complete any paper work necessary and pass it along to the meet management.

LR: How did you become involved in officiating?

JP: Becoming a track and field official resulted from my participation in the sport while in school. When out of school and following my profession, I decided to become active in promoting sports competition and gravitated to the sport I know best – that was track and field. I volunteered to work at all levels and continued working in management, administration, and as a competition official, which led to involvement at the national level and eventually to being Chair of the National Officials Committee in USATF.

RESOURCES

Regulatory Bodies
Children's/Interscholastic
National Federation of State High School
Associations (NF)
11724 Plaza Circle
P.O. Box 20626
Kansas City, MO 64195
Phone: (816) 464-5400 Fax: (816) 464-5571
Internet: www.nfhs.org

Collegiate
National Collegiate Athletic Association
(NCAA)
6201 College Blvd.
Overland Park, KS 66211-2422
Phone: (913) 339-1906 Fax: (913) 339-1950
Internet: www.ncaa.org

National
USA Track & Field
One RCA Dome, Ste. 140
P.O. Box 120
Indianapolis, IN 46206-0120
Phone: (317) 261-0500 Fax: (317) 261-0481
Internet: www.usatf.org

International
International Amateur Athletic Federation
(IAFF)
17, Rue Princess-Florestine
Case Postale 359
98007 Monte Carlo
Monaco
Phone: (377-93) 10-888 Fax: (377-93) 15-9515
Internet: www.iaaf.org

TRACK & FIELD RULES BOOKS
USA Track & Field annually updates and publishes a rules book. Contact USATF for ordering information. Cost is $17.00. Collegiate rules are covered in the National Collegiate Athletic Association (NCAA) publication "NCAA Track & Field/Cross Country – Men's and Women's Rules," available through the NCAA. Cost of the 1999 edition is $5. Rules books pertinent to interscholastic track and field competition are available through the National Federation of State High School Associations.

TRACK & FIELD: A BRIEF HISTORY

One of the oldest of competitive sports, track and field contests can be traced back to the original Olympic Games of ancient Greece. Like gymnastics, track and field events were adopted by the Romans after the fall of Greece. After the fall of Rome, however, the sport virtually disappeared.

Modern track and field re-emerged in England, where the first scholastic meets were held in the early 1800s. The Royal Military Academy of England sponsored the first organized track and field meet in 1849. The first championship meet was held in England in 1866 under the auspices of the Amateur Athletic Club.

Interest in track and field competition in the United States developed slowly over the first half of the 19th century. However, the sport did not attain nationwide popularity until after the Civil War, spurred in part by the organization of the New York Athletic Club, which sponsored indoor meets beginning in 1868. Track and field competition attained international prominence when it was included in the modern Olympic Games, which were revived in 1896. Olympic competition spawned the formation of the International Amateur Athletic Federation (IAAF) in 1913. Created to standardize track and field competition at the international level, the IAAF continues as the governing body of the sport today.

Initially, track and field events were considered suitable solely for male athletes. Competition for women was not formally organized until 1921. Women's track and field competition at the Olympic level was introduced in 1928.

Runners positioned for the start of the 110-meter hurdles at the 1896 Olympics in Athens

TRACK & FIELD OFFICIATING SELF-TEST

1. True or false: In relay races, the length of the passing zone is 20 meters.

2. True or false: In the high jump, a competitor is eliminated after three consecutive failed jumps.

3. What is the height, in inches, of a hurdle in the senior men's 400-meter event?
   a. 30; b. 33; c. 36; d. 42

4. The _____ is responsible for procuring the track and getting the necessary officials.
   a. meet director; b. surveyor; c. clerk of course; d. marshal

5. True or false: A standard outdoor running track is 400 meters in length.

6. After a false start, runners are recalled by the sound of:
   a. a refiring of the starter's gun; b. a single whistle toot; c. an air horn

7. Who has the final decision over the declaration of fouls or questions of contest?
   a. Head track/field judge; b. Games committee; c. Meet referee; d. Clerk of course

8. The diameter of the throwing circle in the discus event is:
   a. 1 meter; b. 1.75 meters; c. 2 meters; d. 2.5 meters

9. True or false: It is legal for a competitor to start a race with his or her fingers on the starting line.

10. In track and field competition, the term *scratch* refers to a competitor who:
    a. is disqualified for false starts; b. fails to appear for an event; c. skips a trial

11.   What is the ruling if the high jump bar vibrates and falls after the jumper is out of the pit?
      a. The jump is good. b. The jump is ruled a miss. c. The jump must be made again. d. There is no ruling.

12.   In track events, staggered starts are used:
      a. when there are three or more competitors; b. for hurdle races; c. for races in which runners must maintain their lanes through the curved portions of the track; d. for 55- and 100-meter sprints.

13.   True or false: In field events, competitors may practice while waiting their turn to compete.

14.   Which three of the following duties are the responsibility of the starter?
      a. Recall runners in case of a false start; b. Ensure that judges and timers are ready to begin; c. Fire the gun after competitors are *set* and motionless; d. Watch for rules violations at the start of the race

TRACK & FIELD OFFICIATING SELF-TEST ANSWERS

1. True; 2. True ; 3. 36; 4. a; 5. True; 6. a; 7. c; 8. d; 9. False (fingers must be behind the starting line); 10. b; 11. b; 12. c; 13. False; all practice is suspended during competition; 14. a, c and d

SCORING THE SELF-TEST

Incorrect Answers	Officiating Aptitude
0	Perfect: You have a solid knowledge of the sport.
1-3	Average: You need to review the track and field rules book.
4-5	Below average: It's been some time since you've seen a track meet.
6+	Far below average: You should consider officiating a different sport.

THE
VOLLEYBALL
REFEREE

VOLLEYBALL OFFICIATING AT A GLANCE

Entry Level: Interscholastic high school and junior high, recreational and youth volleyball

Minimum Age: None

Certification: State (high school athletic) association certification required for interscholastic officiating in most states (see Section V).

Average Pay: Varies widely by area; junior varsity ranges from $15 to $20, and high school varsity from $30 to $40 a day per match.

Schedule: Interscholastic girls volleyball is played in the fall; boys compete in spring. Combined with recreational and summer outdoor leagues, the volleyball official can work practically year round.

The widespread popularity of beach volleyball led to its inclusion in the Olympic Games, beginning in the summer of 1996.

VOLLEYBALL: GENERAL INFORMATION

At most levels of competition, six players comprise a volleyball team. In some forms of the sport, however, teams of two or four compete. The object of the game is to send a ball over a raised net and within the boundaries of the opposing team's court in such a manner that it is either impossible to return or hits the ground in the process. In National Association for Girls and Women in Sports (NAGWS) competition, players are permitted to play the ball with any part of the body above the knee. USA Volleyball (USAV) and Federation Internationale de Volleyball (FIVB) rules allow players to contact the ball with any part of the body. Volleyball matches consist of individual games. In interscholastic and USA Volleyball competition, the first team to win two of three games wins the match. At the collegiate level, three of five games take the match.

OFFICIATING VOLLEYBALL

One of the biggest challenges facing the volleyball official is keeping up-to-date on the latest rules changes. Like gymnastics, the rules of volleyball are changed in Olympic years. A ball handling technique that is illegal one year might become legal the next. Volleyball officials also must be conversant with a variety of hand and card signals used in the game.

Volleyball officials need to be alert and quick-minded in order to follow the ball while simultaneously taking in the manner in which players contact it. Officiating volleyball also requires good communication skills as the first referee must work in concert with the second referee, as well as the support personnel required in a typical match.

VOLLEYBALL OFFICIALS

Volleyball officials include the first and second referees, a scorekeeper, and two line judges. Two additional line judges are often employed in major tournaments and championship matches.

The first referee, referred to as the *up* referee or *1R*, maintains a position on a raised platform or stand that is positioned at one end of the net. The second referee, known as the *down* referee or *2R*, stands just outside the court at the other end of the net. The up referee exercises overall control of the game and has the power to overrule decisions made by other officials during the match. The line judges assist the referees in determining whether the ball falls within the boundaries of the court.

SEASONS OF PLAY

Volleyball matches are scheduled throughout the year. High school and junior high women's teams play in the fall and winter; high school and junior high men's teams compete in the spring. College women's teams compete from September through December, and college men's teams play from January through May. Junior Olympic matches are scheduled from March through July for both boys and girls. USAV adult men's and women's matches run from November through May. Additional officiating opportunities are available for summer outdoor leagues, beach volleyball, tournaments, and recreational leagues throughout the year.

UNIFORMS & EQUIPMENT

Junior high and high school officials wear black and white, vertically striped shirts and black pants or shorts. At the collegiate level, volleyball officials wear white shirts and blue pants. The approved uniform for USAV-certified officials is a white shirt, dark navy slacks or shorts, and white shoes and socks.

Additional equipment requirements for volleyball officials include a whistle, red and yellow cards, a coin for the toss to determine which team will serve first, an air pressure gauge, and a measuring chain to check the height of the net.

Thomas Blue

COMPETITION LEVELS & CERTIFICATION REQUIREMENTS

Junior high and high school volleyball is governed by state high school athletic associations in accordance with rules set forth by the National Federation of State High School Associations. The certification of junior and high school volleyball referees is regulated by specific state high school associations. Typically, prospective officials are required to pass a written volleyball rules examination and attend local volleyball association meetings. Prospective officials are cautioned that significant differences exist between National Federation and USA Volleyball rules; it is vital to review the correct rules book before taking any written examination. The earnings of junior and high school level officials vary by state and are specifically determined by local school districts and/or state associations. Typical event fees for officials at this level range from $15 to $25 at the junior varsity level and from $35 to $40 at the varsity level.

Collegiate level volleyball competition is sponsored by the National Collegiate Athletic Association (NCAA), the National Association of Intercollegiate Athletics (NAIA), and the National Junior College Athletic Association (NJCAA). An annual written rules examination is required for prospective referees of women's volleyball at the collegiate level. The test is based on the rules books published by the National Association for Girls and Women in Sports (NAGWS) and USA Volleyball (USAV). There are minor differences between NAGWS and USAV rules. Annual attendance at a pre-season clinic also is required. USAV referees are employed by individual college conferences for men's competition. Collegiate-level earnings vary throughout college divisions, ranging from $40 at junior colleges to approximately $250 at NCAA Division I schools.

USAV Youth/Junior Olympics programs are organized for individuals from 12 through 18 years old. USAV also conducts adult volleyball programs throughout the United States. USA Volleyball has established six referee classifications: Junior Olympic, Provisional, Regional, Junior National, USA-National, and Provisional USA-International Referee. All referees must be registered with USA Volleyball and their corresponding Regional Volleyball Associations (RVA) for each season, attend volleyball clinics, and pass written referee and scorekeeper tests. Prospective officials are observed during sanctioned competition and rated based on their performance. USAV officials earn from $65 to $70 a day during adult playoff tournaments and approximately $125 a day during Junior Olympic tournament competition.

Volleyball scorekeepers are certified by USAV and Regional Volleyball Associations. USAV has established scorekeeper classifications which include Junior, Provisional, Regional, Junior National, USA-National, USA-International, Regional Outdoor, and USA-National Outdoor.

VOLLEYBALL: A BRIEF HISTORY

Volleyball is a competitive and recreational team sport that was invented in 1895 by William A. Morgan, a YMCA physical education director in Massachusetts. Originally called *mintonette*, the game was created to serve as a less strenuous form of exercise for Morgan's older clients. The game later was renamed by Alfred T. Halstead of Springfield College. Volleyball became a major international sport after its introduction to the Europeans by American soldiers during the World Wars. In 1947, the Federation Internationale de Volleyball (FIVB), the international governing body of the sport, was formed. Team volleyball became an Olympic sport in 1964. Two-person-team beach volleyball made its Olympic debut in 1996.

The United States Volleyball Association, established in 1928, was the original national governing body in the United States. Today, USA Volleyball is recognized by the U.S. Olympic Committee as the national governing body of the sport and serves as the exclusive representative of the United States to the FIVB.

Volleyball is unique in its adherence to an unusually formal pre-game protocol that originated when the game was introduced as an Olympic sport. The customary pre-game ceremony includes the introduction of individual players and referees to the spectators and the playing of the national anthem. Although this pre-game ritual is more frequently incorporated as part of advanced competition, volleyball officials at all levels are encouraged to include it.

COMPENSATION

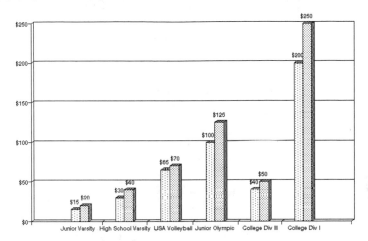

VOLLEYBALL OFFICIATING
COMPENSATION BY COMPETITION LEVEL: EVENT FEES

The graph above reflects average event fee ranges for volleyball officials at various levels of competition. Officials working one game per
week can expect to earn amounts ranging somewhere between the
high and low range for their level. At the lower levels of competition,
it is not uncommon for officials to work more than one game per
week, thereby increasing their earnings. For example, an interscholastic official can easily pull in $70-plus per week by working
two high school games per week, which translates into over $240 per
month. Not bad for roughly 20 or 30 hours of work per month.
Compare this to a part time job paying a minimum wage of $4.75 per
hour, which would yield less than $400 over a month for 80 hours
of work.

As you move up the officiating ladder to higher levels of competition,
your pay goes up accordingly. College and amateur-level officials
earn substantially more than interscholastic officials. At nearly all
levels of competition, officials receive a higher event fee for championship and playoff games than for the regular season. At present,
the top earnings for volleyball officials occur in NCAA Division I. At
this level, referees earn an average of $250 per match during the reg-
ular season and as much as $475 in championship competition.

VOLLEYBALL
LEVELS OF COMPETITION

AMATEUR

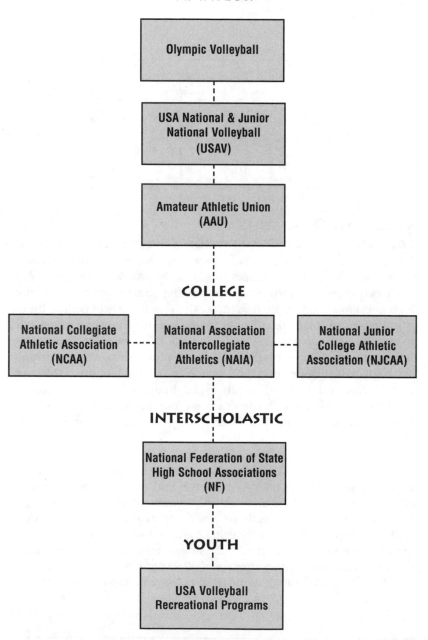

Olympic Volleyball

USA National & Junior National Volleyball (USAV)

Amateur Athletic Union (AAU)

COLLEGE

National Collegiate Athletic Association (NCAA)

National Association Intercollegiate Athletics (NAIA)

National Junior College Athletic Association (NJCAA)

INTERSCHOLASTIC

National Federation of State High School Associations (NF)

YOUTH

USA Volleyball Recreational Programs

OFFICIAL PROFILE:
TOM BLUE
NATIONAL RULES INTERPRETER,
USA VOLLEYBALL

LR: How did you begin your career as a volleyball referee?

TB: The truth is that I broke my ankle. I had been a player and referee since 1965, and I broke my ankle in 1980. I still wanted to stay close to the sport, so I began to spend a lot more time officiating at this point.

LR: What is the best part of being a volleyball official?

TB: Definitely making and keeping associations with everyone in the sport, including the players, coaches, and officials. The camaraderie is terrific. It's also a great thing to see people grow in the sport. For example, I watched a kid go from playing in a junior volleyball league to eventually becoming a coach for the U.S. Olympic men's volleyball team.

LR: And your least favorite aspect of officiating?

TB: When one group of people does not respect the other group, it is difficult. As in when the players don't respect the officials. The officials are there to make sure the game runs smoothly and is played fair, for everyone's benefit.

LR: Tom, tell me about a typical "day in the life."

TB: I'll give you an overview of a typical weekend match for collegiate volleyball. I generally leave some time Friday afternoon. I take off early from work and catch a flight to the city I need to be in. If the match is within three hours by car, I drive instead of fly. Work and flight scheduling takes a lot of planning, so luckily my wife is a travel agent! I arrive in a city, get a rental car, and check into a hotel.

I then show up at the match at least an hour before it starts to check the equipment and court. It's good to be early so you are not in a hurry when you are at the site. The match usually lasts between one and three hours, depending on the teams. With evenly matched teams, the games tend to last longer. Matches are scheduled for Friday evenings and Sunday early afternoons. Saturdays are free. After the match is over Sunday, I fly home.

LR: Could you please share some of your memorable experiences?

TB: Being a referee at the Olympics is very interesting and exciting. However, the things I remember most about officiating, regardless of the level of competition, are being in situations that I have not experienced before and having to make decisions. It's a constant learning process, and that is what makes it so interesting.

LR: Any advice for the newcomer?

TB: Learn the sport completely. Learn to see the sport from all different perspectives – spectator, athlete, coach, and referee. Keep up with the sport and what is happening in and around it. Always remember that it is the players who decide the outcome of a match – you are just there to make it fair.

RESOURCES

Regulatory Bodies
Children's/Interscholastic
National Federation of State High School
Associations (NF)
11724 Plaza Circle
P.O. Box 20626
Kansas City, MO 64195
Phone: (816) 464-5400 Fax: (816) 464-5571
Internet: www.nfhs.org

Collegiate
National Collegiate Athletic Association
(NCAA)
6201 College Blvd.
Overland Park, KS 66211-2422
Phone: (913) 339-1906 Fax: (913) 339-1950
Internet: www.ncaa.org

Amateur
USA Volleyball (USAV)
3595 E. Fountain Blvd., Ste. I-2
Colorado Springs, CO 80910-1740
Phone: (719) 637-8300 Fax: (719) 597-6307
Internet: www.volleyball.org/usav

American Alliance for Health, Physical
Education, Recreation and Dance (AAHPERD)
1900 Association Dr.
Reston, VA 22091
Phone: (703) 476-3400 Fax: (703) 476-9527
Internet: www.aahperd.org

International
Federation Internationale de Volleyball (FIVB)
12 Ave. de la Gare
Case Postale
1001 Lausanne
Switzerland
Phone: (41-21) 345-3535 Fax: (41-21) 345-3545
Internet: www.fivb.ch

VOLLEYBALL RULES BOOKS
Volleyball Rules Books and Case Books are available through the National Federation of State High School Associations (NF). Cost of the 1998-99 NF Volleyball Rules Book and the Case Book is $5 each. The National Association for Girls and Women in Sports (NAGWS) Rules Book is available from AAHPERD (American Alliance for Health, Physical Education, Recreation and Dance) Publications, P.O. Box 704, Waldorf, MD 20604, (800) 321-0789. Cost is $8.95 plus shipping. The USAV Rules Book and the USAV/NAGWS Case Book are available through the USAV publications department. Cost of the rules book is $6.95; cost of the case book is $5.95.

VOLLEYBALL OFFICIATING SELF-TEST

1. How many players comprise a volleyball team in a high school or collegiate match?

2. How many hits per team are allowed before the ball must be sent over the net to the opponent?

3. True or false: A block counts as one hit.

4. What is the minimum number of officials required at a volleyball match?

5. True or false: It is legal to let the ball come to rest in the setter's hand when setting up for a spike.

6. Where must a player stand when serving?

7. True or false: A back row player cannot attack the ball in front of the 10-foot line if the ball is contacted when it is completely above the upper edge of the net.

8. If two players contact the ball at the same time, who can play the ball next?
    a. Either player; b. The player on the right; c. Another player on the team; d. The coach; e. a and c

9. Does the simultaneous contact described in Question 8 count as one or two hits?

10. True or false: The line judge can overrule a call made by the referee.

11. True or false: A blocker can cross over the plane of the net and block the opposing team's attempt to set the ball (the opposing team's second hit).

12. What is the height of the net in women's competition? In men's competition?

13. If a team has the serve and is caught out of rotation, what is the official ruling?

14. In what year was volleyball invented?

15. In which two Olympic Games did the U.S. men's indoor team win the gold medal?

16. What medal did the U.S. women's volleyball team win during the 1984 Olympic Games?

17. If Team A sends the ball over the net and it touches the antenna before traveling over the net and landing in Team B's court, which team wins the volley?

18. If Team A spikes the ball and it touches Team B's blocker's hands before falling outside the court, which team wins the volley?

19. How many points are required to win a set?

20. True or false: A team must win by two points.

VOLLEYBALL OFFICIATING SELF-TEST ANSWERS

1. Six; 2. Three; 3. False; 4. Two (NAGWS/USAV require five: R1, R2, scorekeeper, two line judges; 5. False; 6. Anywhere behind the end line; 7. True; 8. e; 9. One; 10. False; 11. False; 12. women's: 7 feet, 4 1/8 inches; men's: 7 feet, 11 5/8 inches; 13. Loss of serve, side out; 14. 1895; 15. 1984 and 1988; 16. Silver; 17. Team B; 18. Team A; 19. 15; 20. True (Under USAV and FIVB rules, a non-deciding set may be won by one point at 17-16.)

SCORING THE SELF-TEST

Incorrect Answers	Officiating Aptitude
0	Perfect: You have a solid knowledge of the game.
1-3	Average: You need to review the volleyball rules book.
4-5	Below average: It's been some time since you've seen a volleyball game.
6+	Far below average: You should consider officiating a different sport.

THE
WRESTLING
OFFICIAL

WRESTLING OFFICIATING AT A GLANCE

Entry Level: Interscholastic high school and junior high, recreational and youth wrestling

Minimum Age: 14 in most states

Certification: State (high school) athletic association certification required for interscholastic wrestling referees in most states (see Section V).

Average Pay: Varies widely by area; at the high school junior varsity level, wrestling referees typically earn $25 per meet. Varsity referees earn $40 per meet and up to $250 per day during post-season tournaments. In NCAA Championship competition, in all divisions, wrestling referees earn $90 per meet.

Schedule: Interscholastic wrestling is a winter sport, beginning in mid-November and continuing through the end of March.

Freestyle is the most widely practiced competitive form of wrestling in the United States.

WRESTLING: GENERAL INFORMATION

Freestyle wrestlers start a match in an upright position. Using strategic holds, lifts, and throws, each competitor attempts to pin the shoulders of his or her opponent to the mat. Wrestlers score points by utilizing strategic movements and specific wrestling holds during the match. They are penalized for illegal holds and inappropriate conduct. A wrestler who pins any part of both shoulders or shoulder blades of his or her opponent to the mat for one-half second (Olympic and international competitions), one second (college), or two seconds (high school) wins the match. If neither wrestler is pinned, a winner is determined based on the tabulation of points scored during the course of the competition. The wrestler awarded the highest number of points during the match wins.

Wrestlers compete against others of approximately the same weight. USA Wrestling, interscholastic, and collegiate athletes are further classed by age. USA Wrestling, high school, and collegiate matches are conducted within a 32-foot diameter circle on a protective mat. A 10-foot diameter circle at the center of the mat is where the wrestlers begin competition. International and Olympic wrestlers compete on a raised platform that measures 6 to 8 m. (or 19 ft., 8 in.) to 26 ft., 3 in., square.

The duration of a wrestling match varies by competition level. A wrestling match is comprised of one to three periods. USA Wrestling matches range from two 90-second periods for 7- and 8-year olds to one five-minute period for wrestlers age 17 and older. High school junior varsity and varsity matches last six minutes and are made up of three two-minute periods. Collegiate matches are seven minutes in duration and are comprised of a three-minute first period, a two-minute second period, and a two-minute third period. Olympic and international matches are comprised of one five-minute period.

Officiating Wrestling
Officiating wrestling matches requires concentration, focus, and the physical stamina required to keep pace with the action. Mat referees, in particular, constantly must reposition themselves in order to watch for pins and illegal holds. Referees must be fully conversant in the rules specific to their level and master the basic hand signals used to convey information to the judge and mat chairman. Experienced wrestling referees have learned the art of keeping the action moving and are a joy to watch.

Wrestling Officials
Wrestling officials include the referee, the mat chairman, the judge, and the mat controller or timekeeper. The mat chairman is the chief official and the only person permitted to communicate with the judge and referee. The mat chairman indicates decisions by raising a wrestler's colors. During a bout, the referee maintains a position on the mat close to the wrestlers. The referee starts and stops each bout and watches for points scored, illegal holds, and stalling by the contestants. The judge, who is empowered to score points independent of the referee, raises a baton to indicate points scored and gives a score sheet to the mat chairman at the end of each match.

During USA Wrestling sanctioned events, two mat judges are employed. The mat judges rotate positions with the referee between matches. An assistant referee and assistant timekeeper may also be present.

The United States Wrestling Officials Association (USWOA) is responsible for the registration, education, and evaluation of more than 2,000 active freestyle and Greco-Roman mat and pairings officials in the United States. The pairings official is charged with tournament operations. He or she determines which competitors will face off during a meet and the order in which they will wrestle (*tournament bracketing*).

Seasons of Play

Interscholastic and collegiate wrestling competitions typically are scheduled from November through March. USA Wrestling sanctioned matches are held throughout the spring and summer. International freestyle and Greco-Roman wrestlers compete in the games of the Winter Olympics.

Wrestling Rules Books

The Wrestling Rules Book, annually updated by the National Federation of State High School Associations (NF), outlines the official rules of high school competition. Cost of the 1998-99 Wrestling Rules Book is $5. The NF Wrestling Case Book and Manual, invaluable both for individuals interested in officiating and for working officials interested in improving their skills, presents specific competition situations and rulings. The NF Case Book and Manual, published every two years, is available for $5.

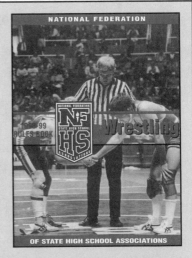

Collegiate level wrestling rules books are available through the National Collegiate Athletic Association for $5 and the USA Wrestling Rules Book and Guide can be purchased from USA Wrestling for $5.

UNIFORMS & EQUIPMENT

Wrestling mat officials wear black pants, black socks, black shoes, black belts, and black and white vertically striped shirts. The referee uses red and green wrist bands to signal the scorekeeper of pins or falls and/or points scored. Each color corresponds to one of the contestants. The referee indicates the number of points scored with extended fingers, raising the right arm (green wrist band) if the wrestler wearing green scored them and raising the left (red wrist band) if the wrestler wearing red scored them.

During tournament-level competition, one wrestler wears a red ankle band and his or her opponent wears a green ankle band to identify themselves to the audience, the referee, and the scoring table. Officials at the international level wear white shirts, pants, and shoes. To indicate points scored, the referee wears a blue band on the right wrist and a red band on the left.

Roger Perlmuter

Wrestling officials at all levels use a whistle to signal the start and stop of competition. Match cards for interscholastic tournament competition are available through the National Federation of State High School Associations. The match cards feature scoring references, signal charts, and instructions for scorers and timekeepers.

COMPETITION LEVELS & CERTIFICATION REQUIREMENTS

United States Wrestling Officials Association (USWOA) members officiate at more than 1,500 USA Wrestling sanctioned events each year, ranging from local tournaments and regional/national events to the Olympic Games. USA Wrestling classes include Bantam for ages seven and eight, Midget for ages nine and 10, Novice for ages 11 and 12, Schoolboy/Girl for ages 13 and 14, Cadet for ages 15 and 16, Junior for students enrolled in grades 9 through 12,

WRESTLING
LEVELS OF COMPETITION*

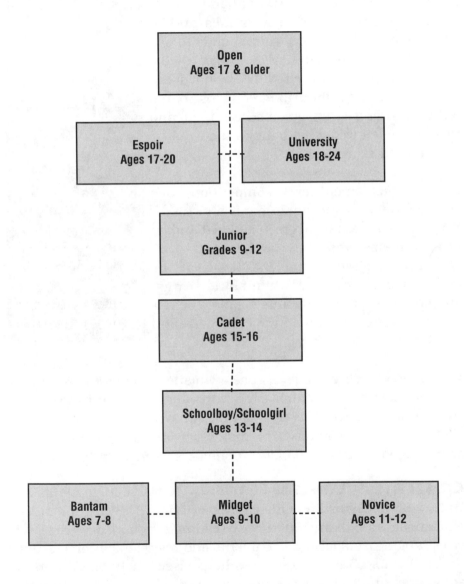

*As recognized by USA Wrestling

Espoir for wrestlers age 17 through 20, University for wrestlers age 18 to 24, and Open for wrestlers 17 and older. The USWOA registers male and female mat and pairings officials beginning at the age of 14. USA Wrestling officials must pass exams, participate in clinics, and accumulate experience to advance through various levels of expertise. Pairings officials levels range from PA (*Pairings Applicant*) through P1E (*Exceptionale*) and Secretariate Internationale. Mat officials classifications range from Mat Applicant (*MA*) through M1E (*Mat Exceptionale*). All USA Wrestling officials work as volunteers.

Interscholastic junior varsity and varsity wrestling, including dual meets and state tournaments, are regulated by specific state high school athletic associations in conformance with the standards set forth by the National Federation of State High School Associations (NF). Individual state high school associations also establish certification requirements for wrestling officials. Most states impose a minimum age limit of 18 for registration and require successful completion of an NF wrestling rules test and rules clinic attendance for certification. High school junior varsity officials typically earn $25 per meet and $75 to $125 per day during tournament competition; varsity officials are paid approximately $40 per meet and can earn from $150 to $250 per day during post-season tournament competition. Interscholastic wrestling tournaments typically are four to eight hours in length. Generally, 12 to 15 tournaments are scheduled each season.

College wrestling teams compete in dual matches and in an annual tournament sponsored by the National Collegiate Athletic Association (NCAA). Wrestling officials at this level are employed by individual colleges and/or conferences, many of which establish conference-specific compensation rates. However, the NCAA hires officials for tournament-level competition. Collegiate-level wrestling officials typically are recruited by college coaches from the ranks of those working at the interscholastic level. Officials at the tournament level are chosen by the NCAA from among those officials recommended by its affiliated members. Although no specific collegiate certification is required, potential officials may be subject to college conference examinations. Collegiate-level officials earn between $50 and $70 per dual meet and from $100 to $150 per day, including travel expenses, during the course of an eight-hour tournament.

COMPENSATION

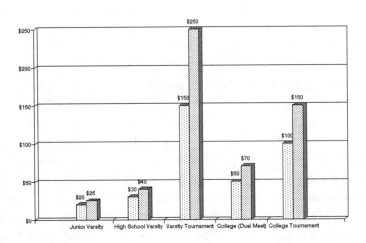

WRESTLING OFFICIATING
COMPENSATION BY COMPETITION LEVEL: MEET FEES

The graph above provides a comparison of meet fees for wrestling referees at various levels. Keep in mind that fees vary widely by area, and referees in some areas may work on a volunteer basis in the early stage of their careers.

At the lower levels of competition, it is not uncommon for wrestling referees to work more than one meet per week. An interscholastic wrestling referee can easily pull in $80 by working two high school meets per week, which translates into $240 per month during the season. Not bad for roughly 24 hours of work per month. Compare this to a part time job paying a minimum wage of $4.75 per hour, which would yield less than $400 over a month for 80 hours of work. Add to this the potential of working post-season tournament competition which pays substantially more than regular season meets.

Unlike most other sports, wrestling referees do not earn substantially more at higher levels and, in some cases, they make even less than high school referees. Referees who advance to the college and amateur level generally are motivated by their love of the sport.

OFFICIAL PROFILE:

BILL BUPP

SUPERVISOR OF OFFICIALS,
MICHIGAN HIGH SCHOOL
ATHLETIC ASSOCIATION

LR: How many years have you been an official?

BB: Twenty-five years as an active official and 10 years as the assistant director of the Michigan High School Athletic Association, responsible for the wrestling program.

LR: What are the best parts and worst parts of being an official?

BB: The opportunity to give back to the athletic program which provided opportunity for me, and the opportunity to be involved with outstanding coaches, officials and athletes. The worst is when sportsmanship is set aside.

LR: What advice would you give to individuals interested in becoming officials?

BB: Study, practice, network, learn from experienced officials, participate in clinics and training opportunities, work in every match you can, at any level.

LR: Would you consider officiating in your sport to be a possible career?

BB: Wrestling officiating is an avocation.

LR: What is the most memorable experience you have had as an official?

BB: Working as much as I cared to, season after season.

LR: Describe a day in the life of a wrestling official.

BB: Rise early, drive to a tournament, work from 10 a.m. until 8 p.m. – on your feet, on your belly, shower and return home. Long, demanding tournament days.

LR: How did you get started in officiating?

BB: My high school coach encouraged me to officiate during practice and I began to officiate in college.

RESOURCES

Regulatory Bodies

Interscholastic

National Federation of State High School
Associations (NF)
11724 Plaza Circle
P.O. Box 20626
Kansas City, MO 64195
Phone: (816) 464-5400 Fax: (816) 464-5571
Internet: www.nfhs.org

Amateur

USA Wrestling (USAW)
6155 Lehman Dr.
Colorado Springs, CO 80918
Phone: (719) 598-8181 Fax: (719) 598-9440
e-mail: usaw@concentric.net
Internet: www.usawrestling.org

Collegiate

National Collegiate Athletic Association
(NCAA)
6201 College Blvd.
Overland Park, KS 66211-2422
Phone: (913) 339-1906 Fax: (913) 339-1950
Internet: www.ncaa.org

International

Federation Internationale des Luttes
Associees (FILA)
Ave. Juste-Olivier
1006 Lausanne
Switzerland
Phone: (41-21) 312-8426
Fax: (41-21) 323-6073
Internet: www.worldsport.com/sports/
        wrestling/home.html

Officials Association

U.S. Wrestling Officials Association
(USWOA)
2612 Hamilton
Glenshaw, PA 15116
Phone: (412) 486-8997

WRESTLING: A BRIEF HISTORY

Wrestling is an ancient sport, depicted on tomb carvings dating from perhaps 3000 BC, described by Homer in the Iliad and the Odyssey, and featured in the Olympic Games of ancient Greece. The sport exists in many forms, including the martial arts, but freestyle (catch-as-catch-can) and Greco-Roman are the two forms most practiced throughout the world and the only two included in modern Olympic competition.

Freestyle wrestling is derived from early Greek wrestling. The most frequently practiced style in United States competition, freestyle allows wrestlers to use their legs to hold and lift opponents. The Greco-Roman style, developed in France, permits no holds below the waist and prohibits the use of the legs for tripping or gripping.

Threatened by fixed *professional* matches sponsored by circuses and carnivals in the United States after World War I, wrestling regained credibility as a sport following its organization by the Amateur Athletic Union (AAU) in 1888 and the Federation Internationale des Luttes Amateurs or International Federation of Amateur Wrestlers (FILA). FILA, founded in 1921, codified rules, set standards, and organized competitions for all amateur wrestlers. The national governing body of amateur wrestling and the United States representative to FILA and to the United States Olympic Committee is USA Wrestling. Today, professional wrestling, still popular in the United States, is more entertainment than competition.

George Hackenschmidt, the Russian Lion, is considered one of the best heavyweights of all time

WRESTLING OFFICIATING SELF-TEST

1. How many weight classes are there in competitive wrestling?

2. What are the two styles of wrestling?

3. How many points can be earned by a takedown?
   a. 3 points
   b. 2 points
   c. 1 point

4. True or false: A wrestling referee wears red and green wrist bands to indicate the start and finish of each round.

5. What is the name given to a maneuver that ends the match after a three-second hold?
   a. takedown
   b. reversal
   c. pin
   d. touch fall

6. How much time is allotted for a rest period?
   a. 30 seconds
   b. 1 minute
   c. 2 minutes
   d. There are no rest periods between periods.

7. What is the name of the organization that oversees the sport of wrestling in the United States?

8. True or false: It is legal for a wrestler to kick the opponent to end a match.

9. True or false: Stalling is not permitted in a wrestling match.

10. True or false: *Injury time* is granted to a wrestler who appears to be hurt.

11. How many officials are required at a match?
   a. 1
   b. 3
   c. 4

12. True or false: A wrestler must be at the exact weight of his weight class precisely one hour before the match begins.

13. True or false: Wrestling is a male only sport.

14. What is the name given to the official who is in charge of the *bracketing* for wrestling matches?
   a. pairings official
   b. grouping official
   c. referee
   d. mat attendant

15. True or false: Wrestling is an Olympic sport.

WRESTLING OFFICIATING SELF-TEST ANSWERS

1. 13; 2. Freestyle (catch-as-catch-can) and Greco-Roman; 3. c; 4. False; 5. c; 6. d; 7. United States Wrestling; 8. False; 9. True; 10. True; 11. c; 12. False; 13. False; 14. a; 15. True

SCORING THE SELF-TEST

Incorrect Answers	Officiating Aptitude
0	Perfect: You have a solid knowledge of the sport.
1-3	Average: You need to review the wrestling rules book.
4-5	Below average: It's been awhile since you've seen a wrestling match.
6+	Far below average: You should consider officiating a different sport.

SECTION IV:
OFFICIATING IN
50 OTHER SPORTS

CONTENTS

AIKIDO

Sports Aikido is based on Tomiki Aikido, an ancient Japanese system of self-defense. The basic philosophy of Aikido is to gain an advantage by using an opponent's actions against him or her. There are four forms of Aikido competition: Kata, Ninidori, Tanto Randori, and Randori Kyoghi.

KATA

Kata is an open event in which competitors are given a time limit (two to three minutes) to perform a Kata (Aikido movement) of their choice. Participants score for correct positioning, posture, coordination, and skillful execution of Aikido movements.

NINIDORI

Ninidori is a competition in which three participants alternate in the role of the defender while the other two act as attackers. A round lasts about one and one-half minutes. Weapons such as Jo, Boken, and Tanto can be used by the aggressors. Ninidori performance is assessed on the participants' defense, use of space, speed, variation of attack, and stamina.

TANTO RANDORI

Tanto Randori is a free fight. For two rounds of two minutes each, an unarmed defender wards off an attacker using a rubber knife; the attacker and the defender switch roles in the second round. The contender who scores a total of two points at any time during a round is declared the winner. Whole points and half points are awarded for successful attacks and defenses. After a score, the referee calls *matte* and the fight is allowed to resume from a starting position. The competitor who wins the most rounds wins the entire event. One overtime round is allowed in the event of a tied score. If this does not break the tie, the contender who exhibits the most style and attempts the most Aikido movements is declared the winner.

RANDORI KYOGHI

Randori Kyoghi is a free fight between two unarmed opponents. Competitors attack and counter-attack using Randori-no-kata forms (or acceptable variations). Scoring and assessment of Randori Kyohgi is the same as used in Tanto Randori; however, the winner is determined without an overtime round.

AIKIDO OFFICIALS

Officials employed in Kata and Ninidori competition include the senior judge, assistant judges (two), scorer, and timekeeper. In Tanto Randori and Randori Kyoghi, officials include the referee, judges, scorer, and a timekeeper. Judges signal scores and penalties with red and white flags. Fouls against a participant may result in warnings, point loss, or disqualification. In Kata competition, scores from each of the assistant judges are given to the senior judge for assessment. After his or her ruling, the Recorder announces the final scores for the event. Judges and contenders alike wear a standard uniform consisting of a loose-fitting gi and a belt. Attacking and defending participants are distinguished by the use of colored belts (usually red and white).

RESOURCES

International Organizations
International Aikido Federation
c/o Dr. Peter Goldsbury
Uskita Hinmachi 3-29 4-Chome Higashi-ku
Hiroshima 732
Japan
Phone: (81-82) 211-1271
Fax: (81-82) 211-1955

Aikido World Headquarters
17-18 Watamatsu-cho Shinjuku-ku
Tokyo 162
Japan

ARCHERY

TARGET ARCHERY

Target archery is the most common form of archery competition for amateurs and professionals alike. Archers shoot from varying distances at straw targets marked with colored, concentric rings. Hits are scored according to their proximity to the target center. Hits within the center area score the most points; the archer accumulating the highest score is the winner. In international tournaments, archers shoot from ranges of 30, 50, 70, and 90 meters for men, and 30, 50, 60, and 70 meters for women. Target archery is an Olympic sport.

FIELD ARCHERY

Field archery competition takes place on a designated course set on natural terrain. The field archery course typically winds through a variety of obstacles such as vegetation, trees, and ponds. Archers shoot at round targets of varying sizes, distances, and angles along the course. As in target archery, the archer or team which accumulates the highest total score is the winner.

CROSSBOW COMPETITION

Competition crossbow events are similar to target archery; however, targets tend to be smaller in size and shooting ranges much shorter than traditional field archery. The two major forms of crossbow archery are match shooting and field archery. Match shooting competitors shoot at mechanical targets from specially built enclosures. Crossbow field competition is similar, but takes place on an open field using stationary targets. The International Armbrust Union (IAU) is the governing body for crossbow competition.

ARCHERY OFFICIALS

In international competitions, officials include the organizing and scoring committees, field captain, and various scorekeepers. The organizing committee sets up the archery event while the field captain oversees the actual competition. Individual scorers, stationed down range near the targets, record the archers' scores for each shot. The scoring committee is responsible for tallying scores for each round.

In field archery, the officials include the field captain, target captain, and scorekeepers. The field captain organizes the start of the match. One person from each of the competing groups is chosen to serve as target captain while the other two competitors act as scorekeepers.

In crossbow competition, a range officer oversees match shooting events. In crossbow field shooting events, a field captain oversees the competition.

RESOURCES

International Organizations
Federation Internationale de Tir a l'Arc (FITA)
Avenue de Cour 135
1007 Lausanne
Switzerland
Phone: 41-21-614-3050
Fax: 41-21-614-3055
e-mail: fita@worldcom.ch
Internet: www.worldsport.com/sports/
         archery/home.html

Internationale Armbrustschetzen Union (IAU)
Central Body
Scholsslirain 9
CH 6006 Luzern
Switzerland

National Organizations
National Archery Association (NAA)
One Olympic Plaza
Colorado Springs, CO 80909-5778
Phone: (719) 578-4576
Fax: (719) 632-4733
e-mail: info@usarchery.org
Internet: www.USArchery.org

National Field Archery Association (NFAA)
31407 Outer I-10
Redlands, CA 92373
Phone (909) 794-2133
Fax (909) 794-8512
e-mail: nfaarchery@aol.com

Federation of Canadian Archers, Inc.
1600 James Naismith Dr.
Gloucester Ontario K1B 5N4
Canada
Phone: (613) 748-5604
Fax: (613) 748-5785

The National Crossbowmen of the USA
P.O. Box 1615
Easton, PA 18044

AUSTRALIAN RULES FOOTBALL

Australian rules football, which has little in common with its American counterpart, is played by two teams of 18 players each on an oval-shaped grass field. Players attempt to score points by kicking the ball, which resembles an American football, through goal posts located at each end of the field. The ball may be kicked or punched up and down the field, but it may not be thrown. Players may tackle an opponent with the ball or block an opponent near the ball. Unlike American football, players do not wear protective gear. Games consist of four, 25-minute quarters, and teams rotate field positions after each quarter.

AUSTRALIAN RULES FOOTBALL OFFICIALS

The officials required in Australian Rules Football include a field umpire assisted by goal and boundary umpires. The field umpire maintains overall control of the game, using a whistle to begin and end play. The goal umpires are positioned near each goal to observe play and use colored flags to signal scores. The boundary umpires alert the field umpire when the ball goes out of bounds.

RESOURCES

International Organization
Victorian Football League (VFL)
VFL House
120 Jolimont Rd.
Jolimont Victoria 3002
Australia

AUTO RACING (CIRCUIT RACING)

Circuit racing is the most popular form of auto racing. It involves racing specially modified cars around a standardized track. Races may run for a set time period or for a specified number of laps. Formula One races are run for either 200 miles or two hours,whichever comes first, while Le Mans races, on the other hand, can last for 24 hours. Sedan, sports car, and vintage car racing are all popular forms of circuit racing. Other forms of racing include: slalom, autocross, hill climb, grasstrack, rallycross, and hill trials. Formula motor car races include: International Formula One, 3000, Three, Ford 1600, Ford 2000, Vauxhall Lotus, CART (Indianapolis), Atlantic, Libre, Vee, and Super Vee.

Other major forms of motor racing are: Stock Car Racing, Rallying, and Drag Racing. Stock car racing uses cars that are highly modified for speed on the inside, but use the outer chassis of stock production models which the general public can purchase. Stripped down and modified cars are used in stock car racing and stadium racing in the United Kingdom. For drag racing, competitors race special, customized autos down a straight course for speed. Minor forms of motor racing include Soapbox Derby, Sport Truck, Hot Rod (Mud, Monster Truck, Tractor Pull), Vintage, and Midget Racing.

Rally racing involves a driver and navigator team. Rally courses are divided into segments which are timed separately. Courses cover constructed circuits, public roads, and unimproved roads. The navigator uses a map to aid the driver in finding the fastest route and avoiding danger. At the end of the race, a competitor's score from all of the stages is tallied. The team that completes all of the segments in the least amount of time is the winner.

AUTO RACING OFFICIALS

A wide array of officials are employed in auto racing. These include a Clerk of Course, Secretary, Stewards, Timekeepers, Scrutineers (and their assistants), Pit Observers, Track Observers, Flag Marshals, Finishing Judges, Handicappers, and Starters. The Clerk of Course organizes and oversees the entire event. Stewards are in charge of interpreting the rules and handling disputes. Official Scrutineers check each car before a race to ensure that it meets regulations. Pit Observers ensure that pit workers' conduct is within specified guidelines. Track Observers monitor the race to ensure safe conditions and appropriate conduct. Blue, yellow, white, red, and black flags are used by the Flag Marshals to signal instructions to the drivers. Handicappers are in charge of evening the odds between cars and assigning handicaps. Starters signal for the drivers to start.

Resources

International Organizations

Federation International du Sport Automobile (FISA)
8 Place de la Concorde
75008 Paris
France

Union International Motornautique (UIM)
Nouveau Stade 11 2 Ave.
Prince Hereditaire Albert MC 98000
Monaco

National Organizations

SCCA Pro Racing Ltd.
Sub of: Sports Car Club of America, Inc.
9033 E. Easter Place
Englewood, CO 80112
Phone: (303) 694-7223
Fax: (303) 694-7391
e-mail: scca@csi.com

U.S. Auto Club (USAC)
4910 W. 16th St.
Indianapolis Speedway, IN 46224
Phone: (317) 247-5151
Fax: (317) 247-0123

BADMINTON

Badminton is a court game in which players volley a shuttlecock (known as the *birdie*) over a tall net using lightweight racquets. The badminton court is divided into sections, the overall size of which is determined by the number of players. Players score by hitting the shuttlecock onto the floor of the opposing player's side of the court. In badminton, play is continuous, although international matches allow a rest between the second and third games. Major badminton competitions include the Thomas Cup for men and Uber Cup for women. Badminton is an Olympic sport of the summer games.

Roger Perlmuter

BADMINTON OFFICIALS

Major badminton matches are typically officiated by a referee or umpire, who may be assisted by one or more line judges. The referee oversees the competition from a raised chair positioned along the sideline at center court. The line judges monitor the sidelines for out-of-bounds infractions.

RESOURCES

International Organization

International Badminton Federation (IBF)
Unit 4, Manor Park
MacKenzie Way
Cheltenham, Gloucestershire GL51 9TX
Great Britain
Phone: (44-1242) 23-4904
Fax: (44-1242) 22-1030
Internet: www.intbadfed.org

National Organizations

USA Badminton
One Olympic Plaza
Colorado Springs, CO 80909
Phone: (719) 578-4808
Fax: (719) 578-4507
e-mail: info@usabadminton.org
Internet: www.usabadminton.org

Badminton Canada
1600 James Naismith Dr.
Gloucester Ontario K1B 5N4
Canada
Phone: (613) 748-5605
Fax: (613) 748-5695
e-mail: badminton@badminton.ca
Internet: www.badminton.ca

BANDY

Like ice hockey, bandy is played on an ice rink by players on skates. Two teams of 11 players each attempt to score points by driving a small plastic ball into their opponent's goal using a curved hockey-like stick. As with ice hockey, one player from each team is designated as a goalkeeper, and his sole function is to prevent the opposing team from scoring. Although the ice rink used in bandy is somewhat larger than that used in ice hockey, players are not permitted to play the ball behind the goals. A bandy game consists of two 45 minute periods.

BANDY OFFICIALS

Competitive bandy requires two or three referees who are assisted by a pair of goal referees. The referees control the competition and are responsible for keeping track of game time. The goal referees monitor action near the goal lines.

RESOURCES

International Organizations

Bandy Federation International
c/o Arne Giving, Secretary General
Elgfaret 23
Hosle N-1347
Norway
Phone: (47) 266-5800
Fax: (47) 266-5883

Svenska Bandyforbundet
(Kopmannagatan 19)
Box 78
S-641 21
Katrineholm
Sweden

BIATHLON

Biathlon combines cross-country skiing and target rifle shooting. Carrying rifles, competitors ski across a course laid out over uneven and/or natural terrain. At each of several designated points along the course, competitors stop to shoot at a series of targets. Participants are scored according to their speed across the course and their marksmanship. One minute is added to a participant's skiing time for each target missed (20-K individual event); for relay and 10-K events, participants ski a 150-meter penalty lap for each target missed. The team or individual with the best combined shooting and skiing scores wins. World championships are held each year. Biathlon is an Olympic sport of the winter games.

U.S. Biathlon Association

BIATHLON OFFICIALS

Biathlon officials include the chief of course who oversees the skiing portion of the competition and the chief of shooting who monitors shooting events. A jury oversees the overall competition. Minor officials are positioned along the course to assist in timekeeping and to record target hits.

RESOURCES

International Organization

International Biathlon Union (IBU)
Airportcenter-Postfach 1
A-5073 Wals-Himmelreich
Austria
Phone: (43-662) 855-5050
Fax: (43-662) 855-0508
e-mail: biathlon@ibu.at
Internet: www.ibu.at

National Organizations

U.S. Biathlon Association (USBA)
29 Ethan Allen Ave.
Colchester, VT 05446
Phone: (802) 654-7833
Fax: (802) 654-7830
e-mail: usbiathlon@aol.com

Biathlon Canada
1600 James Naismith Dr.
Gloucester Ontario K1B 5N4
Canada
Phone: (613) 748-5608
Fax: (613) 748-5762
e-mail: rickn@biathloncanada.ca
Internet: www.biathloncanada.ca

Bobsled Racing

Bobsledding is a high-speed winter downhill event in which teams compete for the fastest time over a measured course. The bobsled features steerable skis and an aerodynamic body shell in which the team rides. Bobsled crews consist of two or four members. Bobsled courses are artificially constructed ice sluices with steeply banked curves. Bobsled racing is a fast and dangerous sport as sleds can easily reach speeds in excess of 90 miles per hour. Amateur bobsled competition is regulated by the Federation Internationale de Bobsleigh et de Tobogganing (FIBT). FIBT events include Olympic, World Cup, International, and Junior International events. Bobsledding is an Olympic sport of the winter games.

Bobsled Officials

Bobsledding competition is officiated by a Jury President, assisted by a jury. Race officials normally are appointed by the FIBT.

Resources

International Organization

Federation Internationale de Bobsleigh et de Tobagganing (FIBT)
Via Piranesi 44B
20137 Milan
Italy
Phone: (39-2) 757-3319
Fax: (39-2) 738-0624
e-mail: fibtsecretariat@mail.asianet.it
Internet: www.bobsleigh.com

National Organization

U.S. Bobsled and Skeleton Foundation (USBSF)
421 Old Military Rd.
P.O. Box 828
Lake Placid, NY 12946-0828
Phone: (518) 523-1842
Fax: (518) 523-9491
e-mail: info@usabobsled.org
Internet: www.usabobsled.org

BOCCIE

Boccie (also known as *boules*) is an Italian lawn bowling game in which players throw boccie balls at a target ball (known as the jack). The objective is to land the ball closer to the jack than the opponents' balls. As in croquet, players may attempt to improve their ball's position by knocking the opponents' ball away from the target. Once all players have thrown their balls, the team with the ball nearest the jack scores. The scoring team is awarded one point for each of their balls that is closer to the target than the opposing team's nearest ball.

BOCCIE OFFICIALS

Boccie seldom requires an official, although an umpire is normally present in major tournaments to supervise measurements between balls. In most cases, players police the game on their own, so long as both teams are in agreement.

RESOURCES

International Organizations

International Boccie Association (IBA)
P.O. Box 170
Utica, NY 13503-0170
Phone: (315) 733-9611

Federation Francaise du Sport Boules
11 Cours Lafayette
69006 Lyon
France

BODYBUILDING

Christy Hoyt

Bodybuilding is both an individual and a two-person team sport. Male and female competitors are classed by weight and judged on muscle group development and symmetry during their performance of mandatory and elective poses. Competition generally is divided into two phases: pre-judging and finals.

Common weight classes for men include Bantam Weight, Light Weight, Middle Weight, Light-Heavy Weight, and Heavy Weight. Women's weight classes include Light Weight, Middle Weight, and Heavy Weight.

BODYBUILDING OFFICIALS

In competition sanctioned by the International Federation of Body Building (IFBB), the chief judge coordinates and controls all aspects of contest registration and/or weigh-in, pre-judging, and finals. Additional officials generally include a panel of nine other judges (representing as many different countries as possible), a judges secretary, two statisticians, and a timekeeper. Officials at this level are selected by the IFBB Judges Committee from nominees forwarded by individual national federations. Requirements for bodybuilding judges at the national level include successful completion of both a written and a practical examination and membership in the National Physique Committee (NPC). In addition, national-level judges are required to accrue five years of judging experience at lower competition levels and/or extensive training in anatomy and kinesiology (the study of the anatomy and physiology of body movement). Attendance at a judges clinic is required for renewal of a judging card.

RESOURCES

International Organization
International Federation of Body Building (IFBB)
P.O. Box 1490
Radio City Station, NY 10101
Phone: (914) 638-9290

National Organization
National Physique Committee (NPC)
P.O. Box 3711
Pittsburgh, PA 15230
Phone: (412) 276-5027

BOWLING

TEN PIN BOWLING

In ten pin bowling, bowlers attempt to knock down 10 wooden pins (arranged in a triangular formation) at the end of the lane. Bowlers alternate turns through 10 frames. Each frame consists of two rolls of the ball, unless a strike is scored on the first roll. One point is scored for every pin knocked over in a single frame, assuming any pins are left standing at the conclusion of the frame. Bonus points are awarded for strikes, which are achieved by knocking over all 10 pins with the first ball of a frame, and for spares, which occur when all 10 pins are knocked down in either two rolls of a frame or the second roll alone. Final scores are decided by the total score of several composite games for competitive matches. Official matches are played on two lanes simultaneously. Bowling is an amateur and a professional sport. Some of the more well known tournaments include the Brunswick World Open, Touring Player's Championship, Firestone Tournament of Champions, Women's U.S. Open, and PBA National Championship.

Other forms of bowling include Duckpins, Ninepins, and Candlepins. Duckpins uses a smaller ball than conventional bowling with an emphasis on accuracy and delicacy over power. In Ninepins, bowlers roll a ball at a diamond formation of nine pins. Ninepins is popular in Northern Europe. Candlepins, similar to Duckpins, is played primarily in New England.

BOWLING OFFICIALS

Bowling requires only a judge who is in charge of conducting meets in accordance with official rules. Scoring is handled by automated equipment. A foul judge may be employed in major tournaments to ensure that bowlers do not gain an unfair advantage by crossing the foul line while releasing the ball.

RESOURCES

International Organization
Federation Internationale des Quilleurs (FIQ)
1631 Mesa Ave., Ste. A
Colorado Springs, CO 80906
Phone: (719) 636-2695
Fax: (719) 636-3300

National Organization
USA Bowling
5301 S. 76th St.
Greendale, WI 53129-0500
Phone: (414) 421-9008
Fax: (414) 421-1194
Internet: www.bowling.org

BOXING

In boxing, two contenders in an enclosed ring attempt to land blows on one another using gloved hands. Boxers fight for a period called a bout, which consists of a series of three-minute rounds. The total number of rounds varies with the level of competition; amateur bouts normally consist of three rounds, while professional bouts run 10 or 12 rounds. Points are awarded on the basis of offense, defense, initiative, and style. A boxer wins a bout through a knock-out (KO) when a boxer is knocked down and cannot get up within 10 seconds or a technical knock-out (TKO) when a boxer is deemed physically unable to continue the fight. In the absence of a knock-out, the winner is determined by the judges' total score. Boxing is both an amateur and professional sport. State and local organizations regulate professional boxing in the United States. The majority of these organizations belong to the World Boxing Association (WBA) and/or the World Boxing Council (WBC). Major tournaments include the World Championships, Golden Gloves Tournament, and the Pan American Games. Boxing is also an Olympic sport.

BOXING OFFICIALS

Boxing is officiated by a referee, assisted by a panel of three to five judges, a timekeeper, and a ring physician. The referee stands in the ring with the contestants and ensures adherence to the rules as well as the safety of the boxers. The judges are responsible for scoring the contestants and declaring a winner. The timekeeper keeps track of time and signals the beginning and end of each round with a bell.

RESOURCES

International Organizations
Association Internationale de Boxe Amateur (AIBA)
P.O. Box 0141
10321 Berlin
Germany
Phone: (49-30) 423-6766
Fax: (49-30) 423-5943
Internet: www.uni-leipzig.dc/~iat/aiba1.htm

World Boxing Council
Geneva 33-DESP 503
Mexico D.I. 06600
Phone: (905) 525-3787
Fax: (905) 569-1911

National Organizations
USA Boxing
One Olympic Plaza
Colorado Springs, CO 80909-5776
Phone: (719) 578-4506
Fax: (719) 632-3426
e-mail: usaboxing@aol.com
Internet: www.usaboxing.org

USA Amateur Boxing Federation, Inc. (USA/ABF)
1750 E. Boulder St.
Colorado Springs, CO 80909

CANOE RACING

Competitive canoe racing exists in many forms. The four major categories include sprint (flat water) racing, slalom (white water) racing, marathon racing, and sailing/poling events.

CANOE SPRINT RACING

In sprint racing (also referred to as flat water racing), one, two, or four racers paddle canoes across smooth waters, such as lakes or lagoons. Distances range from 500 to 10,000 meters for men and 500 to 5000 meters for women. Individual and team events include men's K1, C1, and C2 and women's K1. World and continental championships are held every year (except in Olympic years). Canoe sprint racing is an Olympic sport of the summer games.

SLALOM RACING

In canoe slalom racing, competitors attempt to race a course set on choppy water using a canoe or a decked kayak. Slalom courses challenge the racers' ability to maneuver a canoe as precisely as possible through a course containing a series of gates which hang over the course. Slalom courses usually are laid out along fast moving mountain rivers or streams. Gates must be cleared in sequence, and many natural and man-made obstacles must be overcome in the process. Events are held for one-person kayaks (men and women) and two-place Canadian canoes (men only). Competitions include K1, C1, and C2 for men, and K1 for women. Canoe slalom racing is an Olympic event.

Wild water canoeing events are similar to slalom racing, except they take place on rougher water. Scores are awarded based on the racer's endurance, strength, and skill.

MARATHON CANOE RACING

Marathon canoe competitions are held on a course approximately 20 miles in length, usually laid out along a river. The winner is the individual or team with the fastest time. Men, women, and children compete separately.

SAILING AND POLING

Canoe sailing takes place on a triangular course approximately 10 miles in length. Canoes used in this event are specially equipped with sails, mast, and centerboard and rely on wind power rather than paddling for forward propulsion. Competitive events are governed by International Canoe Federation (FIC) and International Yacht Racing (IYRU) rules. Poling is a special type of canoe race in which contestants use a long pole to propel the canoe forward and maneuver it around buoys.

CANOE RACING OFFICIALS

A wide variety of officials are employed in canoe racing. Typically, a chief judge is in overall charge of the event and is assisted by a panel of judges who score the competitors. Other officials include starters, timekeepers, safety officials, and various minor officials who are spotted along the course.

RESOURCES

International Organization

Federation Internationale de Canoe (FIC)
Dozsa Gyorgy ut 1-3
1143 Budapest
Hungary
Phone: (36-1) 363-4832
Fax: (36-1) 157-5643
Internet: www.worldsport.com/sports/
          canoeing/home.html

National Organizations

American Canoe Association (ACA)
7432 Alban Station Blvd., Ste. B-232
Springfield, VA 22150
Phone: (703) 451-0141
Fax: (703) 451-2245
e-mail: acadirect@aol.com
Internet: www.aca_paddler.org

U.S. Canoe and Kayak Team
421 Old Military Rd.
P.O. Box 789
Lake Placid, NY 12946
(518) 523-1855
Fax: (518) 523-3767
e-mail: usckt@aol.com
Internet: www.worldsport.com/sports/
          canoeing/home.html

Canadian Canoe Association
1600 James Naismith Dr.
Gloucester Ontario K1B 5N4
Canada
Phone: (613) 748-5623
Fax: (613) 748-5700

CRICKET

Cricket is a round ball game played by two teams of 11 players each. Similar in some respects to baseball, the cricket batsman attempts to score runs by hitting a ball thrown by the pitcher (referred to as the *bowler*); the fielding team, in turn, attempts to prevent runs by forcing the batter to make an out. Teams alternate fielding and bowling, and the side with the most runs after a given number of innings is the winner. In some cases, a single cricket match is played over the course of several days. Cricket is played by both men's and women's teams.

CRICKET OFFICIALS

Cricket is officiated by a pair of umpires who are responsible for ruling on outs, dead balls, boundary violations, fouls, and penalties. One umpire stands behind the batting wicket, and the other stands near the bowling wicket. Umpires use hand signals to instruct the players. Unlike most sports where official rulings are made spontaneously, cricket umpires do not rule a batter out unless a verbal appeal is made by the opposing team.

RESOURCES

International Organization

World Cricket League
301 W. 57th St., Ste. 5D
New York, NY 10019
Phone: (212) 582-8556
Fax: (212) 582-8531
e-mail: cricket@porus.com

CROQUET

Croquet is an outdoor lawn game in which players use mallets to propel wooden balls through a series of wickets (hoops) which are laid out on a court that measures roughly 80 feet in width by 100 feet in length. After passing the ball through each wicket twice, players must play the ball off of a stake located in the center of the court. Players may gain an advantage by playing their ball off an opponent's ball. The first team to complete the course wins. United States Croquet Association (USCA) recognizes two forms of Croquet: the six-wicket (one stake) game and the nine-wicket (two-stake) game. Although numerous variations of the game have evolved in the United States, the British Croquet Association has refined the game under a single governing body.

Roger Perlmuter

CROQUET OFFICIALS

A single referee is used in competitive matches and has final say in all disputes.

RESOURCES

International Organization
British Croquet Association United Kingdom
The Croquet Association
Hurlington Club
Ranelagh Gardens London SW6 3PR
England

National Organization
United States Croquet Association (USCA)
11585-B Polo Club Rd.
Wellington, FL 33414
Phone: (561) 753-9141
Fax: (561) 753-8801
e-mail: uscroquet@compuserv.com

CURLING

Rick Patzke, USA Curling

Curling involves two teams of four players each. The teams compete on a rectangular field of ice, sliding stones across the field toward a circular target. Points are awarded for each stone that stops closest to the target center. Brooms are often used to sweep a clear path ahead of the moving stone to improve accuracy and increase range. An inning (also known as an *end*) is called once all 16 stones (eight per team) have been played. A curling match consists of eight, 10, or 12 innings. Curling is a popular sport in Scotland, The Netherlands, Canada, and parts of the United States.

CURLING OFFICIALS

An umpire oversees all measurements after each shot and has the final decision on any disputes.

RESOURCES

International Organization
World Curling Federation (WCF)
81 Great King St.
Edinburgh EH3 6RN
Great Britain
Phone: (44-131) 556-4884
Fax: (44-131) 556-9400
Internet: www.worldsport.com/sports/
        curling/home.html

National Organization
USA Curling
1100 Center Point Dr.
P.O. Box 866
Stevens Point, WI 54481-0866
Phone: (715) 344-1199
Fax: (715) 344-6885
Internet: www.usacurl.org

CYCLING (BICYCLE RACING)

Road racing is the most well-known form of bicycle racing. Cyclists compete on a set route for a specified number of laps or on a linear course, often between two towns. Thousands of contestants can compete in a single race. The cyclist who completes the course with the lowest time wins. Road racing events include stage races and circuit races. The most famous cycle road race is the Tour de France.

Track races are held on indoor and outdoor velodromes (oval tracks) for .2 kilometer to .5 kilometer events. Championships are generally held outdoors and can range from 800 meter sprints to 100 kilometer distance races. The cyclist with the lowest time wins. Other events include the Point-to-Point, Madison Racing, Human and Motor Pacing, individual and team pursuits, hill climbs, and roller races. Bicycle Motocross (BMX) racing takes place on a dirt track with many sharp turns and bumps. Cyclists wear padding and helmets to protect against injury. Mountain biking is a recent addition to the Olympic sport roster.

CYCLING OFFICIALS

Bicycle road racing requires a variety of officials; typically a referee or chief judge exercises overall control of the event with the assistance of several minor officials such as timekeepers, equipment examiners, starters, and lap scorers.

RESOURCES

International Organization
Union Cycliste Internationale (UCI)
37 Route de Chavannes
Case Postale 84
1000 Lausanne 23
Switzerland
Phone: (41-21) 622-0580
Fax: (41-21) 622-0588

National Organization
USA Cycling, Inc.
One Olympic Plaza
Colorado Springs, CO 80909-5775
Phone: (719) 578-4581
Fax: (719) 578-4596
Internet: www.usacycling.org

DARTS

Players stand behind a toe-line and use three darts each to strike a circular dart board mounted to a wall. The dart board is marked by concentric rings which are divided into multiple scoring areas. Darts is played by singles, doubles, or teams of virtually any size. The winner is the first side to reduce its starting score to zero.

DARTS OFFICIALS

With the exception of some championships, there is usually no official. However, in major tournament play a referee may be employed to mediate disputes.

RESOURCES

National Organization

American Darts Organization (ADO)
652 S. Brookhurst Ave., Ste. 543
Anaheim, CA 92804
Phone: (714) 254-0212
Fax: (714) 254-0214
Internet: www.infohwy.com/darts

EQUESTRIAN EVENTS

Competitive equestrian (horse riding) events include dressage, eventing (*three-day event*), and show jumping.

DRESSAGE

Dressage riders guide their horses through a specified series of gaits and movements (including walks, halts, trots, submissions, piaffes, pirouettes, and passages) using a variety of seat and

Rachel Jelen

leg signals. Dressage events challenge the physical control of the horse, as well as the cooperation and communication between horse and rider. Dressage requires that the horse's motions be graceful, smooth, and precise. The horse and rider with the most points is the winner.

EVENTING (THREE-DAY EVENT)

A rider and horse compete over three days of eventing that consists of dressage, cross-country, and show jumping with each event scheduled on a different day. Eventing competition challenges the speed, endurance, jumping ability, and obedience of the horse, as well as the focus and control of the rider. Successful competition requires that the horse and rider work in unison. Both individuals and teams may compete. Team eventing is an Olympic sport.

SHOW JUMPING

Show jumping competition takes place on a specially constructed course featuring various obstacles to test both the horse's jumping ability and the rider's control. Course difficulty varies depending on the level of competition. Judges assess penalties that count against the competitor's overall score; normally, the competitor with the fewest faults is the winner. Occasionally, a horse and rider will compete for the fastest time or the highest score. Both individuals and teams compete in sport jumping. Grand Prix show jumping is part of the Olympic Games.

EQUESTRIAN OFFICIALS

A jury is used to judge dressage competition. At the international level, dressage events are judged by a five-member jury. Three judges stand on the short end of the arena and one on each side. Judges award points for successful movements and assess penalties for errors. At lower levels of competition, only two judges may be employed.

Eventing is officiated by a ground jury which is composed of a president, two judges, technical delegates, an appeals committee, a course designer, veterinary officials, timekeepers, and jump judges.

Show jumping is officiated by a panel of judges, assisted by stewards, timekeepers, a veterinarian official, and an appeals committee.

RESOURCES

International Organization

Federation Equestre Internationale (FEI)
Ave. Mon-Repos 24
Case Postale 157
1000 Lausanne 5
Switzerland
Phone: (41-21) 312-5656
Fax: (41-21) 312-8677
Internet: www.worldsport.com/sports/
equestrian/home.html

National Organizations

American Horse Shows Association
4047 Iron Works Pkwy.
Lexington, KY 40511
Phone: (606) 258-2472
Fax: (606) 231-6662
Internet: www.ahsa.org

U.S. Equestrian Team
Pottersville Rd.
Gladstone, NJ 07934
Phone: (908) 234-1251
Fax: (908) 234-9417
Internet: www.uset.com

U.S. Dressage Foundation (USDF)
P.O. Box 6669
Lincoln, NE 68506-0669
Phone: (402) 434-8550
Fax: (402) 434-8570

Canadian Equestrian Federation
1600 James Naismith Dr.
Gloucester Ontario K1B 5N4
Canada
Phone: (613) 748-5632
Fax: (613) 747-2920

FENCING

Competitive fencing involves two participants who face off using blunted weapons including the foil, epee, and saber. To score, a fencer must hit his or her opponent's target area(s) with either the point of the weapon, or, in the case of the saber, the cutting edge. Fencing takes place on a court (known as a piste) measuring six feet in width by 46 feet in length. Protective garments are worn to minimize the risk of injury to the participants. Fencing is an Olympic sport of the summer games.

FENCING OFFICIALS

Fencing typically is officiated by a president who is assisted by four judges, all of whom must hold amateur fencing status. The president rules on fouls and penalties and ensures that the participants adhere to proper protocol during the event. In some cases, electronic scoring equipment is used to keep track of hits and monitor the fencers' positions within the piste.

RESOURCES

International Organization
Federation Internationale d'Escrime (FIE)
Ave. Mon-Repos 24
Case Postale 2743
1002 Lausanne
Switzerland
Phone: (41-21) 320-3115
Fax: (41-21) 320-3116
Internet: www.fie.ch

National Organization
U.S. Fencing Association (USFA)
One Olympic Plaza
Colorado Springs, CO 80909-5774
Phone: (719) 578-4511
Fax: (719) 632-5737
Internet: www.usfa.org
e-mail: usfencing@aol.com

FIELD HOCKEY

Field hockey is similar to ice hockey. However, unlike ice hockey, field hockey is played on a grass field, players run rather than skate, and a ball is used in place of a puck. Using hockey-like sticks, two teams of 11 players score points by propelling the ball across the goal line. The team scoring the most goals during two periods of play wins the match. Although played by both men and women, girls and women dominate the sport in the United States. Field hockey competition is regulated internationally by the Hockey Rules Board in conjunction with the International Hockey Federation and nationally by the United States Field Hockey Association (USFHA).

FIELD HOCKEY OFFICIALS

Field hockey is officiated by two umpires, each controlling play on his or her side of the field. Umpires do not change sides during the course of a match. Common infractions include advancing the ball with any part of the body, dangerous use of the stick, and hitting the ball in any manner that could result in dangerous play. Unique to field hockey is the obstruction rule, which prohibits players from shielding the ball with any part of the body. Most field hockey scoring opportunities result from penalty corners.

RESOURCES

International Organization
Federation Internationale de Hockey (FIH)
Boite Postale. 5
1210 Brussels
Belgium
Phone: (32-2) 219-4537
Fax: (32-2) 219-2761
Internet: www.fihockey.org

National Organization
U.S. Field Hockey Association
One Olympic Plaza
Colorado Springs, CO 80909-5773
Phone: (719) 578-4567
Fax: (719) 632-0979
e-mail: usfha@usfieldhockey.com
Internet: www.usfieldhockey.com

GOLF

Golf is a game in which players attempt to hit a small ball into a series of holes using special clubs. Golf is played on specially constructed courses featuring a variety of obstacles such as ponds and sand traps. Players use heavy clubs to drive the ball from one hole to the next, and lightweight clubs to putt the ball into the cup from the putting green. Golf courses feature a total of 18 holes, typically laid out over several acres.

The most common types of golf include match play and stroke play. The object of both forms is to play the ball from a teeing area into a hole in the fewest strokes possible. In stroke play, the winner is the player who accumulates the fewest total strokes at the completion of the round. In match play, the player or side that wins the most holes is the winner, regardless of the total number of strokes used.

GOLF OFFICIALS

In the game of golf, the rules official is responsible for the determination of fair play and the ethical conduct of the players. Should a questionable situation arise, the rules official has final say. The United States Golf Association is the governing body for the sport of golf and is responsible for choosing the rules officials who preside in the large USGA Tournaments. Nearly all golf rules officiating is performed on a volunteer basis; however, Professional Golf Association (PGA) officials are compensated for their work.

RESOURCES

National Organizations

United States Golf Association (USGA)
P.O. Box 708
Far Hills, NJ 07931-0708
Phone: (908) 234-2300
Fax: (908) 234-9687

Professional Association of Golf Officials
1735 Market St., Ste. 3420
Philadelphia, PA 19103
Phone: (215) 979-3200
Fax: (215) 979-3201

HANDBALL

Roger Perlmuter

Handball is a court ball game played by two players or teams. Using gloved hands, players alternate striking a small rubber ball against the court walls in such a way that it is difficult for the opposing side to return it. Only the serving side can score points. Like racquetball, handball is played on one-, three-, or four-wall courts. The first side to accumulate 21 points is the winner.

HANDBALL OFFICIALS

Competitive handball tournaments are officiated by a referee, who exercises overall control of the event. A line judge and scorekeeper may also be employed, depending on the level of competition.

RESOURCES

National Organization
United States Handball Association
2333 N. Tucson Blvd.
Tucson, AZ 85716
Phone: (520) 795-0434
Fax: (520) 795-0465
e-mail: handball@ushandball.org
Internet: www.ushandball.org

JAI ALAI (PELOTA)

Jai Alai is a fast and dangerous ball game that originated in Spain. Similar to court handball, it is played on a three-wall court. Singles, doubles, triples, and teams attempt to hit the ball (*pelota*) against the front wall of the court (*frontis*) with a basket-like racquet (*cesta*). The object of the game is to score points by throwing the ball so that the opposing side can not return it. Games are played to a specified number of points or length of time; six-point games are popular for betting. The winner is the player or team with the greatest number of points.

JAI ALAI OFFICIALS

Officiating in Jai Alai is handled by a panel of three judges; during competition, judges are positioned along the length of the court at specified intervals. Jai Alai judges carry racquets to protect themselves from the ball, which can reach speeds in excess of 150 miles per hour.

RESOURCES

International Organization
Federacion Internacional de Pelota
Vasca Sede Central
Aldamar, 5-1 Dcha
San Sebastian 20003
Spain
Phone: (34-4) 342-8415
Fax: (34-4) 342-8309

National Organizations
National Association of Jai Alai Frontons
Highway US-92
P.O. Box 2630
Daytona Beach, FL 32015

KORFBALL

Korfball is a team sport similar in some respects to basketball. The game is played by two teams of eight players each, who attempt to score points by shooting a soccer-like ball into a raised goal. Unlike basketball, korfball players may not dribble the ball, and physical contact with other players is prohibited.

KORFBALL OFFICIALS

Korfball is officiated by a referee with the assistance of two linesmen. The referee enforces game rules, signals starts and stops of play, and settles disputes. The linesmen rule on ball out-of-play violations as well as fouls.

RESOURCES

International Organization
International Korfball Federation
P.O. Box 1000
Bunnik 3980 DA
Holland
Phone: (31-34) 057-0655
Fax: (31-34) 056-7025

National Organization
U.S. Korfball Federation
1636 S. Florence Place
Tulsa, OK 74104
Phone: (918) 742-0354

LACROSSE

Lacrosse is a team sport in which players use a netted stick (*crosse*) to throw or bat the ball into a netted goal. The game is played on a large field by 10-member teams in men's competition or 12-member teams in women's competition. Each team fields one goal tender who is assisted by three defensive players. Other positions include mid-fielders and offensive players, known as *attackers*. The game is won by the team which accumulates the highest score.

LACROSSE OFFICIALS

Lacrosse is officiated by a team of three field referees who work in conjunction with a chief bench official. Additional personnel are required for timekeeping and scoring.

RESOURCES

National Organization

U.S. Lacrosse
113 W. University Pkwy.
Baltimore, MD 21210
Phone: (410) 235-6882
Fax: (410) 366-6735
Internet: www.lacrosse.org

LUGE

U.S. Luge Association

In luge competition, participants lie feet first and on their backs as they maneuver a small sled down a steeply banked, ice-covered course. Luge sleds easily can reach speeds of 70 miles per hour. Similar in some respects to bobsled competition, luge courses generally offer more twists and turns. Luge is an Olympic sport of the winter games.

LUGE OFFICIALS
Luge requires a host of officials including a Race Director and various starting and finishing officials. Scoring is handled by a three-member jury that works in conjunction with a representative of the Federation Internationale de Luge de Course (FIL).

RESOURCES

International Organization
Federation Internationale de Luge de Course (FIL)
Rathausplatz 9
83471 Berchtesgaden
Germany
Phone: (49-8652) 699-60
Fax: (49-8652) 699-69

National Organization
U.S. Luge Association (USLA)
35 Church St.
Lake Placid, NY 12946-1805
Phone: (518) 523-2071
Fax: (518) 523-4106
e-mail: usaluge@usaluge.org
Internet: www.usaluge.org

MARTIAL ARTS

JU JITSU

Ju jitsu is a form of unarmed self-defense that stresses the use of mental and physical skills to defeat an opponent, as opposed to the application of brute force. In Ju jitsu, competitors attempt to gain an advantage by redirecting their opponent's physical moves against them, typically by upsetting their balance and throwing them to the mat. Ju jitsu competition includes *nage-waza*, which is initiated from a standing position, and *ne-waza*, which begins from a sitting position. Both forms of competition are divided into specific weight categories for both men and women.

JU JITSU OFFICIALS

Ju jitsu officials include a senior judge assisted by two four-corner judges. The senior judge, positioned within the competitive arena, is responsible for starting and stopping the event, and awarding points.

JUDO

Judo evolved out of Ju jitsu as a form of unarmed self-defense. Judo competition consists of two primary elements: *nage-waza* (throwing techniques), and *katame-waza* (chokes, holds and pins on the mat). Judo competition favors strength, speed, balance, timing, and leverage. Contests are won by competitors who display superior throwing and holding techniques. Judo competition is classified by age, rank, and weight. Judo is an Olympic sport.

JUDO OFFICIALS

Competitive judo is officiated by a referee who is assisted by a pair of judges. The referee is positioned on the mat within the competitive arena, while the judges observe the action from the corners of the mat.

KARATE

Karate is an unarmed combat sport that uses kicks and strikes with the hands, feet, elbows, and knees. Competitive karate is essentially a sparring match in that all blows and punches are pulled to avoid injury. For form matches, competitors perform a sequence of movements and are awarded points based on their technique. In free-fights, competitors earn points for movements that the judges think would be an effective technique against an opponent. There are four major types of karate: Japanese, Chinese (*Gong Fu*), Okinawan, and Korean (*Taekwondo*).

KARATE OFFICIALS

Karate events are officiated by a referee who exercises overall control of the competition. The referee starts and stops the match, awards points, and issues penalties and warnings to the participants. The referee is assisted by a judge, who is assigned to observe the contest and relay signals to the referee. An arbitrator may offer an opinion in the event of questionable technique.

KENDO

Kendo is an Oriental form of fencing in which two competitors in protective gear face off with bamboo swords. Competitors employ different forms of footwork for their attacks and counter attacks. A single kendo bout usually is limited to five minutes.

KENDO OFFICIALS

Kendo competition is officiated by a chief judge who is assisted by a pair of assistant judges and a line judge. The chief judge starts and ends the match; any of the three judges may rule on misconduct and signal points. Kendo officials signal their calls with colored flags. The line judge monitors the competition for out-of-bounds violations.

TAEKWONDO

Korean karate, also called *Taekwondo*, is a martial art that emphasizes kicking techniques. (For competition description, see Karate.) Taekwondo is an Olympic sport.

TAEKWONDO OFFICIALS

(See Karate Officials)

RESOURCES

International Organizations
International Judo Federation (IJF)
101-1 Ulchi-Ro, 21st Fl. Doosan Bldg., I-KA
Chung-ku Seoul
Korea
Phone: (82-2) 759-6936
Fax: (82-2) 754-1075
Internet: www.ijf.org

World Union of Karatedo Organizations
Headquarters
Senpaku Shinko Building 1-15-16
Toranomon Minato-ku
Tokyo 105
Japan
Phone: (81-3) 503-6638

World Taekwondo Federation (WTF)
635 Yuksam-dong Kangnam-ku
Seoul 135-081
Korea
Phone: (82-2) 566-2505
Fax: (82-2) 553-4728
e-mail: wtf@unitel.co.kr
Internet: www.wtf.or.kr

National Organizations
USA Judo
One Olympic Plaza
Colorado Springs, CO 80909
Phone: (719) 578-4730
Fax: (719) 578-4733
Internet: www.usjudo.org

Judo Canada
1600 James Naismith Dr.
Gloucester Ontario K1B 5N4
Canada
Phone: (613) 748-5640
Fax: (613) 748-5697
e-mail: info@judocanada.org

USA Karate Federation
1300 Kenmore Blvd.
Akron, OH 44314
Phone: (330) 753-3114
Fax: (330) 753-6967
e-mail: usakf@imperium.net

American Amateur Karate Federation
1930 Wilshire Blvd., Ste. 1208
Los Angeles, CA 90057
Phone: (213) 483-8261

USA National Karate-Do Federation, Inc.
8351 15th Ave., NW
P.O. Box 77083
Seattle, WA 98177-7083
Phone: (206) 440-8386
Fax: (206) 367-7557
Internet: www.usankf.org

American Taekwondo Association (ATA)
6210 Baseline Rd.
Little Rock, AR 72209
Phone: (501) 568-2821
Fax: (501) 568-2497

U.S. Taekwondo Union
One Olympic Plaza
Colorado Springs, CO 80909-5792
Phone: (719) 578-4632
Fax: (719) 578-4642
e-mail: ustumedia@aol.com
Internet: www.ustu.com

MOTORCYCLE RACING

Motorcycle racing encompasses a wide variety of competitive events. International competition is governed by the Federation Internationale Motorcycliste (FIM), while local, regional, and national races are governed by individual organizations with their own competitive levels. Some of the more popular forms of motorcycle racing include road racing and circuit (track) racing, which involves high-performance, often streamlined motorcycles. These events are generally held on paved or otherwise smooth surfaces with speed being the primary objective. Other forms of motorcycle racing include ice racing and motocross; in these events, the skill and ability of the rider are emphasized over the speed and horsepower of their equipment.

MOTORCYCLE RACING OFFICIALS

As with most motorized racing competition, a clerk of course is responsible for organizing the event, while a panel of judges is responsible for scoring the contestants. In addition, various timekeepers and track/equipment officials are also employed to ensure adherence to safety and equipment regulations.

RESOURCES

International Organization
Federation Internationale Motorcycliste (FIM)
19 Chemin William-Barbery
CH-1292 Chambesy Geneva
Switzerland
Phone: (41-22-75) 819-6061
Fax: (41-22-75) 819-2180

National Organization
American Motorcyclist Association (AMA)
13515 Yarmouth Dr.
Tickerington, OH 43147
Phone: (614) 856-1900
Fax: (614) 856-1920

NETBALL

Netball is a round ball court game similar in many respects to basketball. The game is played by two teams of seven players each. Points
are scored by shooting the ball through the opposing team's hoop.
However, unlike basketball players who are free to move about the
court, netball players must remain within specific areas. Netball players may pass the ball, but are prohibited from running with it. Netball
usually is played by women.

NETBALL OFFICIALS

Netball is officiated by a pair of umpires, each of whom monitors one
half of the court; umpires are responsible for ruling on fouls and
mediating disputes.

RESOURCES

International Organization

International Federation of Netball Associations
99 Awaba St.
Mosman New South Wales 2088
Australia
Phone: (44-39) 428-2609

PADDLEBALL

Roger Perlmuter

Paddleball is an indoor court ball game played by doubles and singles. Players use wooden paddles to volley a small rubber ball against the vertical walls of the court. The serving side attempts to score points by making it difficult for the opposing side to return the ball. The first player or side to score 21 points wins the game. Paddleball matches consist of three games; the best two out of three games wins the match.

PADDLEBALL OFFICIALS

Competitive paddleball is officiated by a referee who is assisted by a scorekeeper. The referee exercises overall control of the match and rules on all scores and fouls. The scorer assists the referee by announcing the score and taking notes of play. A line judge may also be employed in major tournaments to assist the referee.

RESOURCES

National Organization
National Paddleball Association (NPA)
P.O. Box 712
Flint, MI 48501

PARACHUTING: SPORT PARACHUTING

Sport parachute jumpers perform stunts and formation hookups, both in free fall and under canopy. Parachutists are judged on their ability to maintain formation, individual style, and accuracy of landing. Jump altitudes vary, depending on the event, from 2,600 feet to in excess of 11,000 feet.

PARACHUTING OFFICIALS

Sport parachuting requires a variety of officials, including a drop zone controller, an international jury, and a panel of judges. The drop zone controller, generally a veteran jumper,

David Dreimiller

acts as the chief safety official at all events. The jury, which consists of members of the Federation International Aeronautique (FAI), in conjunction with the panel of judges, is responsible for scoring the participants.

RESOURCES

International Organization

Federation International Aeronautique
10-12 Rue du Capitaine Menard
Paris 75015
France
Phone: (33-14) 579-2477
Fax: (33-14) 579-7315

National Organizations

United States Parachute Association
1440 Duke St.
Alexandria, VA 22314
Phone: (703) 836-3495
Fax: (703) 836-2843
Internet: www.uspa.org

Star Crest Association
c/o Bill Newell, President
3418 Mona Way
Bakersfield, CA 93309
Phone: (805) 831-7771

U.S. BASE Association
321 W.Durian Ave.
Coalinga, CA 93210-1915
Phone: (213) 678-0163

Canadian Sport Parachute Association
4185 Dunning Rd.
Navan, Ontario K4B 1J1
Canada
Phone/Fax: (613) 835-3731
e-mail: cspa@travel/net.com

PENTATHLON

David Dreimiller

Modern pentathlon is a multi-sport event that combines swimming, pistol shooting, cross-country running, equestrian, and fencing events into a single competition. The pentathlon takes place over three or four days and is played by teams of three members each. Each team member must compete in each event in order to receive a score for that event. Each participant's score is tallied after each event; the team that accumulates the most points wins. Both men and women compete in the modern pentathlon at the international, national, and club levels. Men only compete at the Olympic level.

PENTATHLON OFFICIALS

Modern pentathlon is officiated by a representative of the Union Internationale du Pentathlon Moderne (UIPM) and a panel of judges. Although the UIPM governs the rules of the pentathlon, each of the five events is controlled by its respective international governing body.

RESOURCES

International Organization
Union Internationale de Pentathlon Moderne (UIPMB)
Stade Louis II, Entrance E
13, Ave. des Castelans
Monte Carlo 98000
Monaco
Phone: (377) 9777-8555
Fax: (377) 9777-8550
e-mail: uipmb@image.dk
Internet: www.pentathlon.org

National Organization
U.S. Modern Pentathlon Association
7330 San Pedro, Box 10
San Antonio, TX 78216
Phone: (210) 528-2999
Fax: (210) 528-2992
e-mail: usmpa@texas.net
Internet: www.uspentathlon.org

POLO

Polo is played on horseback by two teams of four players who attempt to score points by propelling a small wooden ball, using a long-handled mallet, through the opposing team's goal. The side scoring the most goals is the winner. A polo game generally lasts 56 minutes and consists of eight seven-minute periods.

Other forms of polo include arena polo and indoor-outdoor polo. Arena polo is played indoors, on a field of dirt, sand, or clay, with three players on each team. Field size, ball type, and length of playing time differ from outdoor polo, but the rules for both are similar. Indoor-outdoor polo is played outdoors, but the game follows the rules of arena polo.

POLO OFFICIALS

Polo is officiated by a pair of umpires on horseback, a referee, two goal judges, and a timekeeper. Generally, each mounted umpire oversees one half of the playing field. Should any disagreement come between the mounted umpires, the referee (who stands off the field) has the final word. The goal judges oversee activity at each goal and signal goals with colored flags. The timekeeper is responsible for signalling the start of each period and also is in charge of keeping score.

RESOURCES

National Organization
U.S. Polo Association
4059 Iron Works Pike
Lexington, KY 40511
Phone: (606) 255-0593
Fax: (606) 231-9738
e-mail: uspalexy@aol.com

RACQUETBALL

Racquetball is a court game similar to handball, except players use short-handled rackets to hit the ball rather than their hands. The game is played by singles or teams on either a one-, three-, or four-wall court. One point is awarded to the serving team for each ball that is unreturned by the opposition. The first player or team to score 15 points wins the game.

RACQUETBALL OFFICIALS

Competitive racquetball games typically are officiated by a referee, who is assisted by a scorekeeper. For smaller matches, the referee is the top official, ensuring that the players are aware of the rules, checking equipment, deciding plays throughout the match, and penalizing players. At higher levels of competition, a pair of line judges often is employed to monitor out-of-bounds infractions.

RESOURCES

International Organization
International Racquetball Federation (IRF)
1685 W. Uintah
Colorado Springs, CO 80904-2921
Phone: (719) 635-5396
Fax: (719) 635-0685
e-mail: rbzine@interserve.com

National Organization
Canadian Racquetball Association
2185 W. 14th Ave.
Vancouver, British Columbia V6K 2V8
Canada
Phone: (604) 734-6600
Fax: (613) 748-5644

ROLLER HOCKEY

Roller hockey is similar to ice hockey in many respects, except that players wear roller skates, and a hard rubber ball is used in place of a puck. Two teams of five players each attempt to score points by striking the ball into the opposing team's netted goal using curved wooden sticks. Each team is composed of one goalie and four floor players. Unlike ice hockey, roller hockey is considered a non-contact sport. A match generally consists of two 20-minute periods.

ROLLER HOCKEY OFFICIALS

Roller hockey is officiated by a referee who is assisted by a pair of goal judges. The referee controls and oversees the competition and uses colored cards to signal penalties and fouls. The goal judges observe play around the goals and signal scores with colored flags. One or more timekeepers and a scorekeeper may also be employed in competitive matches.

RESOURCES

International Organization
Federation Internationale de Roller Skating (FIRS)
Rambla Cataluna, 80 (piso 1)
08008 Barcelona
Spain
Phone: (34-3) 487-5348/5593
Fax: (34-3) 487-6916

ROWING (CREW)

The most common form of competitive rowing is the regatta in which teams compete for the best time over a measured course in specially constructed boats. Boats are rowed by either a single oarsman or teams of two to eight oarsmen, depending on the length of the craft. In some cases, a coxswain (who does not row) is present to call the strokes, ensuring that the oarsmen act in unison. In regatta racing, each boat operates from its own marked lane; in river head races, there are no lanes.

ROWING OFFICIALS

Regatta racing is conducted under the auspices of the Regatta Committee, while a separate Race Committee oversees the actual competition. Other officials are responsible for checking equipment and monitoring the competition along the course.

RESOURCES

International Organization

Federation Internationale des Societes
d'Aviron (FISA)
Case Postale 18
Ave. de Cour 135
1000 Lausanne 3
Switzerland
Phone: (41-21) 617-8373
Fax: (41-21) 617-8375
e-mail: fisa@ping.ch

National Organization

United States Rowing Association (U.S. Rowing)
Pan American Plaza, Ste. 400
201 S. Capitol Ave.
Indianapolis, IN 46225
Phone: (317) 237-5656
Fax: (317) 237-5646
e-mail: usrowing@aol.com
Internet: www.usrowing.org

RUGBY

Rugby is an aggressive and physically demanding kicking, passing, and tackling game that originated in England. Two forms of the sport exist: rugby league, a sport dominated by professionals; and rugby union, played exclusively by amateur athletes. Both versions are played with an oval-shaped

ball on a field with goal posts set at either end. Rugby league is played by 13-member teams. Rugby union is played by 15-member teams. Points are scored by kicking the ball through the goal posts or moving it across the goal line.

RUGBY OFFICIALS

Rugby is officiated by a referee who works on-field and exercises overall control of the game. In some cases, additional officials, known as *touch judges,* are employed to monitor out-of-bounds violations.

RESOURCES

International Organization

International Rugby Football Board (IRFB)
Huguenot House
35/38 St. Stephen's Green
Dublin 2
Ireland
Phone: (353-1) 662-54-44
Fax: (353-1)676-93-34
Internet: www.irfb.com

National Organizations

USA Rugby
3595 E. Fountain Blvd., Ste. M22
Colorado Springs, CO 80910
Phone: (719) 637-1022
Fax: (719) 637-1315
e-mail: usarugby@rmii.com
Internet: www.usarugby.org

Western Rugby Football Union of the U.S.
Dr. William L. Sexton, President
1405 E. Meadow Lane
Kirksville, MO 63501-2635
Phone: (660) 626-2324
Fax: (660) 626-2965
e-mail: wls@fileserver5.kcom.edu

SHOOTING: PISTOL/RIFLE

PISTOL

Competitive pistol shooting includes rapid-fire and free shooting events. In rapid fire competition, participants fire groups of five shots at targets that rotate into and out of view in a matter of seconds. Scores are based on the number of hits per target and their proximity to the target center. In free shooting competition, participants fire at their leisure at fixed targets; although the targets used in free style event do not move, they typically are set up much further away. In both events, only .22 caliber pistols are permitted.

RIFLE

In competitive rifle shooting, participants attempt to score hits on a stationary circular target from ranges of ten to 300 meters. Various weapon categories exist in competitive rifle shooting, including small and large bore and air rifle events. Competitors shoot from a variety of positions including standing, kneeling, and prone. Running game target shooting is a variation of rifle shooting in which competitors fire at a moving target, typically the silhouette of a wild boar. Competitors shoot from a standing position. Rifle shooting is an Olympic sport.

SHOOTING OFFICIALS

A single referee generally oversees pistol shooting events. He or she also rules on misfires and malfunctioning pistols. In rifle shooting events, a jury judges the competition, along with various minor officials who keep track of scores and work in the target area. In all shooting events, a chief range or safety official is present to guard against accidents.

RESOURCES

International Organization

Union International di Tir (UIT)
Bavariaring 21
80336 Munich
Germany
Phone: (49-89) 53-4293 or 53-1012
Fax: (49-89) 53-9481
Internet: www.worldsport.com/sports/
        shooting/home.html

National Organization

USA Shooting
One Olympic Plaza
Colorado Springs, CO 80909-5762
Phone: (719) 578-4670
Fax: (719) 635-7989
Internet: www.usashooting.org

SHOOTING: TRAP SHOOTING

National Skeet Shooting Association

In competitive trap shooting, participants fire a shotgun at saucer-shaped clay *pigeons*, which are launched into the air by a mechanized *trap*. Trap shooting challenges the shooter's timing and accuracy with a moving target. The most common competitive forms of trap shooting are Olympic trench shooting, down the line, and skeet shooting.

TRAP SHOOTING OFFICIALS

At the international level, competitive trap shooting events require a variety of officials including: a jury panel, a referee and assistants, along with scorekeepers and trap operators. The jury controls the overall event, while the referee rules on individual shots. The scorekeeper notes the competitors' misfires and misses. Trap operators load and prepare the traps. Outside of international competition, a referee and his or her assistants oversee events.

RESOURCES

International Organization

Amateur Trapshooting Association (ATA)
601 W. National Rd.
Vandalia, OH 45377
Phone: (513) 898-4638
Fax: (513) 898-5472

National Organization

National Skeet Shooting Association
5931 Roft Rd.
San Antonio, TX 78253-9261
Phone: (210) 688-3371
Fax: (210) 688-3014
e-mail: nssa.nca.hdqtrs@internetmci.com

SKATING: ICE FIGURE SKATING

Figure skaters perform graceful, dance-like movements, often set to music, as they glide across a smooth surface of ice. Men and women compete separately and together in a series of compulsory and free style movements. Points are awarded based on the skater's artistic presentation and technique. In all events, the individual or team ranked first by the most judges wins. Competitive figure skating includes singles skating, pairs skating, ice dancing, and precision skating. Figure skating is a professional and an Olympic sport.

SINGLES SKATING

Singles skating combines compulsory and free skating periods with an original program of eight movements. In the compulsory period, skaters attempt to accurately trace and retrace a sequence of 41 movements. The original program allows a skater to arrange eight separate movements as he or she sees fit. Each skater chooses his or her music and must execute movements within the allotted time. For the free skate period, competitors choose and choreograph their own movements. Skaters are judged on their precision, creativity, technique, choreography, and originality.

PAIRS SKATING

In pairs skating, two skaters (male and female) compete together through compulsory and free skate periods. Skating pairs are given a limited amount of time in which to perform their routines, which must be executed in complete harmony. Pairs skating often is characterized by the incorporation of ambitious movements such as lifts.

ICE DANCING

Ice dancing combines figure skating and ballroom dancing steps. In competitive ice dancing, skating pairs perform compulsory dances, an original set, and a free dance. Ice dancing involves the use of special steps and rules of competition that differ from singles and pairs skating. For example, ice dancers must keep one skate in contact with the ice at all times, and no high lifts are allowed. In addition, ice dancing pairs may separate only briefly during the performance.

PRECISION SKATING

Precision skating is a team sport. Precision skating emphasizes the skaters' ability to successfully execute maneuvers and stay in formation. Teams are judged on their speed and footwork as well as the originality, composition, and presentation of their routines.

SKATING OFFICIALS

Competitive figure skating is officiated by referees and judges, assisted by secretaries and a timekeeper. The referee oversees the event and ensures that competitions are in accordance with the rules. A panel of judges scores the competition, while the secretaries keep track of individual scores.

RESOURCES

International Organization

International Skating Union (ISU)
Chemin de Primerose 2
CH-1007 Lausanne
Switzerland
Phone: (41-21) 612-6666
Fax: (41-21) 612-6677
e-mail: info@isu.ch
Internet: www.isu.org

National Organizations

U.S. Figure Skating Association
20 First St.
Colorado Springs, CO 80906-3697
Phone: (719) 635-5200
Fax: (719) 635-9548
e-mail: usfsa1@aol.com
Internet: www.usfsa.org

Canadian Figure Skating Association
1600 James Naismith Dr.
Gloucester Ontario K1B 5N4
Canada
Phone: (613) 748-5635
Fax: (613) 748-5718
e-mail: cfsa@cfsa.ca
Internet: www.cfsa.ca

SKATING: ICE SPEED SKATING

Ice speed skaters compete on an oval-shaped course for the fastest time over a specified distance. Speed skating events include Olympic speed skating, pack skating, and short track skating. In Olympic speed skating, two skaters compete against one another, and points are awarded for each event according to a skater's time and use of technique. For pack skating events, several competitors race at once through a series of elimination races called heats. The first four skaters of the final heat qualify for the championship race. In short track speed skating, racers skate in the same manner as standard speed skating, only over a smaller course. Short track competition includes individual events, pursuit, and relay races. Speed skating is an Olympic sport.

SPEED SKATING OFFICIALS

The exact number and type of officials required for speed skating events varies with the competition. In most cases, a referee oversees the event, while a judge or panel of judges scores the competition. Various minor officials, including starters, timekeepers, and lap counters, may also be employed.

RESOURCES

International Organization

International Skating Union (ISU)
Chemin de Primerose 2
CH 1007 Lausanne
Switzerland
Phone: (41-21) 612-6666
Fax: (41-21) 612-6677
e-mail: info@isu.ch
Internet: www.isu.org

National Organizations

U.S. Speedskating
P.O. Box 450639
Westlake, OH 44145
Phone: (440) 899-0128
Fax: (440) 899-0109

Amateur Speed Skating Union of the U.S.
(ASU)
1033 Shady Lane
Glen Ellyn, IL 60137
Phone: (630) 790-3230
Fax: (630) 790-3235
Internet: www.mit.edu/jeffrey/speedskating/
asu.html

Canadian Amateur Speed Skating
Association
1600 James Naismith Dr., Ste. 312
Gloucester Ontario K1B 5N4
Canada
Phone: (613) 748-5669
Fax: (613) 748-5600
e-mail: ssc@speedskating~canada.ca
Internet: www.speedskating~canada.ca

SKATING: ROLLER SKATING

Competitive roller skating includes artistic and speed skating events. Artistic roller skating is similar to figure skating, except that it is performed on roller skates. Artistic events include compulsory and free skating routines, pair skating, and dance skating. Skaters may compete as singles or pairs.

Competitive speed roller skating is similar to ice speed skating. For indoor competitions, skaters race on an oval track. Outdoor competitions take place on a flat or banked oval track or suitable pathway. Men and women skate separately and are further divided by age group. Relay events (both indoor and outdoor) are also held for teams of two, three, and four skaters.

Roller Derby is another form of speed roller skating. Competitors skate en masse around a banked oval track, scoring points by lapping their opponents. Roller derby skaters are permitted to jostle one another and make frequent use of physical contact to impede an opponent's forward progress. Teams of men and women may compete.

ROLLER SKATING OFFICIALS

Officiating in artistic roller skating is similar to ice figure skating. Speed roller skating is officiated by a panel of judges. Supplemental officials include a starter, timekeeper, and lap scorer.

RESOURCES

International Organization
Federation Internationale de Roller-Skating (FIRS)
Rambla Cataluna 80, piso 1
08008 Barcelona
Spain
Phone: (34-3) 487-5348 or 487-5593
Fax: (34-3) 487-6916
Internet: www.firs.org

National Organization
USA Roller Skating
4730 South St.
P.O. Box 6579
Lincoln, NE 68506
Phone: (402) 483-7551
Fax: (402) 483-1465
Internet: www.usacrs.com

Skibob Racing

Skibob racing is a winter downhill racing event in which competitors maneuver skibobs over a circuitous course marked with a series of gates. The skibob resembles a mountain bike outfitted with skis in place of wheels. Like the luge sled, the skibob is completely dependent on gravity for forward movement. International skibob competition includes downhill, slalom, parallel slalom, giant slalom, and Super-G events.

Skibob Racing Officials

Skibob races are officiated by a variety of officials including a race director, FISB judge, and a chief judge. The race director exercises overall control of the event while the judges score the competition. A multitude of minor officials are required for such tasks as starting the race, recording scores, timekeeping, and monitoring the course and equipment.

Resources

International Organization
Federation Internationale de Skibob (FISB)
FISB Generalsekretariat
Lutherstrasse 27
D4100 Duisburg 1
Germany
Phone: (49-20) 333-4087
Fax: (49-66) 266-2532

SKIING

Competitive skiing consists of four broad categories including Alpine, Nordic, Freestyle, and Biathlon. Alpine skiing includes the downhill, the slalom, the giant slalom, and Super-G events. Freestyle events include the ballet, aerials, and moguls. Ski jumping, cross-country, and combined events are part of the Nordic group. The Biathlon is a combination of cross-country skiing and rifle shooting (see Biathlon).

SKIING OFFICIALS

Competitive skiing events typically are regulated by an organizational committee which is assisted by a clerk of course, starter, judges, timekeepers, and a jury. The organizational committee supervises the event. The clerk of course and his or her assistant(s) prepare and tend the course. The judges oversee the skiers during the competition, while the jury rules on any disputes.

RESOURCES

International Organization
Federation Internationale de Ski (FIS)
Blochstrasse 2
3653 Oberhofen Thunersee
Switzerland
Phone: (41-33) 244-6161
Fax: (41-33) 243-5353
Internet: www.worldsport.com/sports/
ski/home.html

National Organizations
U.S. Ski and Snowboard Association
1500 Kearns Blvd.
P.O. Box 100
Park City, UT 84060-0100
Phone: (435) 649-9090
Fax: (435) 647-2630
Internet: www.usskiteam.com or
www.ussa.org

Cross Country Canada
1600 James Naismith Dr.
Gloucester Ontario K1B 5N4
Canada
Phone: (613) 748-5662
Fax: (613) 748-5703
e-mail: xcski@cdnsport.ca

SPEEDBALL

Speedball is an outdoor round ball game played by two teams of 11 players each. Competition takes place on a field approximately the same size as a football field. The game is played with a regulation soccer ball, which players attempt to kick into their opponent's goal in order to score. Unlike soccer, speedball players are allowed to pass the ball with their hands. Speedball games consist of four 10-minute quarters.

SPEEDBALL OFFICIALS

Speedball is officiated by a referee, assisted by a pair of linesmen, a scorekeeper, and a timekeeper. The referee controls the game, while the linesmen watch for fouls and signal when the ball goes out of play.

RESOURCES

At present, there is no recognized governing body for speedball. However, both the National Association for Girls and Women in Sport (NAGWS) and its parent organization, the American Alliance for Health, Physical Education, Recreation and Dance (AAHPERD), have actively promoted the game for a number of years.

American Alliance for Health, Physical Education,
Recreation and Dance (AAHPERD)
1900 Association Dr.
Reston, VA 22091
Phone: (703) 476-3410
Fax: (703) 476-8316

National Association for Girls and Women in Sport (NAGWS)
1900 Association Dr.
Reston, VA 22091
Phone: (703) 476-3453
Fax: (703) 476-9527
Internet: nagws@aahperd.org

SQUASH

Squash is an indoor game similar to handball in which two or four players compete in an enclosed court. Players use squash rackets to hit a small rubber ball against a vertical wall with the objective of keeping the ball in continuous play while making it difficult for the opposing side to return. While squash has long been played with a hard ball, the use of a softer ball has gained popularity in recent years.

Roger Perlmuter

SQUASH OFFICIALS

Squash officials include a referee, a pair of judges, and a marker; the referee is the chief official, while the marker is responsible for announcing scores. The judges rule on disputes.

RESOURCES

International Organization

World Squash Federation (WSF)
6 Havelock Rd.
Hastings East Sussex TN34 1BP
Great Britain
Phone: (44-1424) 42-9245
Fax: (44-1424) 42-9250
e-mail: squash@wsf.cablenet.co.uk
Internet: www.squash.org

National Organizations

U.S. Squash Racquets Association (USSRA)
23 Cynwyd Rd.
P.O. Box 1216
Bala-Cynwyd, PA 19004
Phone: (610) 667-4006
Fax: (610) 667-6539
e-mail: ussquash@us-squash.org
Internet: www.us-squash.org/squash

Professional Squash Association
56 Spooner Rd.
Chestnut Hill, MA 02467
Phone: (617) 731-6874
Fax: (617) 277-1457
e-mail: psajn@aol.com

Squash Canada
1600 James Naismith Dr.
Gloucester Ontario K1B 5N4
Canada
Phone: (613) 748-5672
Fax: (613) 748-5681
e-mail: squash.canada@bpg.ca

TABLE TENNIS

Roger Perlmuter

Commonly known as ping-pong, table tennis essentially is an indoor version of tennis. Players use small paddles to volley a ping-pong ball back and forth across a net stretched over the center of the table. As in regulation tennis, the serving side attempts to score points by making the ball difficult to return. Play is continuous, and the first player or team to score 21 points wins. Matches are won by the player or side taking the best of three (or five) games. Major tournaments include the World Championship, the National Team Championship, and the National Open. Table tennis is an Olympic sport.

TABLE TENNIS OFFICIALS

Competitive table tennis is officiated by an umpire who is in charge of each game and has final say in any disputes.

RESOURCES

International Organization

International Table Tennis Federation (ITTF)
53 London Rd.
St. Leonards-on Sea
East Sussex TN37 6AY
Great Britain
Phone: (44-1424) 72-1414
Fax: (44-1424) 43-1871
e-mail: hq@ittf.cablenet.co.uk
Internet: www.ittf.com

National Organization

USA Table Tennis
One Olympic Plaza
Colorado Springs, CO 80909-5769
Phone: (719) 578-4583
Fax: (719) 632-6071
e-mail: usatt@iex.net
Internet: www.usatt.org

TEAM HANDBALL

Team handball is a round ball game played by two teams of seven players each. While court handball is played on a relatively small indoor court, team handball courts are much larger in size and have no walls. In team handball, teams alternate offensive and defensive roles with the offense attempting to maneuver the ball into the opponent's goal. Players may throw, pass, or dribble the ball with their hands, but may not kick it. The object of the game is to score more goals than the opposing team. Team handball is an Olympic sport.

TEAM HANDBALL OFFICIALS

Team handball officials include a pair of referees, a scorekeeper, and a timekeeper. One referee is positioned near the defender's goal; the other follows the action from behind the offensive team. Referees rotate positions with each change of possession.

RESOURCES

International Organization
Federation Internationale de Handball (IHF)
Lange Gasse 10
Case Postale 312
4020 Bale
Switzerland
Phone: (41-61) 272-1300
Fax: (41-61) 272-1344
e-mail: ihf@magnet.ch
Internet: www.worldsport.com/sports/handball/home.html

National Organization
U.S. Team Handball Federation
1903 Powers Ferry Rd., Ste.230
Atlanta, GA 30339
Phone: (770) 956-7660
Fax: (719) 956-7976
e-mail: info@usateamhandball.org
Internet: www.usateamhandball.org

TRIATHLON

David Dreimiller

Triathlon competitions are composed of individual and team events in swimming, cycling, and running. All events are held in continuous order with athletes making a transition from one event to the next. Three course lengths are used: short, long, and Iron Man courses. Course length varies by level of competition. Triathlon is an Olympic sport of the summer games.

TRIATHLON OFFICIALS

The triathlon requires a number of officials to keep track of the event. These include a race director, referee, swim officials, running officials, cycle officials, timekeepers, scorekeepers, transition judges, marshals, and finish judges. The race director organizes the event while the referee observes each event and ensures that players follow the rules. The marshals direct the competitors on their respective cycle and race courses.

RESOURCES

International Organization
International Triathlon Union (ITU)
1154 W 24th St.
North Vancouver British Columbia V7P 2J2
Canada
Phone: (604) 926-7250
Fax: (604) 926-7260
e-mail: ituhdq@axionet.com
Internet: www.triathlon.org

National Organization
USA Triathlon
3595 E. Fountain Blvd., Ste. F-1
Colorado Springs, CO 80910
Phone: (719) 597-9090
Fax: (719) 597-2121
e-mail: usatriathlon@usatriathlon.org
Internet: www.usatriathlon.org

WATER POLO

Water polo is a round ball game played in a swimming pool by two teams of seven players each. Players attempt to score points by throwing the ball into their opponents' goal net. The ball may be thrown with one or both hands; however, only the goalie is allowed to punch the ball. The game is played in four seven-minute periods. Water polo is an Olympic sport.

WATER POLO OFFICIALS

Water polo is officiated by a pair of referees, assisted by goal judges. Referees stop and start the game, decide fouls and exclusions, and can play the advantage in order to see who gains from an illegal play – the offenders or the innocent party. Both referees use whistles and colored flags to signal rulings. Goal judges use colored flags to signal goals.

RESOURCES

International Organization
Federation Internationale de Natation Amateur (FINA)
Ave. de Beaumont 9
Rez-de-Chaussee
1012 Lausanne
Switzerland
Phone: (41-21) 312-6602
Fax: (41-21) 312-6610
Internet: www.fina.org

National Organizations
U.S. Water Polo
1685 W. Uintah
Colorado Springs, CO 80904-2921
Phone: (719) 634-0699
Fax: (719) 634-0866
e-mail: uswpoffice@uswp.org
Internet: www.uswp.org

Water Polo Canada
1600 James Naismith Dr.
Gloucester Ontario K1B 5N4
Canada
Phone: (613) 748-5682
Fax: (613) 748-5777
e-mail: susanfh@rtm.cdnsport.ca

WATER SKIING

Water skiers, pulled across the water by powerboats, compete in a variety of events. Competitive water skiing includes the slalom, ski jumping, and trick riding. In the slalom, skiers negotiate a specified course, using progressively shorter tow lines as the speed of the boat increases. In ski jumping, participants compete for distance after launching from a fixed ramp. In trick riding, skiers execute a variety of maneuvers, often on a single ski. In championship competition, the skier with the best overall score in all three events is the winner. Water skiing is included in the Pan American Games.

WATER SKIING OFFICIALS

Water skiing is officiated by a chief judge who works in conjunction with a panel of judges which monitor the individual skiing events.

RESOURCES

International Organization

International Water Ski Federation (IWSF)
P.O. Box 2038
Medellin
Colombia
Phone\Fax: (00574) 260-4526
e-mail: iwsf@intic.net

National Organization

American Water Ski Association (AWSA)
799 Overlook Dr., SE
Winter Haven, FL 33884
Phone: (941) 324-4341
Fax: (941) 325-8259
e-mail: usawaterski@worldnet.att.net
Internet: www.usawaterski.org

WINDSURFING

In windsurfing, competitors complete a set course as they maneuver sailboards across open water. Wind surfers must complete the course using wind power alone. The three major forms of windsurfing are: course racing, slalom racing, and wave riding. In course racing, competitors race around an irregular M-shaped course that challenges the surfer's ability to navigate his or her craft regardless of wind direction. In slalom events, wind surfers navigate a series of buoys, often in a figure eight pattern. Wave performance competitions are held in waves with a minimum velocity of 12 knots. Individuals compete, one-on-one, in three events: jumps, transitions, and surfing. High scores are given to the most diverse, innovative, and challenging moves. The winner of each event advances to the next round. Other forms of windsurfing are Freestyle Windsurfing (of which Speed Sailing is a part), Bodyboarding and Skimboarding. In freestyle, surfers find as many different ways to sail on a board as possible. Like skateboarding, they can perform on the edge of the rail, inside the broom, and do pirouettes for a competition. Freestyle was especially popular before the advent of smaller boards in the mid-1980s. In speed sailing, competitors attempt to break world records for speed on specially built courses. Races are held in some of the windiest locations on earth. (And competitors often use some of the smallest boards available). A delegate from the World Speed Sailing Committee must be present to confirm all world record attempts.

WINDSURFING OFFICIALS
Windsurfing is officiated by a race director who is assisted by a panel of judges. In wave performance, events are often scored by different

factors that take into account wind and wave conditions. Prior to the race, the race director chooses if and which factors should be used. A panel of judges observes the actual events. Each judge must be a windsurfing expert in addition to being well versed in the rules and procedures of competition.

RESOURCES

International Organization
World Boarding Association
Feldafinger Platz 2
Munchen 71 D-8000
Germany
Phone: (49-8) 978-1074

National Organization
U.S. Windsurfing Association (USWA)
P.O. Box 978
Hood River, OR 97031
Phone: (541) 386-8708
e-mail: uswa@aol.com

YACHT RACING (SAILING)

In traditional yacht racing, competitors attempt to maneuver their craft over a designated course in the least amount of time. The yachts used in competition include catamarans, dinghies, and keel boats. Dinghies and keel boat races are divided into class categories.

Categories include: *one design* events in which all boats are identical, *development class* events that allow only certain kinds of sail craft, and *formula races* which only govern the specific measurements a boat must conform to. Competitions are held for both daylight and night events (for individuals and teams). Seven races are held for each class. The six best race scores count as a crew's final score. Yacht racing is an Olympic sport. Boats allowed in Olympic events are: Soling, Tornado, Star, Flying Dutchman, 470, keel boats (two- and three-person), dinghies (two-person and single, and two-person high performance), catamarans (two-person), International Europe Class, sailboards (see Windsurfing), and Lechner 390 boats.

Other forms of yacht racing are: offshore yacht racing and ice yachting. For offshore yachting, sea-going keel yachts are raced over offshore courses. Events can be short afternoon races or eight-month-long, around-the-world events.

Ice yachting (iceboating) is a sport in which small crafts, similar to sailboats, are raced across a smooth surface of ice using the force of the wind to propel them. Most courses consist of two buoys located 1.6 km (1 mile) apart. Three counterclockwise laps through the course constitute a race.

YACHT RACING OFFICIALS

Races are organized by a race committee which also gives instructions on starting, finishing, and sailing as well as scoring. Referees or umpires are not used in yacht racing (except in special matches) due to the unique conditions under which yacht racing occurs. A great deal of responsibility is placed on the competitors who are expected to monitor both themselves and others in a match. For example, a crew must raise its flag and attempt to inform the offending yacht of its intention to protest. An offending yacht may suffer point penalties and is required to withdraw from the event. Protests against a yacht must be made within the time limit specified for the race. In national races, protests are ruled on by a race committee or subcommittee. Appeals are sent to the national yacht racing authority. In international events, protests are decided by an IYRU panel, and no appeals are allowed.

RESOURCES

International Organizations

International Yacht Racing Union (IYRU)
27 Broadwell
Waterloo, London SE1 9PL
Great Britain
Phone: (44-71) 928-4670
Fax: (44-71) 401-8304

International Sailing Federation (ISAF)
Ariadne House, Town Quay
Southhampton SO14 2AQ
United Kingdom
Phone: (44-1703) 635-111
Fax: (44-1703) 635-789
e-mail: sail@isaf.co.uk
Internet: www.sailing.org

National Organizations

United States Sailing Association
15 Maritime Dr.
P.O. Box 1260
Portsmouth, RI 02871-1260
Phone: (401) 683-0800
Fax: (401) 683-0840
Internet: www.ussailing.org

U.S. Yacht Racing Union (USYRU)
8516 Sand Point Way, NE
Seattle, WA 98115

Canadian Yachting Association/
Windsurfing Canada
1600 James Naismith Dr., Ste. 504
Gloucester Ontario K1B 5N4
Canada
Phone: (613) 748-5687
Fax: (613) 748-5688
e-mail: sailcanada@sailing.ca
Internet: www.sailing.ca

SECTION V:
DIRECTORY OF
STATE ATHLETIC
ASSOCIATIONS

ALABAMA
HIGH SCHOOL
ATHLETIC ASSOCIATION

Sports
Baseball, basketball, football, gymnastics, soccer, softball, volleyball, wrestling

Registration of Officials
-Contact the AHSAA for referral to a local officials association
-Contact your local officials association for registration and testing details

Contact Information
Alabama High School Athletic Association
926 Pelham St.
P.O. Box 5014
Montgomery, AL 36103-5014
Phone: (334) 242-5654 Fax: (334) 240-3389

Distinguished Service Awards
Presented to Officials by the Alabama High School
Athletic Directors and Coaches Association

	Years of Service			Years of Service			Years of Service
1990:						**1996:**	
Billy Henderson	50		Joe Fowler	36		Bill Gaulden	33
			C.P. Newdome	36		Jon Ramsey	32
1991:			Johnny Purter	36		Luther Redden	31
Ed Balzli	51					Max Wilkes	31
Doc Blanchard	44		**1994:**				
Wayne Boteler	49		J.C. Brewer	35		**1997:**	
Glenn Hawkins	46		Fred Hughes	37		Jack Burton	
Scotty Sauers	45		Herman Keeney	35		John Christy	
			Mickey Kirkland	36		James Crawford	
1992:			Fred Thomas	38		Nancy Green	
Willie Scoggins	42		Gaynes Waters	42		Mike Griffin	
Sam Short	42					Lem Jones	
James Stallworth	41		**1995:**				
Holley Stanley	40		Perry Canada	39		**1998:**	
			William Jessie	35		J.D. Cartwright	
1993:			W.L. Smith	37		Melvin Grant	
Pat Adkison	36		Bill Talbot	36		Hugh Gunter	
Ormond Brown	36					Glenn Padgett	

ALASKA SCHOOL ACTIVITIES ASSOCIATION

Sports
Baseball, basketball, cross-country running, cross-country skiing, football, girls gymnastics, hockey, rifle, soccer, softball, swimming and diving, track and field, tennis, volleyball, wrestling

Registration of Officials
-Contact the ASAA for an application
-Fees: one sport, $35; each additional sport, $10

Requirements for Officials
-Submit an application for each sport in which certification is requested
-Achieve minimum score of 75% on part I of examination

Contact Information
Alaska School Activities Association
4120 Laurel St., Ste. 102
Anchorage, AK 99508
Phone: (907) 563-3723 Fax: (907) 561-0720

ARIZONA INTERSCHOLASTIC ASSOCIATION

The Arizona Interscholastic Association has been established to advance the best interests of interscholastic competition. The association aids officials, coaches, and players in acquiring thorough knowledge about the playing rules of all sports. The AIA encourages the fostering of spirit and the promotion of sportsmanship and fair play.

Sports
Baseball, basketball, football, soccer, softball, track and field, volleyball, wrestling

Registration of Officials
-Contact the AIA for registration materials
-Registration deadline is June 15 annually
-Registration fees: one sport, $30; each additional sport, $10; interstate reciprocity (per sport), $10; late fee (after June 15 annually), $25 (late fee does not apply to new officials)

Requirements for Officials
-Must be 18 years of age and cannot be enrolled in high school
-Rules meetings are required for each individual sport: 10 meetings, 1 area clinic, 1 general meeting, 1 intersquad scrimmage
-Exam score must be above 70%

Classification of Officials
-Classification levels are based on test scores:
Level 1: Minimum test score of 90%
Level 2: Minimum test score of 85%
Level 3: Minimum test score of 80%
Level 4: Minimum test score of 70%
Level 5: Must have previous experience

Contact Information
Arizona Interscholastic Association
John Reigar, Commissioner of Officials
2606 West Osborn Rd.
Phoenix, AZ 85017-9141
Phone: (602) 257-0272 Fax: (602) 254-9141

ARKANSAS ACTIVITIES ASSOCIATION

The Arkansas Activities Association had its beginnings in 1904 when it was formed by seven high schools. As a part of the National Federation of State High School Associations, the AAA is comprised of 476 public and private schools in the state and oversees administration of the rules and regulations for all activities.

The Arkansas Officials Association is a part of the Arkansas Activities Association and registers officials in the sports of football, volleyball, basketball, baseball, softball, and gymnastics, with soccer to be added.

Sports
Baseball, basketball, football, gymnastics, softball, volleyball

Registration of Officials
-All applicants should register in June
-Contact the AAA for an application

Requirements for Officials
-18 years of age and graduated from high school
-Good physical condition
-Endorsement of school head coach, administrator, or another official

Classification of Officials
-Ratings are determined based on age, exam scores, attendance of rules meetings, clinics and business meetings, and number of games officiated:
Division 5: Entry level; age 18
Division 4: Must be 19; minimum 70% exam score
Division 3: Must be 21 (18 for baseball); minimum 75% exam score
Division 2: Must be 22 (19 for baseball); minimum 80% exam score
Division 1: Top level; minimum age 25 (21 for baseball)

Contact Information
Arkansas Activities Association
3920 Richards Rd.
North Little Rock, AR 72117
Phone: (501) 955-2500 Fax: (501) 955-2600

CALIFORNIA INTERSCHOLASTIC FEDERATION

The State of California is large enough that 10 geographic sections are necessary to register all officials in the state. For information on the official's associations in each CIF Section, please contact the appropriate CIF Section Commissioner from the list below.

Contact Information
California Interscholastic Federation
Jack Hayes, Executive Director
664 Las Gallinas Ave.
San Rafael, CA 94903
Phone: (415) 492-5911 Fax: (415) 492-5919

Northern
Darold Adamson
30 Greenville Circle, #A
Chico, CA 95928
Phone: (530) 345-9133 Fax (530) 345-0826

North Coast
Paul Gaddini
P.O. Box 2907
Dublin, CA 94568
Phone: (925) 828-4900 Fax (925) 828-5700

Sac-Joaquin
Pete Saco
2405 S. Stockton Rd., #2
Lodi, CA 95420
Phone: (209) 334-5900 Fax (209) 334-0300

San Francisco City
Anne Heinline
300 Seneca Ave., Rm. 2
San Francisco, CA 94112
Phone: (415) 452-4932 Fax (415) 452-4935

Oakland City
Jerry Luzar
1025 Second Ave.
Oakland, CA 94606
Phone: (510) 879-8311 Fax (510) 879-1835

Central Coast
Nancy Lazenby Blaser
1691 Old Bayshore Hwy., Ste. 200
San Jose, CA 95112
Phone: (408) 441-9505 Fax (408) 441-9509

Central
Jerry Laird
2555 Clovis Ave.
Clovis, CA 93612
Phone: (209) 292-7580 Fax (209) 292-3838

Los Angeles City
Barbara Fiege
P.O. Box 3307
Los Angeles, CA 90051
Phone: (213) 743-3640 Fax (213) 746-6390

Southern
Dean Crowley
P.O. Box 488
Cerritos, CA 90702
Phone: (562) 860-2414 Fax (562) 860-1692

San Diego
Jan Jessop
6401Linda Vista Rd.
San Diego, CA 92111
Phone: (619) 292-8165 Fax (619) 292-1375

COLORADO HIGH SCHOOL ACTIVITIES ASSOCIATION

The Colorado High School Activities Association was established in 1921 to shape and expand the interscholastic programs offered in the secondary schools of Colorado. The CHSAA is a non-profit organization that has been the governing body for all of Colorado's 285 member schools for 75 years and continues today to promote a meaningful and well-rounded educational experience.

Sports
Baseball, basketball, football, girls field hockey, girls gymnastics, girls lacrosse, ice hockey, soccer, softball, speech, swimming, track and field, volleyball, wrestling

Registration of Officials
-Contact the CHSAA for clinic dates
-Fees: $25 to $50, depending on the sport

Requirements for Officials
-Attend mandatory rules clinics and meetings
-Must pass the National Federation rules test
-Dues must be paid to the officials association for each sport

Contact Information
Colorado High School Activites Association/Officials Office
14855 E. 2nd Ave.
Aurora, CO 80011
Phone: (303) 364-1337 Fax: (303) 367-4101

Colorado Sports Officiating Organizations Partners/Presidents

Baseball
George Demietriou (CHSBUA)
4925 Fathing Dr.
Colorado Springs, CO 80906
Phone: (719) 535-1893 (W)
(719) 540-0420 (H)

Ice Hockey
Ray Streicher
3134 Whileaway Circle W.
Colorado Springs, CO 80917
Phone: (719) 540-1614 (W)
(719) 597-3955 (H)

Speech
Stephen Larue
674 S. Emerson St.
Denver, CO 80209
Phone: (303) 556-6199 (W)
(303) 777-9185 (H)

Basketball
Steve Stone (Board #4)
950 Ute Lane
Gunnison, CO 81230
Phone: (970) 641-2429 (W)
(970) 641-3495 (H)

Lacrosse
Saskia Van Woudenberg
(CWLOA)
825 Pearl St.
Denver, CO 80209
Phone: (303) 766-2000 (W)
(303) 777-3843 (H)

Swimming
Kathy Christy (CASO)
320 Waco Court
Colorado Springs, CO 80919
Phone: (970) 565-8000 (W)
(719) 593-1966 (H)

Field Hockey
Lisa Ellsworth (CFHUA)
1341 S. Pennsylvania St.
Denver, CO 80210
Phone: (909) 698-2092 (H)

Larry Jackel
16100 E. Smoky Hill Rd.
Aurora, CO 80015
Phone: (303) 693-1700 (W)
(303) 693-2991 (H)

Track & Field
T.J. Henderson
434 Steele St.
Denver, CO 80206
Phone: (303) 333-6435 (H)

Football
J.J. Klikus (CFOA)
6878 Grapewood Circle
Colorado Springs, CO 80918
Phone: (719) 578-6177 (W)
(719) 260-7296 (H)

Soccer
Mary Van Allen,
Interim President (HSSO)
21035 Capella Dr.
Monument, CO
Phone: (719) 481-3821 (H)

Volleyball
Anita Rentas (CVOA)
4025 Hickory Hill Dr.
Colorado Springs, CO 80906
Phone: (719) 382-1610 (W)
(719) 576-2740 (H)

Girls' Gymnastics
Cindy Staudt (CHSGGJA)
9774 Kipling St.
Westminster, CO 80021
Phone: (303) 420-2508 (H)

Softball
John Fochi (CHSSBUA)
6122 Dudley Court
Arvada, CO 80004
Phone: (303) 982-0662 (W)
(303) 456-5781 (H)

Wrestling
Daryn Klassen (CWOA)
1544 Peach Court
Brighton, CO 80601
Phone: (303) 659-0895 (W)
(303) 659-8817 (H)

CONNECTICUT INTERSCHOLASTIC ATHLETIC CONFERENCE

The Connecticut Interscholastic Athletic Conference is a non-profit corporation organized to direct and control both boys and girls athletics in the secondary schools of Connecticut. Interscholastic athletics are considered to be an integral segment of the total educational program in Connecticut.

Sports
Boys: football, cross country, soccer, basketball, ice hockey, indoor track, swimming, wrestling, baseball, golf, tennis, outdoor track, lacrosse
Girls: cross country, field hockey, soccer, swimming, basketball, gymnastics, indoor track, softball, tennis, outdoor track

Registration of Officials
-To become an official in the state of Connecticut a person must apply through the individual Officials Associations. For more information, contact the CIAC.

Requirements for Officials
-All officials must be 18 years of age

Contact Information
Connecticut Interscholastic Athletic Conference
30 Realty Dr.
Cheshire, CT 06410
Phone: (203) 250-1111 Fax: (203) 250-1345

Connecticut Interscholastic Athletic Conference
Networking Contacts

Baseball
Walter Zalaski
34 Farms Village Rd.
Simsbury, CT 06078

Boys Basketball
Joseph Tonelli
24 Ricardo Rd.
West Haven, CT 06516

Girls Basketball
Nick Zeoli
20 Meeker Rd.
Wilton, CT 06897

Field Hockey
Paula Fitzgerald
156 McVeagh Rd.
Westbrook, CT 06498

Football
Joseph Tonelli
24 Ricardo Rd.
West Haven, CT 06516

Gymnastics
Eugene Primavera
100 Black Rock Turnpike
Redding, CT 06896

Ice Hockey
Robert Broderick
34 Farms Village Rd.
Simsbury, CT 06070

Softball
Raymond Marr
124 N. Maple St.
Enfield, CT 06082

Soccer
Ed Ferrigno
355 High St.
Willimantic, CT 06226

Swimming
Nick Zeoli
395 Danbury Rd.
Wilton, CT 06897

Volleyball
Bill McAllister
115 Howard Ave.
Ansonia, CT 06401

Wrestling
Bill McAllister
115 Howard Ave.
Ansonia, CT 06401

DELAWARE SECONDARY SCHOOL ATHLETIC CONFERENCE

For information about becoming an official in the state of Delaware, please contact:

Delaware Secondary School Athletic Association
Robert A. Depew, Executive Director
P.O. Box 1402
John G. Townsend Building
Dover, DE 19901-2899
Phone: (302) 739-4181 Fax: (302) 739 4221

DISTRICT OF COLUMBIA INTERSCHOLASTIC ATHLETIC ASSOCIATION

The District of Columbia Interscholastic Athletic Association (DCIAA) was established in 1991 to replace and supersede the District of Columbia Interhigh League, which primarily consisted of the public senior high schools in Washington, D.C. The D.C. Interhigh League was establised in 1892. In 1958, the D.C. Interhigh League joined as a member of the National Federation of High School Associations.

Sports
Baseball, basketball, cheerleading, crew, cross country, football, golf, soccer, softball, tennis, track and field, volleyball, wrestling

Registration of Officials
-Contact the individual officiating organizations for clinic dates and fees

Requirements for Officials
-Attend mandatory rules clinics and meetings
-Must pass the National Federation rules test
-Dues must be paid to the officials association for each sport

Contact Information
District of Columbia Public Schools Department of Athletics
District of Columbia Interscholastic Athletic Association
Truesdell Elementary School
800 Ingraham St. NW
Washington, DC 20011-2925
Phone: (202) 576-7167 Fax: (202) 576-8505

District of Columbia Interscholastic Athletic Association
Sports Officiating Organizations Commissioners

Baseball
Phillip Morgan
5819 Eighth St. NE
Washington, DC 20011
Phone: (202) 529-1916 (H)
Pager: (202) 405-0360

Basketball
Joe Marosy
16601 Lescot Terrace
Rockville, MD 20853
Phone: (301) 924-5884 (H)
      (301) 650-6627 (W)

Football
Eastern Board of Officials (EBO)
Thomas Beard
746 Quebec Place NW
Washington, DC 20010
Phone: (202) 882-4287 (H)

Washington District
Football Officials Association
(WDFOA)
Alan Ferraro
15328 Durant St.
Silver Spring, MD 20905
Phone: (301) 384-4562 (H)

Soccer
Alan Ceceilo, Treasurer
1007 Venice Dr.
Colesville, MD 20901-2065
Phone: (301) 622-3608 (H)

Softball
Phillip Morgan
5819 Eighth St. NE
Washington, DC 20011
Phone: (202) 529-1916 (H)
Pager: (202) 405-0360

Track and Field
Harold Plummer
3117 Bellbrock Court
Temple Hills, MD 20748
Phone: (301) 630-9592 (H)

Volleyball
Fletcher Tinsley
4530 Natahala Dr.
Clinton, MD 20735
Phone: (301) 297-7039 (H)

FLORIDA HIGH SCHOOL ACTIVITIES ASSOCIATION

The Florida High School Activities Association is dedicated to providing educational activities through which Florida's students learn by doing.

Sports
Baseball, basketball, cross-country running, football, soccer, softball, track, volleyball, wrestling

Registration of Officials
-Contact the FHSAA for registration requirements and information

Contact Information
Florida High School Activities Association
Robert W. Hughes, Commissioner
515 N. Main St.
P.O. Box 271
Gainesville, FL 32602-1173
Phone: (352) 372-9551 ext. 290 Fax: (352) 373-1528

GEORGIA HIGH SCHOOL ASSOCIATION

The mission of the Georgia High School Association shall be the promotion of education in Georgia from a mental, physical, and moral perspective; to promote the study of public speaking; to standardize and encourage athletic participation; and to promote an appreciation for music and other fine arts through regional and statewide competitions.

Sports
Baseball, basketball, football, gymnastics, soccer, softball, swimming, volleyball, wrestling

Registration of Officials
-Contact the GHSA for a registration application

Classification of Officials
Registered
-18 years of age and a high school graduate
-File an application and be accepted by a local GHSA-sanctioned association
-Attend annual GHSA rules clinic
-Score at least 75% on part I, part II, and mechanics examinations annually
-Officiate minimum number of contests required in sport of registration
Approved
-Serve at least two years as **Registered** official
-Attend required rules interpretation clinics
-Officiate minimum number of contests required in sport of registration
Certified
-Serve a minimum of two years as **Registered** official and two years as **Approved** official
-Score at least 85% on part II of National Federation exam
-Officiate minimum number of contests required in sport of registration

Contact Information
Georgia High School Association
P.O. Box 271
Thomaston, GA 30286
Phone: (706) 647-7473 Fax: (706) 647-2638

HAWAII
HIGH SCHOOL
ATHLETIC ASSOCIATION

Registration of Officials
-Contact the HHSAA for referral to a local officials association
-Contact your local officials association for registration and testing details

Contact Information
Hawaii High School Athletic Association
Keith Amemiya, Executive Director
P.O. Box 62029
Honolulu, HI 96839
Phone: (808) 587-4495 Fax: (808) 587-4496

IDAHO HIGH SCHOOL ACTIVITIES ASSOCIATION

The Idaho High School Activities Association believes that sports officials play an important role in the development of young people. The officials of the IHSAA are expected to exhibit a high degree of moral character and should always display conduct which is a credit to the officials of Idaho, the Association, and the sports program.

Sports
Baseball, basketball, football, softball, track, volleyball, wrestling

Registration of Officials
-Contact the IHSAA for a registration form
-Registration dates: Fall sports, September 1; Winter sports, November 1; Spring sports, April 1
-Fees: $30

Certification Requirements
-18 years of age
-Cannot be enrolled in high school
-Score 70% or higher on part II of the National Federation exam

Classification of Officials
Nonvarsity
-Must fulfill the above requirements for certification
Varsity
-State rules meeting attendance is mandatory
-Must attend two local meetings
-Must score 80% or higher on part II of the National Federation exam
-Must have a recommendation from the district commissioner

Contact Information
Idaho High School Activities Association
P.O. Box 4667
Boise, ID 83711
Phone: (208) 375-7027 Fax: (208) 322-5505

Football Officials
District I: Referee Roger Stewart, Umpire Rick Rasmussen, Linesman Terry Gorton, Line Judge Jim White, Back Judge Shane Anderson; District II: Referee Doug Thornton, Umpire Dan Davenport, Linesman Gary Allen; Line Judge Dan Storey, Back Judge Corky Fazio; District III: Referee Tim Gridley, Umpire Bob Ranells, Linesman Tim Messuri, Line Judge Jerry Helgeson, Back Judge Dan Yraguen; District IV: Referee Reed Tucker, Umpire Brent Larsen, Linesman Mel Hine, Line Judge Kenny Lively, Back Judge Art Watkins; District V: Referee Doug Carlson, Umpire Arne Jones, Linesman Greg Harding, Line Judge Gary Carlson, Back Judge Jeff Wakely; District VI: Referee Chris Gardner, Umpire Alan Gardner, Linesman Nate Chipman, Line Judge Tad Pearson, Back Judge Hugh Foster

Girls Basketball Officials
District I: Bill Bopp, Doug Olin, Scott Peterson; District II: Greg Billups, Dean Roy, Darren Malm; District III: Kay Engelking, Tim Gridley, Dallas Flischer, Randy Powell; District IV: Allan Howa, Tim Campbell, Steve Thoms, Vint Turner; District V: Doug Carlson, Gregg Harding, Gary Carlson; District VI: Lynn Smith, Brant Kerbs, Brent Martin

Boys Basketball Officials
District I: Steve Hudson, John Poznick, Shannon Pooler; District II: Darren Malm, Dean Roy, Warren Beckman; District III: Perry Kerfvoot, Darren Krzesnik, Matt Stong, Larry Lincoln; District IV: Jerry Hall, Randy Winn, Gary Krumm, Robert Ketterling; District V: Doug Carlson, Gary Carlson, Greg Harding; District VI: Hugh Foster, Kent Marboe, Lynn Smith

Wrestling Officials
District I: Merrill Owens, Bob Grigg; District II: Gary Canady, Dan Lejameyer; District III: Gary Kamo, Paul Schaffeld; District IV: Craig Maki, Kelly Kidd; District V: Arne Jones, Travis Spahr; District VI: Greg Scheer, Roger Hansen

Track Officials
Starters: Ben Allen, Chris Mattocks, Warren "Moke" Strong, Bruce Sweeney; Referees: Bob Ranells, Jerry Kleinkopf; Chief Field Judge Pat Shanafelt

State Volleyball Tournament Officials
A-1/A-2: District I, Tammy Holdahl; District II, Sally Greene; District III, Kelly Chapple; District IV, Laurie Howard; District V, Jeff Horrocks; District VI, Norm Kane; A-3/A-4: District I, Don Friis; District II, Sharon Rausch; District III, Richard Gaona; District IV, Heidi Peck; District V, Nancy Bealer; District VI, Stacy Fonua

ILLINOIS HIGH SCHOOL ASSOCIATION

The Illinois High School Association provides an Officials Manual to help promote uniformity in officiating and to improve conditions under which athletic contests are held. The IHSA requires all officials to attend a rules interpretation meeting to ensure that a high standard of officiating is maintained in the state of Illinois.

Sports
Basketball, soccer, swimming, track and field, boys baseball, boys football, boys gymnastics, wrestling, girls gymnastics, girls softball, volleyball

Registration of Officials
-Contact the IHSA for an application form
-Fee: $30

Certification Requirements
-Must be 17 years of age
-Must submit favorable character references which outline potential officiating abilities
-Must receive a passing grade of 80% on preliminary exam
-Must attend rules interpretation meetings

Classification of Officials
-Once registered an individual is considered a **Recognized Official**
-Promotion to a **Certified Official** is based on requirements specifically established for each sport

Contact Information
Illinois High School Association
H. David Fry, Executive Director
2715 McGraw Dr.
P.O. Box 2715
Bloomington, IL 61702-2715
Phone: (309) 663-6377 Fax: (309) 663-7479
e-mail: fry@ihsa.org
Internet: www.ihsa.org

Illinois High School Association Officials
Assigned to State Finals in Multiple Sports

Donna Anfield
Joseph Antonini
John Babler
Richard Bartlett
John Bati
Kerry Baugher
Wayne Bigham
Carolyn Bishop
Nereo Blasevich
Stan Block
Henry P. Bowman
Don Brady
Preston Brewer
Randy Brickman
Raymond Brooks
Victor Buehler
Howard Burns
Peg Campana
Rey Carlberg
Dot Carter
Richard Carter
Phillip Coady
Donald Cobb
Walter Cocking
Greg Cole
James Collins
Robert Conte
Tony Costantino
Randy Cox
Wilton (Bingo) Crotz
Ted C. Daniels
Steve Davidson
Stan Decker
Richard Deitz
George Dekan
Jean W. DesMarteau
Frank DeVrieze
Charles Dhooge
Kevin Donlan
Samuel Donnelly
Kelly Douglas
Donald Drumm
Walter Elmore
Ron Fahnestock
Nick Finck
William Finedore
Gene Fowler
Thomas J. Fangella
Donald Frits

James Gannaway
Harold Garrett
Thomas Garrey
Roger Garrison
Becky Gillespie
Robert Graham
Larry Hackett
Kirby Hamm
Robert Hardt
Jim Harmison
A.G. (Frenchie) Haussler
Robert Hearns
Melvin Hebert
Richard Henley
D. Bradley Hill
Shelby Himes
David Hockersmith
Frans Hoogland
Dan Hopcus
Reuben Horna
Clive Hornstein
Ken Hungate
Denise Izatt
Willie Jackson
Leo Johnson
James A.B. Jones
Gene Jordan
Margaret Kelso
Amos Kent
Richard Kessler
Lois Klatt
Alfred Kleinaitis
Mel Klitzing
Ted Knapp
Jessie B. Knighten
Otho T. Kortz, Jr.
Judith Kretzschmar
Norman Kruger
Thomas Landi
David Laning
James Lapetina
Gene Lash
William Laude
Richard Leiber
Larry Leitner
George Lewerenz
John Lipe
Richard Lippert

Jack Lulay
Frank (Jay) Lyons
Charles McCarthy
Marlen McGinnis
Ernie McKinnon
Donald McVeain
Mark Madorin
Robert Mann
Bert Marett
James Mathis
Lee Mieure
Joseph Moroney
Kenneth Morrow
Larry Nemmers
Haig Nighohossian
Ed Norfleet
Michael Oliver
Jean Pankonin
Barry Pepper
Jim Pownall
Randall Pozzi
Joe Przada
Roger Quinlan
Frank Rago
Arthur E. Rawers
Robert Redman
Ferris Reid
Donald Rheinecker
Patricia Ritchie
Richard Rokop
Edward Rubin
David Rubini
Alfred Scheel
Ronald Scott
Ted Search, Jr.
Larry Sholl
Steve Siomos
W. Burdell Smith
Joseph M. Starcevic
John Sullivan
Joe Thompson
Richard Thompson
Lynette Trout
Alex Westhoff
Larry Wilcoxen
Wasyl Wowk
Robert L. Wright
Fred (Brick) Young

392

INDIANA HIGH SCHOOL ATHLETIC ASSOCIATION

In 1903, a group of Indiana High School principals met in Richmond to discuss the organizing of the High Schools of the state into a single association for the purpose of controlling athletic activities. The result was a body of suggested rules and regulations called the "Richmond Agreement." Although there was no central organization having executive power to enforce the rules, the way was, nevertheless, paved for the birth of the Indiana High School Athletic Association before the year was over.

Sports
Baseball, basketball, football, gymnastics, soccer, softball, swimming, track, volleyball, wrestling

Registration of Officials
-Contact the IHSAA to receive an application
-Registration deadlines vary for each sport
-Fee: $35

Requirements for Officials
-Applicant cannot be a high school student
-Character references will be contacted by the Association
-Score of 75% or higher on open book exam
-Attendance at rules interpretation meetings is mandatory

Classification of Officials
Registered: An official who has been registered less than three years
Certified: An official who has been licensed three or more years and scored 90% or above on most recent certification test
Professional: An official who has been recommended by the local association for which he/she participates

Contact Information
Indiana High School Athletic Association
Attn: Theresia Winns
9150 Meridian St.
P.O. Box 40650
Indianapolis, IN 46240-0650
Phone: (317) 846-6601 Fax: (317) 575-4244

IOWA HIGH SCHOOL ATHLETIC ASSOCIATION

The Iowa High School Athletic Association takes pride in the training and certification of its officials. A dedication to high professional standards and a proper attitude toward the advocation of officiating is expected by all IHSAA officials in the pursuit of a successful organization.

Registration of Officials
-Registration due by May 1
-Request an application form from the IHSAA
-Fee: $35

Certification Requirements
-Must pass an unsupervised rules examination with a score of at least 75%
-Registration is complete at the receipt of a registration card prepared by the IHSAA

Classification of Officials
Temporary
-Score of 75% or higher on unsupervised rules exam
Approved
-Score of 70% or higher on supervised rules examination
-After one year as an **Approved** official an official may apply for **Recognized** certification
Recognized
-Score of 85% or higher on supervised rules examination
-Must receive 80 points on the promotional scale
Certified
-Must officiate at the **Recognized** level for two years
-Must achieve at least a 90% on supervised rules examination
-Must receive 85 points on the promotional scale
Superior
-Must officiate at the **Certified** level for one year
-Must receive at least a 95% on supervised rules examination
-Must receive 90 points on the promotional scale

Contact Information
Iowa High School Athletic Association
P.O. Box 10
Boone, IA 50036-0100
Phone: (515) 432-2011 Fax: (515) 432-2961

Iowa High School Athletic Association
Officials Hall of Fame

Charles Adair
Jack Anderson
Kenneth Anderson
Leo Barcus
Everett Barr
Larry Barr
Roger Barr
Dale Barringer
Lawrence (Doc) Bates
Ben Beckerman
Tim Bell
Bob Bender
Len Benhart
Garry Bixby
Larry Blaker
Randy Blum
Richard Blumeyer
Henry Boone
R.L. Braunschweig
Howard Browne
Gary Christiansen
Ron Clinton
Wayne Clinton
Richard Colson
Paul Colenbrander
Dan Conry
Wes Cranston
Bud Demitroff
Richard Dotson
G.L. (Jud) Eichorn
Finn Eriksen
Bill Evans
Don Farnsworth
Joe Ferguson
Art Fish
Arlo Flege
Jim Fox
Eli Fredin
Waldo Geiger
Dick Geith
Gene Glab
Connie Goodman
Maurice Goodside
John Grace
Claison Groff
Ray Hamad

Ray Hammersley
Jim Hanlon
Cal Harms
Merle Harris
Henry Hasbrouck
Roger Heathman
Maynard Henderson
Ralph Hibbs
George Hicks
Bob Hildebrand
Don Holmes
Art Huinker
Al Huppert
Jim Jagim
Delbert Jensen
Phil Johnson
Willis Johnson
Ron Jurgens
John Kenney
Bob Klieman
Clifford (Bud) Knox
Rich Koolbeck
Don Koster
Bob Krall
Ken Kreykes
D.C. (Bill) Lamm
Richard Lashier
Bob Lee
Bud Legg
Richard Legg
Eugene (Dutch)
    Leonard
Wayne Lichty
Bob Locker
Ray Lounsberry
John Lowry
Max Lynn
Roy Martin
Q.S. McClannahan
Jim McElliot
Dr. Robert McNiel
Ralph Messerli
Jim Mumper
Henry Nissen
James Nora
George Norris

Carroll Oberman
Charles O'Brien
Bernie O'Connor
Bob Oldis
Jack Padilla
Arnold (Bud) Paulsen
Dale Petersen
Lanny Peterson
Larry Peterson
Barney Phillips
H.S. (Mike) Phillips
Bruce Pickford
William Praska
Richard Preston
L. Kirby Range
Jim Reese
Gordon Rhum
Ted Rideout
Earl Robinson
M.M. Rogers
August (Gus) Rump
Bernie Saggau
Richard Sampson
Harold Schmickley
James Schneekloth
Rollie Schrank
Bill Sears
T. Kendall Sexton
Leonard Shillinglaw
Bob Siddens
Ray Smalling
Paul Somers
Dwight Spangler
Elmer Starr
Fred Stoeker
Ron Sturch
Bennett Toay
Bob Tvrdik
A.W. Vanderwilt
John Van Why
Bob Vrbicek
Mel Walker
Martin Wierda
Dr. Everett Williams
Fred Winter
Richard Wulkow

1998 Inductees
Marvin Bell
Harold Baeth
Dennis Brumm
Terry Curtis
Russ Kraai
Randy Krejci
Jim Jensen
Hugh Norman
Don Proctor
George Stone

1999 Inductees
Jack Boal
Charles Brittian
Randy Bruns
Father Craig Collison
Mike Exline
Pete Hanson
Steve Janssen
Vernard Keerbs
Bill Roths
Earl Shostrom

KANSAS STATE HIGH SCHOOL ATHLETIC ASSOCIATION

The Kansas State High School Athletic Association was established in 1910 to contribute to the education of the high school boys and girls of Kansas. The KSHSAA has elevated the standards of good sportsmanship while encouraging the growth of good citizenship for both the students and adults involved with this outstanding organization.

Sports
Football, volleyball, soccer, basketball, wrestling, girls gymnastics, baseball, softball

Registration of Officials
-Request a registration card from KSHSAA, or register at a rules meeting
-Fee: $30

Requirements for Officials
-All registering officials must attend rules meetings for the sport in which they are registering
-Applicants must pass the National Federation exam for each sport they want to officiate

Classification of Officials
Level One
-Must be registered with the KSHSAA
-Must achieve a 90% or higher on the rules test
-Must attend all rules meetings
Level Two
-Must have met all **Level One** requirements
-Must attend an officiating clinic approved by KSHSAA
Level Three
-Must have been an official for the two previous years
-Must have attended rules meetings for two years
-Must score 90% or higher on the rules tests for three consecutive years
-All applicants must attend all series of area supervisor meetings

Contact Information
Kansas State High School Athletic Association
520 SW 27th St.
P.O. Box 495
Topeka, KS 66601-0495
Phone: (913) 235-9201 Fax: (913) 235-2637

KENTUCKY HIGH SCHOOL ATHLETIC ASSOCIATION

The Kentucky High School Athletic Association believes that officiating is an important part of the athletic program. For this reason, considerable time, effort, and money is spent on clinics, films, and materials designed to increase the knowledge and improve the techniques for officials.

Sports
Baseball, basketball, fast-pitch softball, field hockey, football, slow-pitch softball, soccer, swimming, track, volleyball, wrestling

Registration of Officials
-Contact the KHSAA office for registration cards and information
-Registration period: Year round
-Fee: first sport $25; each additional sport $15
-After the registration card is received by the KHSAA, prospective applicants will be sent a rules book and part I of the National Federation exam

Requirements for Officials
-Must be a graduate of an accredited high school
-Must be 18 years of age
-Must receive at least a 70% on part I of the exam given for applicants' particular sport
-Must attend a minimum of four local association meetings

Classification of Officials
Registered
-Paid registration fee; scored at least 70% on part I of exam
Approved
-Registered for one year
-Attended required rules meetings
-Scored at least 80% on part II of the National Federation exam
Certified
-Eligible 6th year of registration
-Scored at least 90% on part II of National Federation exam

Contact Information
Kentucky High School Athletic Association
2280 Executive Dr.
Lexington, KY 40505-4808
Phone: (606) 299-5472 Fax: (606) 293-5999

LOUISIANA HIGH SCHOOL ATHLETIC ASSOCIATION

Sports
Basketball, football, softball, soccer, volleyball, wrestling

Registration of Officials
-All officials must register through a local officials association
-Contact the LHSAA for an application form
-Fee: $20

Classification of Officials
Registered
-Attend the state rules clinic
-Submit a recommendation from an officials association
-Register with a local association
-Officiate 10 junior varsity games, supervised by an experienced official
-Score 70% or higher on the exam
Approved
-Must be a **Registered** official for two years
-Attend the state rules clinic
-Score 80% or higher on the exam
Certified
-Must be an **Approved** official for at least two years
-Attend the state rules clinic
-Score 90% on the exam

Contact Information
Louisiana High School Athletic Association, Inc.
7905 Wrenwood Blvd.
Baton Rouge, LA 70809-1774
Phone: (225) 925-0100 Fax: (225) 925-5801

MAINE PRINCIPALS' ASSOCIATION

The Maine Principals' Association was established to improve and enhance the educational opportunities for students. The MPA provides a strong interscholastic program that will provide its students with the leadership and opportunities to ensure all students are well prepared for life after graduation.

Sports
Baseball, basketball, field hockey, football, gymnastics, ice hockey, soccer, softball, swimming, wrestling

Registration of Officials
-Contact the MPA for information on becoming an official in the state of Maine

Contact Information
Maine Principals' Association
Richard W. Tyler, Executive Director
16 Winthrop St.
P.O. Box 2468
Augusta, ME 04338-2468
Phone: (207) 622-0217 Fax: (207) 622-1513
Internet: www.mint.net/~mpa

MARYLAND PUBLIC SECONDARY SCHOOLS ATHLETIC ASSOCIATION

Registration of Officials
-Contact the MPSSAA for registration information

Requirements for Officials
-Be at least 18 years old and a high school graduate
-Be a member in good standing with an MPSSAA-recognized officials group
-Attend an MPSSAA-sponsored rules interpretation clinic
-Pass the National Federation exam
-Pay the MPSSAA registration fee

Contact Information
Maryland State Department of Education
200 W. Baltimore St.
Baltimore, MD 21201-1595
Phone: (410) 767-0376 Fax: (410) 333-2379

Maryland Public Secondary Schools Athletic Association
Rules Interpreters

Baseball
Tom O'Hara
(410) 335-5107 (H)
(410) 244-1700 (W)

Basketball
Bill Burroughs
(301) 884-3371 (H)
(410) 767-0375 (W)

Field Hockey
Joan Salmon
(410) 256-9118 (H)

Football
Joe Warren
(301) 262-2264 (H)
(301) 918-8100 (W)

Boys Lacrosse
Jim Bateman
(410) 343-0910 (H)
(410) 252-2111 (W)

Girls Lacrosse
Sue Diffendorffer
(410) 783-1450 (H)

Soccer
Steve Malone
(410) 761-1394 (H)

Softball
Ted Kotowski
(301) 384-3662 (H)

Track & Field
Steve Smith
(410) 665-7157 (H)
(410) 887-4266 x478 (W)

Volleyball
Stacey Weitzell
(410) 255-1246 (H)
(410) 789-4101 (W)

Wrestling
Bob Newton
(410) 661-6119 (H)
(410) 887-4888 (W)

MASSACHUSETTS INTERSCHOLASTIC ATHLETIC ASSOCIATION

The mission of the Massachusetts Interscholastic Athletic Association is to serve member schools and the maximum number of their students by providing leadership and support for the conduct of interscholastic activities which will enrich the educational experiences of all participants. The MIAA will promote interschool activities that provide *lifelong* and *life-quality* learning experiences to students while enhancing their achievement of educational goals.

Sports
Alpine skiing, baseball, basketball, cross-country skiing, cross-country track, field hockey, football, golf, gymnastics, ice hockey, lacrosse, soccer, softball, swimming, tennis, track and field, volleyball, wrestling

Registration of Officials
-Contact the MIAA for registration information

Requirements for Officials
-Information available through the MIAA

Classification of Officials
-Information available from MIAA

Contact Information
Massachusetts Interscholastic Athletic Association
83 Cedar St.
Milford, MA 01757
Phone: (508) 478-5641; (508) 478-1449 Fax: (508) 634-3044
Internet: www.mec.edu/miaa

michigan high school athletic association

MICHIGAN HIGH SCHOOL ATHLETIC ASSOCIATION

The Michigan High School Athletic Association was established in 1924. It became a not-for-profit organization in 1972 and serves as the only high school association in the nation to publish a newsletter exclusively for athletic officials.

Sports
Baseball, basketball, competitive cheerleading, cross country, football, gymnastics, ice hockey, soccer, softball, swimming, track, volleyball, wrestling

Registration of Officials
-Registration dates vary for each sport
-Fee: $15 registration fee plus $7 per sport
-Contact the MHSAA for more information

Requirements for Officials
-Requirements vary for each sport
-All sports officials are required to attend rules meetings to be eligible to officiate MHSAA tournaments

Classification of Officials
-Officials are classified by ratings established by the MHSAA
-Officials are listed as **Approved**, **Supplemental, or General**, according to their quantity of varsity ratings over the most recent three-year period

Contact Information
Michigan High School Athletic Association
1661 Ramblewood Dr.
East Lansing, MI 48823
Phone: (517) 332-5046 Fax: (517) 332-4071

MINNESOTA STATE HIGH SCHOOL LEAGUE

For information about becoming an official in the state of Minnesota, please contact:

Minnesota State High School League
Dorothy E. McIntyre, Associate Director
2100 Freeway Blvd.
Brooklyn Center, MN 55430-1735
Phone: (612) 560-2262 Fax: (612) 569-0499
e-mail: dmcintyre@mshsl.org

MISSISSIPPI HIGH SCHOOL ACTIVITIES ASSOCIATION

The Mississippi High School Athletic Association accomplished a worthwhile and constructive task in its efforts to elevate the standards of sportsmanship, to develop a higher standard of scholarship, and to encourage pride in scholastic achievement. Much credit for these accomplishments is due to the men/women who have given unselfishly of their time and effort in behalf of the program.

Sports
Football, baseball, basketball, track and field, cross country, tennis, golf, volleyball, softball, soccer, wrestling, swimming, powerlifting, cheerleading

Registration of Officials
-Contact the MHSAA for an informational packet
-Registration dates vary for each sport
-Fee: $20

Requirements for Officials
-Any person age 18 or older is eligible to become an official
-Application must include references
-Applicants are required to attend rules interpretation meetings annually
-Must complete a five-day training session

Classification of Officials
-Ratings are based on a point system:
Certified Official: 85 points
Approved Official: 65 points
Recognized Official: All other officials
-Points are awarded based on exam scores and meeting attendance

Contact Information
Mississippi High School Activities Association
P.O. Box 244
Clinton, MS 39060-0244
Phone: (601) 924-6400 Fax: (601) 924-1725

MISSOURI STATE HIGH SCHOOL ACTIVITIES ASSOCIATION

The Missouri State High School Activities Association is a voluntary, non-profit educational organization through which its member schools work cooperatively. Interscholastic activities are intended to provide opportunities to supplement the educational curriculum and to provide learning outcomes that contribute to the development of good citizenship.

Sports
Football, basketball, soccer, volleyball, track and field, baseball, water polo, wrestling, softball, swimming

Registration of Officials
-Send a written request for application with a $15 test packet fee for each sport
-Registration deadlines: Fall sports, October 1; Winter sports, January 15; Spring sports, April 15
-Fee: One sport, $30; each additional sport, $15

Requirements for Officials
-Must pass rules test with a score of 75% (passing grade on part II of National Federation exam required annually for baseball, basketball, football, volleyball, and wrestling officials)
-Annual attendance of rules interpretation meetings for each sport registered
-Annual attendance of mechanics clinics, if offered

Classification of Officials
-Officials are rated by school coaches the day after the athletic contest in which they officiated:
1. **Superior:** Top 20% of officials
2. **Above Average:** Top 40% of officials
3. **Fair:** Competent in some areas, but needs improvement
4. **Below Average:** Needs considerable improvement
5. **Unsatisfactory** (When a "5" rating is returned by a coach, a letter outlining reasons for that rating must be included.)

Contact Information
Missouri State High School Activities Association
Becky Oates, Executive Director
1808 Interstate 70 Dr. SW
P.O. Box 1328
Columbia, MO 65205-1328
Phone: (573) 445-4443 Fax: (573) 445-2502

Missouri State High School
Activities Association Networking Contacts

Baseball
Al Flischel
6565 N. Brown Station Rd.
Columbia, MO 65202

Basketball
Mike Weir
2402 W. Broadway
Columbia, MO 65201

Football
Dale Pleimann
23000 Coonce Lane
Hartsburg, MO 65039

Soccer
Jan Gettemeyer
12190 Parkwood Place
Maryland Heights, MO 63043

Softball
Al Flischel
6565 N. Brown Station Rd.
Columbia, MO 65202

Swimming
Bill Pohlman
710 Stump Rd.
Des Peres, MO 63131

Track and Field
Dick Ault
1107 Vine St.
Fulton, MO 65251

Volleyball
Cathy Viets
Rt. 1, Box 99
Mora, MO 65345

Water Polo
Robert Higgins
8781 Bridgeport
St. Louis, MO 63144

Wrestling
Dale Pleimann
23000 Coonce Lane
Hartsburg, MO 65039

MONTANA HIGH SCHOOL ASSOCIATION

The Montana Officials Association was established to promote good fellowship among its members; to elevate the standards of officiating; to secure understanding among the interscholastic athletic officers; and to foster a high standard of ethics and further the interests of all sports.

Sports
Baseball, basketball, football, softball, soccer, volleyball, wrestling

Registration of Officials
-Fee: $44
-Contact the MOA for more information

Requirements for Officials
-Must be 18 years of age
-Can no longer be a student in high school
-Must take a nationwide exam on a given day

Classification of Officials
Apprentice
-Must score 70% on open book National Federation exam
Certified
-Must serve as an **Apprentice** for two consecutive years
-Must score 80% on open book National Federation exam
-Must have received a favorable recommendation
Master
-Must have served as a **Certified** official for two consecutive years
-Must score 80% or higher on closed book National Federation exam
-Must have officiated a certain number of varsity games
-Must have received a favorable evaluation

Contact Information
Montana High School Association
(Montana Officials Association)
One S. Dakota Ave.
Helena, MT 59601
Phone: (406) 442-6010 Fax: (406) 442-8250

NEBRASKA SCHOOL ACTIVITIES ASSOCIATION

NEBRASKA SCHOOL ACTIVITIES ASSOCIATION

The Nebraska School Activities Association was formed to regulate the competition of athletic events between schools. The NSAA provides an informational booklet for people interested in becoming an official; the Association feels very strong about the proper training of its officials and promoting sportsmanlike conduct.

Sports
Basketball, football, gymnastics, soccer, softball, swimming, volleyball, wrestling

Registration of Officials
-Contact the NSAA for an application
-Fee: $15 to $20

Requirements for Officials
-Must attend rules meetings
-Must pass an open book exam annually

Classification of Officials
Registered
-Attend state-sponsored rules interpretation meeting
-Score 80% or higher on open book exam
-Take a supervised test and score at least 65%
Approved
-Fulfill all requirements of **Registered** official for two years
-Attend state-sponsored rules interpretation meeting
-Score 85% or higher on open book exam
-Take a supervised test and score at least 75%
-Officiate required number of contests (varies by sport)
Certified
-Fulfill all requirements of an **Approved** official for two successive years
-Attend state-sponsored rules interpretation meeting
-Submit open book test and score 90% or higher
-Take supervised test and score 80% or higher

Contact Information
Nebraska School Activities Association
8230 Beechwood Dr.
Lincoln, NE 68505-0447
Phone: (402) 489-0386 Fax: (402) 489-0934

NEVADA INTERSCHOLASTIC ACTIVITIES ASSOCIATION

The Nevada Interscholastic Activities Association recognizes the many educational values to be derived from participation in all forms of interscholastic activities. Contact the NIAA for information about becoming an official.

Sports

Baseball, basketball, football, golf, soccer, softball, swimming, tennis, track, volleyball, wrestling

Contact Information

Nevada Interscholastic Activities Association
Dr. Jerry Hughes, Executive Director
One E. Liberty St., #505
Reno, NV 89501
Phone: (702) 688-6464 Fax: (702) 688-6466

NEW HAMPSHIRE INTERSCHOLASTIC ATHLETIC ASSOCIATION

The New Hampshire Interscholastic Athletic Association was formed in 1947 to organize, supervise, and coordinate a state-wide athletic program. In addition to the administration of athletics, the Association has formulated standards of officiating to ensure competition is equalized.

Sports
Baseball, basketball, cross country, field hockey, football, golf, gymnastics, ice hockey, indoor track, lacrosse, outdoor track, skiing, soccer, softball, spirit, tennis, volleyball, wrestling

Registration of Officials
-Fee: $3
-For more information on registration procedures, please contact NHIAA

Contact Information
New Hampshire Interscholastic Athletic Association
James W. Desmarais, Executive Director
251 Clinton St.
Concord, NH 03301-8432
Phone: (603) 228-8671   Fax: (603) 225-7978
e-mail: info@nhiaa.org
Internet: www.nhiaa.org

NEW JERSEY STATE INTERSCHOLASTIC ATHLETIC ASSOCIATION

The New Jersey State Interscholastic Athletic Association grew out of a meeting in 1918 in the Council Chambers of City Hall in Newark, New Jersey. The NJSIAA has grown to over 425 member schools and also conducts State Championships in over 30 sports.

Sports
Baseball, basketball, bowling, fencing, field hockey, football, golf, gymnastics, ice hockey, lacrosse, skiing, soccer, softball, swimming, tennis, cross country, track, volleyball, wrestling

Registration of Officials
-Contact the NJSIAA for registration procedures

Requirements for Officials
-Candidates must pass the National Federation exam
-Applicants must attend a rules interpretation meeting

Classification of Officials
-Officials are evaluated on a system established by the individual chapters of the NJSIAA

Contact Information
New Jersey State Interscholastic Athletic Association
Rt. 130
P.O. Box 487
Robbinsville, NJ 08691
Phone: (609) 259-2776 Fax: (609) 259-3047

NEW MEXICO OFFICIALS ASSOCIATION

The New Mexico Officials Association was established in 1952 as a subsidizing member organization within the New Mexico Activities Association structure. The NMOA provides a professional training program for its officials. The program is considered to be one of the top programs in the country.

Sports
Baseball, basketball, football, soccer, softball, volleyball, wrestling

Registration of Officials
-Contact the NMOA for an application
-Fee: $40 first year; $35 thereafter

Requirements for Officials
-Must fill out application form and profile
-Contact the NMOA for more information

Classification of Officials
-Information provided in NMAA registration packet

Contact Information
New Mexico Officials Association
6600 Palomas NE
Albuquerque, NM 87109
Phone: (505) 821-1887 Fax: (505) 821-2441

New Mexico Officials Association
Board of Directors

Ralph Ortiz, President
Tom Powers, Vice President
Dick Rodriguez, Baseball
Oscar Payen, Basketball
Ric Maxey, Football

Kenneth Roberts, Soccer
I.D. Cato, Softball
Frank Rael, Volleyball
Allen Lyon, Wrestling
Gary Spitzberg, Supervisory

NEW YORK STATE PUBLIC HIGH SCHOOL ATHLETIC ASSOCIATION

The NYSPHSAA is organized into 11 athletic areas called Sections. Sixteen state officials organizations are under contract to service the member schools of these sections. For information on becoming a certified official in any of these 16 sports, please contact:

New York State Public High School Athletic Association
Walter Eaton, Assistant Director
88 Delaware Ave.
Delmar, NY 12054-1599
Phone: (518) 439-8874 Fax: (518) 475-1556
e-mail: w.eaton@nysphsaa.org

State Officials Organizations Contacts

Baseball
Rob Lang
NYS Baseball Umpires Association
672 N. Shore Rd.
Peck's Lake
Gloversville, NY 12078
Phone: (518) 725-0859

Boy's Basketball
Richard Park
NYS Basketball Officials Association
PO Box 162
Aguebogue, NY 11931
Phone: (516) 722-3041
Fax: (516) 548-7032

Girl's Basketball
Dr. George Roney
NYS Girls Basketball Officials Association
117 George St.
Vestal, NY 13850
Phone: (607) 754-5381

Field Hockey
Priscilla Nellissen
NYS Certified Field Hockey Officials Association
Box 546
Round Lake, NY 12151
Phone: (518) 899-6003

Football
Paul Weatherup
NYS Association of Certified Football Officials
3604 E. Genesee St.
Syracuse, NY 13214
Phone: (315) 446-0402

Boy's Gymnastics
Wayne Suddaby
NYS Gymnastics Officials Association
7717 W. Sorrell Hill
Baldwinsville, NY 13027
Phone: (315) 635-3346

Girls Gymnastics
Gail Caspare
NYS Officials of Girl's Gymnastics
27 Taconic Rd.
Millwood, NY 10546
Phone: (914) 941-7957

Ice Hockey
Horton Shaw
NYS Congress of National Ice Hockey Officials
Chapters Association
50 Parkway Dr.
Rye, NY 10580
Phone: (914) 967-7467

Boys Lacrosse
Skip Spensieri
NYS Lacrosse Officials Association
216 Saratoga Ave.
Ballston Spa, NY 12020
Phone: (518) 885-4753

Girls Lacrosse
Cheryl Silverman
NYS Certified Officials of Girl's Lacrosse
1 Ridge Lane
Ballston Lake, NY 12019
Phone: (518) 877-5857

Soccer
Neil Riddel
NYS Certified Officials of Soccer
RD 2 Box 270
Otego, NY 13825
Phone: (607) 988-9117

Softball
James Berkery
NYS Softball Officials Organization
20 Massachusetts Ave.
Cohoes, NY 12047
Phone: (518) 237-6682

Swimming
Stephen S. Morris
NYS Certified Swimming Officials Association
2665 Freshour Rd.
Canandaigua, NY 14424
Phone: (716) 394-1067

Track & Field
Mary Onken
NYS Certified Track & Field Officials
Association
74 Edgewood Dr.
Central Valley, NY 10917
Phone: (914) 928-2420
Fax: (914) 782-5931

Volleyball
Linda Matthews
NYS Certified Volleyball Officials Association
504 Dutch Hill Rd.
Frankfort, NY 13340
Phone: (315) 733-6144

Wrestling
Fred Brown
12 Fenner St.
Cazenovia, NY 13035
Phone: (315) 655-5803

NORTH CAROLINA HIGH SCHOOL ATHLETIC ASSOCIATION

The North Carolina High School Athletic Association was formed to provide adequate and well-trained officials for all member school interscholastic athletic contests. The officiating program is a branch of the North Carolina High School Athletic Association.

Sports
Baseball, basketball, football, lacrosse, softball, soccer, swimming, track, volleyball, wrestling

Registration of Officials
-Contact the NCHSAA for registration information
 Registrations are effective beginning April 1
-Fees: $10 to $30

Requirements for Officials
-All NCHSAA officials must belong to a state-approved booking agency
-All NCHSAA officials must take the National Federation exam

Classification of Officials
Class 1
-A grade of 90 or higher on the examination
-90 to 100 points on the promotional scale*
Class 2
-A score between 80 and 89 points on the exam
-80 to 89 promotional points*
Class 3
-A score between 70 and 79 on the exam
-70 to 79 points on the promotional scale*
Class 4
-A grade of 60 to 69 on the exam
-60 to 69 points on the promotional scale*
*Points can be earned on the promotional scale for clinic attendance, varsity experience, and years of experience.

Contact Information
North Carolina High School Athletic Association
P.O. Box 3216
Chapel Hill, NC 27515-3216
Phone: (919) 962-2345 Fax: (919) 962-7812
Official's Information Line: (919) 962-7747
Internet: www.nchsaa.unc.edu

1995 State Football Championship Officials

1A: Referee Lawrence Whiteside, Umpire Reggie Kerns, Linesman Don Causey, Line Judge Ed Sigmon, Back Judge Tommy Larrimore; 2A: Referee David Hendrix, Umpire Keith Roden, Linesman Anthony Ellerbee, Line Judge Wade King, Back Judge Mike Sorrells; 3A: Referee Bert de la Rua, Umpire Thomas Speller, Linesman James Lloyd, Line Judge Coy Headen, Back Judge John Jeffries; 4A: Referee Jim Dargan, Umpire Richard Luther, Linesman Don Brinkley, Line Judge Randall Morrison, Back Judge Jim Rouse

1995 State Men's Soccer Championship Officials

1A/2A: Beady Stevenson, Ruben Ortiz-Velazquez, Thomas Rowlee; 3A: John Schmitz, Richard Hirsch, David Alston; 4A: Paul James, Terry Boose, Jerry Morrison

1995 State Volleyball Championship Officials

1A/2A: Greg Fletcher, Joyce Sparks, Marie Lewis, Irene Lewis; 3A/4A: Wayne Sheldon, Don Carr, Marlene Stout, Gayle Hughes

1995-96 State Basketball Championship Officials

Men's 1A: Roger Smith, Brad Sorg, Phil Duggin; Men's 2A: Jack Huss, Mark Dreibelbis, Tim Rhoney; Men's 3A: Dan Stryffeler, Roger Rickman, Mike Nobles; Men's 4A: J.R. Creech, Harry Edwards, Anthony Mitchell; Women's 1A: Alan McCracken, Ken O'Connor, Roger Trantham; Women's 2A: Ron Fly, Kenny Parrish, David Fulghum; Women's 3A: Mike Parnell, Al McRae, Richard Scott; Women's 4A: Maurice Everette, Lonnie Blue, W.C. Clary

1996 State Women's Soccer Championship Officials

1A/2A/3A: McRae Smith, Bob Bowen, Bob Foreman; 4A: Kevin Bowers, Hector Villagran, Alexander Vlahos

1996 State Baseball Championship Officials

4A: Neil Buie, Tom King, Brad Allen, Don Kitts, Chuck Wright, Mike Parnell; 3A: Doug Fagan, Larry Richards, Randy Dulin, Chris Padgett, Brad Sorg, Jeff Riviera, Dusty Rhodes, Buddy Rego; 2A: Harry Edwards, Bryant Woodall, Eddie Gray, John Josey, Jerry Lincoln, Dale Gibson; 1A: Larry Howard, Rob Castle, Henry Stanck, Pete Goswick, Clark Hunslinger, Todd Teele, James Horne, Oscar Pace, Tom Satterthwaite, Steve Broadwell, Roger Rickman, Bill Harman

1996 State Fast and Slow Pitch Softball Championship Officials

Donald Alford, Jerry Bitzenhoper, Mike Chalk, Russell Hill, Joe Wolfe, Phillip King, Lonnie O'Dom, Floyd Quick, Kevin Williams, William Johnson, Thomas Payne, Diane Atkins, Keith Brewington, Jeff Cohn, Donnie Jackson, Adam Johnson, Arnold Marshburn, Chris Parisher, Todd Smith, Johnny Davis, David Mansfield, Donnie Peaks, Wayne Beasley, Dan Brown, P.D. Debnam, David Jewel, Ken Pike, J.C. O'Neal, Dianne Renner, Mike Thompson, Diane Hudson, Ron Parr, Charlie Vincent

NORTH DAKOTA HIGH SCHOOL ACTIVITIES ASSOCIATION

The North Dakota High School Activities Association sponsors local workshops for several sports to ensure athletic events are conducted in an ethical and sportsmanlike manner. The NDHSAA also requires all officials to attend rules clinics to provide the highest quality of officiating.

Sports
Baseball, basketball, football, gymnastics, hockey, soccer, swimming, volleyball, wrestling

Registration of Officials
-Fee: $35, first sport (college student fee: $20; high school student fee: $15); $10 each additional sport+
-Contact the NDHSAA for an application

Requirements for Officials
-All officials must attend rules clinic conducted by NDHSAA

Classification of Officials
Apprentice
-Score of 70 to 74 on exam
-Attend rules clinic and officiating workshop, if available
Registered
-Must have met requirements of **Apprentice** official for one year
-Score between 75 and 89 on exam
-Attend rules clinic and officiating workshop, if available
Certified
-Must have met requirements of **Registered** official for two years
-Score 90 or higher on the exam
-Attend rules clinic and officiating workshop, if available

Contact Information
North Dakota High School Activities Association
134 NE Third St.
P.O. Box 817
Valley City, ND 58072
Phone: (701) 845-3953 Fax: (701) 845-4935

OHIO
HIGH SCHOOL
ATHLETIC ASSOCIATION

The Ohio High School Athletic Association is a voluntary, unincorporated, not-for-profit organization established for public and private High Schools. The OHSAA has sponsored over twenty State Championship sports since its humble beginnings of only one, in 1908.

Sports
Baseball, basketball, field hockey, football, gymnastics, ice hockey, soccer, softball, swimming and diving, track and field, volleyball, wrestling

Registration of Officials
-Contact the OHSAA for an informational packet
-Registration deadlines vary for each sport
-Fee: $35

Requirements for Officials
-Must be 18 years of age; cannot be enrolled in high school
-Rules meetings attendance requirements vary for each sport
-An open book exam is given, and a score of 75% or higher must be achieved
  for certification

Classification of Officials
Class 1: Certified to officiate 7th, 8th, 9th grade and high school events
Class 2: Eligible to officiate 7th, 8th, 9th grade and high school contests
  except varsity football, basketball and volleyball
Class 3: Restricted to 7th, 8th, 9th grade, and non-school officiating
Class 4 (Retired): Not permitted to officiate high school contests

Contact Information
Ohio High School Athletic Association
Clair Muscaro, Commissioner
4080 Roselea Place
Columbus, OH 43214-3070
Phone: (614) 267-2502 Fax: (614) 267-1677

Networking Contacts

Dave Bell
2378 Dresden Rd.
Zanesville, OH 43701
(614) 453-0335

James D. Fox
534 Oakridge Dr.
Youngstown, OH 44512
(216) 758-5623

Ohio High School Athletic Association
Officials Hall of Fame Inductees

1989
- Don Bachman
- Carel Cosby
- Fred Dafler
- Norman Kies
- Jack McLain
- Bill Newman
- Joe Pangrazio
- A.H. (Jack Rhoads)
- Fred Vicarel
- Howard Wirtz

1990
- James Allen
- Jordan Besozzi
- Glen Hursey
- James Oberlander
- Bob Overly
- Horace Rainsberger
- Harold Rolph
- Evan Reese
- George Wilson

1991
- Frank Allen Deuschle
- Sam V. DiBlasi
- Robert Richard Diller
- Sam Fausto
- Kenneth W. Fox
- Donald G. Mack
- James J. Mains, Jr.
- C. Mel McAfee
- Clarence "Pat" McMillin
- Ginny Lee Powers

1992
- Thomas N. Ballaban
- Allan Berger
- Carolyn Ann Bowers
- Frederick E. Cope
- Merlin S. Eidemiller
- Frank D. "Dick" Hyland
- A.J. "Tony" Montonaro
- Joseph A. Romano
- Allen F. Veigel
- Donald N. Welsh

1993
- Charles H. "Charlie" Bennett
- Gene Bennett
- Bobby Christian
- Owen Donahue
- Warren H. Jones
- Anthony L. Mieczkowski
- Charles "Mike" Mileusnich
- Don Rushing
- Glen Sample
- Irvin "Bud" Shopbell

1994
- Ronald Althoff
- Robert W. Brown, Jr.
- Howard Cross
- Hy Davis
- Ron Duncan
- Chalmer G. Hixson
- Robert Morrison
- Octavio "Tubby" Sirgo
- Lewis William Spurrier
- Joseph Blair Yanity, Jr.

OKLAHOMA SECONDARY SCHOOL ACTIVITIES ASSOCIATION

The Oklahoma Secondary School Activities Association believes that strict and fair enforcement of rules during extra-curricular activities is a must. The OSSAA deeply appreciates the service of each game official; without game officials, the athletic contests could not continue.

Sports
Baseball, basketball, football, soccer, fast-pitch softball, slow-pitch softball, volleyball, wrestling

Registration of Officials
-Contact the OSSAA for enrollment information
-Fee: $25 for first sport, $15 each additional sport

Requirements for Officials
-Must score a minimum of 75% on the National Federation test for the sport in which enrolled
-High school seniors may enroll as officials but are not eligible to work high school games

Contact Information
Oklahoma Secondary School Activities Association
P.O. Box 14590
Oklahoma City, OK 73113
Phone: (405) 840-1116 Fax: (405) 840-9559

OREGON SCHOOL ACTIVITIES ASSOCIATION

Sports
baseball, basketball, football, soccer, softball, volleyball

Registration of Officials
-Contact the OSAA office for the name of the sports commissioner responsible
  for local officials association that trains, evaluates, and certifies its members

Requirements for Officials
-Must be 18 years of age
-Must become a member of a local Oregon officials association

Classification of Officials
Varsity Level
-Must pass a closed book exam each year with at least 75% on the National
  Federation rules exam
-Must attend local association training sessions
Non-varsity Level
-Following third attempt at closed book exam, must pass an open book exam
  with at least 75% on the National Federation rules exam
-Must attend local association training sessions

Contact Information
Oregon School Activities Association
Wes Ediger, Executive Director
25200 SW Parkway Ave.
Wilsonville, OR 97070
Phone: (503) 682-6722 Fax: (503) 682-0960
e-mail: tonih@osaa.org
Internet: www.osaa.org

Volleyball Championship Officials 1995
4A: Brenda Skinner, Naomi Burke; 3A: Paula Martin, Anna Farley; 2A: Roger Keiffer, Larry Osborn; 1A: John Wallin, Delma Stuck

Soccer Championship Officials 1995
4A Boys: Referee Jim Stanhope, Linesmen Bob Thayer, Darren Placek; 4A Girls: Referee Harry Garabedian, Linesmen Dick Homer, John Plechl; 3A Boys: Referee Jim Sernoffsky, Linesmen Hal Williams, Ken Johnson; 3A Girls: Referee Richard Canaday, Linesmen Fred Parrish, Padman Senthirajah

Basketball Championship Officials 1996
4A Boys: Bill Judd, Greg Adrian; 4A Girls: Jerry McMahon, Don Wescott; 3A Girls: Mike Surplus, Robert Freeman

Baseball Championship Officials 1996
4A: Gary Carter, Rich Strnad, Rick Brincefield; 3A: Lysle Thomas, Dave Holloway, Bill Middleton; 2A: Duane Collins, Kip Johnson, Norm Sack

Softball Championship Officials 1996
4A: Bob Phillips, Deb Madore, T.J. Evans; 3A: Sue Hand, Terry Stephens, Mark Boren; 2A: Don Alexander, Ted Crowley, Rick Waddell

PENNSYLVANIA INTERSCHOLASTIC ATHLETIC ASSOCIATION

Sports
Baseball, basketball, field hockey, football, girls gymnastics, girls lacrosse, soccer, softball, swimming and diving, track and field, volleyball, wrestling

Registration of Officials
-Fee: $25
-Contact the PIAA for an official's application

Requirements for Officials
-Must be 18 years of age or older and a high school graduate
 Must score at least 75% on a sports examination
-Must become affiliated with a local officials' chapter

Contact Information
Pennsylvania Interscholastic Athletic Association
550 Gettysburg Rd.
P.O. Box 2008
Mechanicsburg, PA 17055-0708
Phone: (717) 697-0374 Fax: (717) 697-7721
Internet: www.piaa.org

Pennsylvania Interscholastic Athletic Association
Officials Representatives

District I
Thomas F. Brady
607 Baldwin Ave.
Norristown, PA 19403

Frances Pierce
1209 Locust St.
Norristown, PA 19401

District II
Robert Spagna
536 Deerfield Dr.
Clarks Summit, PA 18411

Maureen S. Williams
54 Crescent Ave.
Wilkes-Barre, PA 18702

District III
Leonard Czarnecki
411 Norman Rd.
Camp Hill, PA 17011

Cynthia K. Rinehart
2150 Derry Rd.
York, PA 17404

District IV
Charles Carr
21 Mill Rd.
Selinsgrove, PA 17870

District V
Ronald D. Beachley
200 Conemech Trail
Box 723
Davidsville, PA 15928

Beverly Jane Buck
RR #5, Box 347G
Stepping Stone Rd.
Somerset, PA 15501

District VI
David Heim
RR #2, Box 245
Hollidaysburg, PA 16648

Kathy E. Getz
659 Highland Ave.
Revloc, PA 15948

District VII
Duane Norton
116 Castle Dr.
West Miffin, PA 15122

Pamela R. Cherubin
2070 Borland Rd.
Pittsburgh, PA 15243

District VIII
Donald Kovach
640 Fernhill St.
Pittsburgh, PA 15226

Sue Frey
318 Waldorf St.
Pittsburgh, PA 15214

District IX
Frank Palaggo
710 Washington St.
New Bethlehem, PA 16316

District X
William C. Sherry
12436 Lakeside Dr.
Conneaut Lake, PA 16316

Julia Taylor
123 Brighton Ave.
Erie, PA 16509

District XI
Herbert R. Welsh
RR #2, Box 224D
New Ringgold, PA 17960

Elisabeth Wilson

RHODE ISLAND INTERSCHOLASTIC LEAGUE

Registration of Officials
-Contact the RIIL for referral to a local officials association
-Contact your local officials association for registration and testing information

Contact Information
Rhode Island Interscholastic League
Bldg. #6, Rhode Island College
600 Mt. Plcasant Ave.
Providence, RI 02908-1991
Phone: (401) 272-9844 Fax: (401) 272-9838

SOUTH CAROLINA HIGH SCHOOL LEAGUE

The South Carolina High School League was established in 1913. The purpose of the League is to formulate and maintain policies that will safeguard the educational values of interscholastic competition; to cultivate high ideals of sportsmanship; to develop and direct a program which will promote, protect, and conserve the health and physical welfare of all participants; and to promote uniformity of standard in all interscholastic competition. The SCHSL is a non-profit organization that has been the governing body of all of South Carolina's member schools for more than 80 years and continues today to promote a meaningful and well-rounded educational experience.

Sports
Baseball, basketball, cheerleading, cross-country, football, golf, soccer, softball, swimming, tennis, track and field, volleyball, wrestling

Officials
The League also serves as a booking agent for the Officials of basketball, football, volleyball, and wrestling. All other officiated sports are booked by local directors. Persons interested in becoming certified officials must meet the following criteria:
- Pay registration fee
- Attend mandatory rules clinics and meetings
- Pass the state rules test
- Pay dues to officials association for each sport

Contact Information
South Carolina High School League
P.O. Box 211575
Columbia, SC 29221-6575
Phone: (803) 798-0120 Fax (803) 731-9679

South Carolina Baseball Officials Association Secretaries
Aiken: R.L. Culbreath; **Beaufort:** Gerald McDougall; **Catawaba:** W.P. Feaster; **Charleston:** Sam Brock; **Coastal:** Mickey Hunter; **Columbia:** Gib Rogers; **Edisto:** Leon Myers; **Greenville:** Tommy Rogers; **Mid-State:** J. Truman Owens; **Pee Dee:** Russel Watson; **Spartanburg:** Danny Rhodes

South Carolina Basketball Officials Association 1998-99 Directors
District 1: D. Mark Hamrick; **District 2:** Jerry Parris; **District 3:** J. Frank Overcash; **District 4:** J. Truman Owens; **District 5:** A.C. Lewis; **District 6:** Dennis Sullen; **District 7:** Leon E. Myers; **District 8:** Raymond Barrett; **District 9:** Thomas Hinton; **District 10:** Johnny Bell; **District 11:** Brian Fink; **District 12:** Alvin H. Stevens; **Commissioner:** Jerome Singleton

South Carolina Football Officials Association Directors
District 1: Ken Phillips; **District 2:** Joel Bullard; **District 3:** Marcus R. Polk; **District 4:** Jack R. Childress; **District 5:** Bruce Hulion; **District 6:** James W. Shire; **District 7:** Terry Wright; **District 8:** Sebastian Hernandez; **District 9:** Rand Bailey; **District 10:** Donald Brooks; **District 11:** Michael Mullinix; **District 12:** W. Brent Boore; **District 13:** Sam O. Owens; **District 14:** Steve Wilson; **Commissioner:** Ronald H. Matthews

South Carolina Soccer Officials Association Directors
District 1: Ray Hansel; **District 2:** Dennis R. Cook; **District 3:** John Hill; **District 4:** Samuel Tucker; **District 5:** Bruce Malick; **District 6:** John Realm; **District 7:** R.C. Price; **Director:** Roger Hazel

South Carolina Softball Officials Association Directors
Aiken: Dwight Smith; **Beaufort:** Gerald McDougall; **Charleston:** Sebastian Hernandez; **Columbia:** Dennis O'Keefe; **Edisto:** Leon Myers; **Grand Strand:** Jeff Linder; **Greenville:** Tommy Rogers; **Mid-State:** J. Truman Owens; **Southern:** Jim Bull; **Spartanburg:** Danny Rhodes; **Sumter:** Ernest Ledbetter; **Director:** Dru Nix

South Carolina Volleyball Officials Association Directors
District 1: Elaine "Sam" Harp; **District 2:** Kim Lorick; **District 3:** James Artis; **District 4:** Mickie Ellis; **District 5:** Sue LeBlanc; **District 6:** Ron L. Hinnant; **District 7:** Jane I. Millen; **District 8:** Marie Dompierre; **District 9:** Becky A. Dunn; **District 10:** Jim Whalen; **Director:** Dru Nix

South Carolina Wrestling Officials Association 1998-99 Directors
District 1: Deno White; **District 2:** Theodore D. "Bo" Willard; **District 3:** Glenn W. Easterby; **District 4:** Charles H. "Hank" Hammond; **Director:** Roger Hazel

SOUTH DAKOTA HIGH SCHOOL ACTIVITIES ASSOCIATION

The South Dakota High School Activities Association recognizes the fact that sports contests become more sophisticated and technical each year. In South Dakota, officials must continually upgrade their skills in order to keep pace with the high school programs which have directed themselves towards excellence.

Sports
Basketball, football, gymnastics, track, volleyball, wrestling

Registration of Officials
-Fee: $25
-Contact the SDHSAA for a registration card

Requirements for Officials
-Specific requirements for individual sports
-All officials must attend a rules meeting

Classification of Officials
Registered
-Attend a rules meeting
-Pass the open book exam with a minimum score of 75%
Certified
-Attend a rules meeting
-Pass the open book exam with a score of 80% or higher
-Must take and pass a supervised test with a score of 75% or higher

Contact Information
South Dakota High School Activities Association
204 N. Euclid
P.O. Box 1217
Pierre, SD 57501
Phone: (605) 224-9261 Fax: (605) 224-9262

1997-98 State Boys Basketball Tournament Officials

AA: Rick Brommer, David Dolan, Bruce Ferrie, Jim Johnston, Tim Plimpton, Gary Reed, Randy Schaefer, Jeff Wilbur; A: Kevin Bad Wound, Jeff DesLauries, Lee Johnson, Mark Koopman, Tom McGough, Jim Philips, Dave Tate, Steve Withorne; B: Everett Gebhart, Bob Krietlow, Keith Kusler, Bob Malloy, Wally Steiner, Gene Struck, Randy Thomas, Marty Weismantel

1997-98 State Girls Basketball Tournament Officials

AA: Mike Begeman, Clyde Hagen, Mary Kapitan, Jim Peterson, Gary Reed, Casper Roth, Larry Stevens, Jeff Wilbur; A: Jeff DesLauries, Lee Johnson, Tom McGough, Randy Stanton, Gene Struck, Jeff Syliaasen, Dave Tate, Steve Withorne; B: Kurt Buckwalter, Sherman Cutler, Burnell Glanzer, Bob Krietlow, Kelly Larson, Bob Malloy, Randy Thomas, Marty Weismantel

1997-98 State Football Championship Game Officials

9B: Burnell Glanzer, Dave Fuller, Ron Weber, Doug Odens; 9A: Randy Kludt, Brad Peters, Glen McCready, Dwight Covey; 11B: Todd Landsman, Jay Larsen, Stewart Olson, Richard Landsman; 11A: Buck Timmins, Randy Oldenkamp, Jim Johnston, Dave Brown; 11AA: Dana Nelson, Keith Hanneman, Darin Berg, Colin Kapitan, Chad Gordon

1997-98 State Gymnastics Tournament Officials

Meet Referee: Mary Lee; Lucy Lindskov, Kelly Busch, Virginia Purcell, Sue Hamre, Jeni Applewick, Ellen Steever, Nadine Thompson, Erica Dahle, Kay Rose, Michelle Brunz, Bobby Schumacher

1997-98 State Volleyball Tournament Officials

AA: Kelley Devine, Susan James, Peggy Kessler, Kim Weed; A: Gary Duffy, Dan Krier, Lisa Link, Deb Schlagel; B: Tammy Carmody, Terry Duffy, Lori Krier, Sandy Neugebauer

1997-98 State Wrestling Tournament Officials

A: Jerry Bussler, Clair Donovan, Jerry Hirrschoff, John Houska, Chet Jones, Gary Maffett, Mike McFarland, Mark Neises, Frank Pavich, Gregg Roach; B: Rick Fink, Greg Harrell, Mike Jorgensen, Tim Pranger, Steve Rounds, Paul Schreiner, Jay Swatek, Casey Thompson, Justin Tupper, Al Van Wyhe

TENNESSEE SECONDARY SCHOOL ATHLETIC ASSOCIATION

Sports
Baseball, basketball, football, soccer, softball, volleyball, wrestling

Registration of Officials
-Contact the TSSAA for an application
-Fee: $30 for first sport; $20 for each additional sport

Requirements for Officials
-Must be 18 years old, a high school graduate, and never have been convicted
  of a felony
-First-time applicants must be recommended by a school principal, coach,
  supervisor, or assigning officer of a local officials group
-Must score at least 70% on open book qualifying exam

Contact Information
Tennessee Secondary School Athletic Association
Terry Hillier
3333 Lebanon Rd.
Hermitage, TN 37076
Phone: (615) 889-6740 Fax: (615) 889-0544
e-mail: thillier@tssaa.org
Internet: www.tssaa.org

TEXAS: SOUTHWEST OFFICIALS ASSOCIATION

Because the state of Texas is so large, there are a number of Officials Associations. The Southwest Officials Association oversees the individual sport's officials organizations. For more information on becoming an official in the state of Texas, please contact:

Contact Information

Southwest Officials Association
1300 W. Mockingbird Lane
P.O. Box 569420
Dallas, TX 75356-9420
Phone: (214) 638-3722 Fax: (214) 638-0976

Texas University Interscholastic League
William D. Farney, Director
1701 Manor Road
Austin, TX 78722
Phone: (512) 471-5883 Fax (512) 471-6589
Internet: www.utexas.edu/admin/uil/

UTAH
HIGH SCHOOL
ACTIVITIES ASSOCIATION

The purpose of the Utah High School Activities Association shall be to administer and supervise interscholastic activities among its member schools according to the Association Constitution and By-Laws. Knowing that student activities are a significant force in the development of skills needed to become a contributing member of society, the UHSAA reaffirms that students are the focus and the reason for the Association. As such, the Association will provide opportunities that: promote sportsmanship and safe competition through standardized eligibility rules; provide interscholastic sports, music, drama, and speech; create learning laboratories where practical life-situations, teamwork, sportsmanship, winning and losing, hard work, leadership, and cooperation are taught; nurture self-realization and build self-confidence; promote, through participation, higher academic achievement, better attendance, lower drop-out rates, and positive citizenship.

Sports
Baseball, basketball, football, soccer, softball, volleyball, wrestling

Registration of Officials
-Contact the UHSAA for registration forms
-Fees: $20 to $30

Requirements for Officials
-The required number of attended rules meetings will be decided by the local associations
-Officials must take an annual open book exam
-All other requirements are to be decided by the local associations

Classification of Officials
-Officials will be given a numerical rating determined by the officials association

Contact Information
Utah High School Activities Association
199 E. 7200 South
Midvale, UT 84047
Phone: (801) 566-0681 Fax: (801) 566-0633

VERMONT PRINCIPALS' ASSOCIATION

The Vermont Principals' Association assists school leaders in the development and governance of those student activities which contribute to a well-rounded educational experience. The VPA works to make children our nation's number one priority.

Sports
Baseball, basketball, cheerleading, cross country, field hockey, football, golf, gymnastics, ice hockey, lacrosse, skiing, soccer, softball, tennis, track, wrestling

Contact Information
Vermont Principals' Association
W. Scott Blanchard, Executive Director
Two Prospect St., Ste. 3
Montpelier, VT 05602
Phone: (802) 229-0547 Fax: (802) 229-4801

VIRGINIA
HIGH SCHOOL
LEAGUE

The Virginia High School League recognizes the need for qualified officials. Officiating is considered to be an integral part of the organization, and a great deal of time and effort are put into the training and certification of the VHSL's officials.

Sports
Baseball, basketball, field hockey, football, gymnastics, lacrosse, soccer, softball, swimming and diving, track and field, volleyball, wrestling

Registation of Officials
-Registration fees change periodically for each sport
-Contact the VHSL for information

Requirements for Officials
-Must be 18 years old or a high school graduate
-Must pass the National Federation exam

Classification of Officials
Registered
-Minimum score of 70% on the exam
-Must not have missed two consecutive rules clinics
Approved
-Minimum score of 70% on the exam
-Meet all requirements determined by the local associations
Certified
-Minimum score of 80% on the exam
-Meet the requirements set by the local associations

Contact Information
Virginia High School League
1642 State Farm Blvd.
Charlottesville, VA 22911-8809
Phone: (804) 977-8475 Fax: (804) 977-5943

WASHINGTON INTERSCHOLASTIC ACTIVITIES ASSOCIATION

The purpose of the Washington Officials Association is to provide qualified officials for WIAA sanctioned regular season and post season events. This shall be accomplished by developing:

1. A registration process that is thorough, accurate, and prompt.
2. A core of knowledgeable sports rules clinicians who are dedicated to interscholastic coaches, participants, and to the game itself.
3. A process to recruit, train, and retain competent officials, particularly from the female and minority segments of the population.
4. A Board of Directors who are leaders and who are responsive to the needs of the associations and boards.

Sports
Baseball, basketball, football, gymnastics, soccer, softball, volleyball, wrestling

Registration of Officials
-Contact the WOA at (425) 746-7102

Requirements and Classification of Officials
-The registration of officials with the WIAA/WOA will be classified as **Registered** or **Certified**

A **Registered** official is one who has paid the WOA registration fee and is a member in good standing with any recognized WOA local association or board

A **Certified** official, in addition to meeting the requirements for a **Registered** official, must also:

-Attend the WIAA/WOA rules clinic annually in that sport
-Meet the meeting attendance requirements from the previous year (Each Association/Board must hold a minimum of six meetings per year)
-Pass the current National Federation test in that sport with a score of 70% or higher

Only **Certified** officials become eligible to officiate varsity and WIAA State Tournaments. These nominations are then compared to the rankings submitted by Associations/Boards for final selection.

Contact Information
Washington Interscholastic Activities Association
4211 W. Lake Sammamish Pkwy. SE
Bellevue, WA 98008-5999
Phone: (425) 746-7102 Fax: (425) 747-9422

WEST VIRGINIA SECONDARY SCHOOL ACTIVITIES COMMISSION

The West Virginia Secondary School Activities Commission knows that quality officiating is an important part of the athletic program. For this reason, considerable time, effort, and money is spent on training programs, clinics, films, testing, promotional, and classification systems to increase the knowledge and improve techniques of the some 3,000 officials in the state.

Sports
Baseball, basketball, football, soccer, softball, swimming, track, volleyball, wrestling

Registration of Officials
-Applicants must attend a training program
-Applicants can register upon verification that the training program has been completed and a physical evaluation is on file with the WVSSAC
-Registrations must be completed by June 15 for all sports

Requirements for Officials
-18 years of age
-Applicants shall not have previously been convicted of a felony
-Officials must attend annual WVSSAC-sponsored rules clinics

Classification of Officials
Class 4
-Less than two years experience
-Score of less than 55% on supervised exam
Class 3
-Minimum two years experience
-40 to 74 promotional points*
Class 2
-Minimum four years experience
-75 to 89 promotional points*
Class 1
-Minimum six years experience
-90 to 100 promotional points*
*Promotional points can be earned through meeting attendance, games or matches worked, experience, coaches' ratings

Contact Information
West Virginia Secondary School Activities Commission
Rt. 9, Box 76
Parkersburg, WV 26101
Phone: (304) 485-5494 Fax: (304) 428-5431

WISCONSIN INTERSCHOLASTIC ATHLETIC ASSOCIATION

The purpose of the Wisconsin Interscholastic Athletic Association is threefold: to organize, develop, direct, and control an interscholastic athletic program which will promote the ideals of its membership and opportunities for their participation; to emphasize interscholastic athletics as a partner with other school activities in the total educational process and formulate and maintain policies which will cultivate high ideals of good citizenship and sportsmanship; and to promote uniformity of standards in interscholastic athletic competition and prevent exploitation by special interest groups of the school program and the individual's ability.

Sports
Baseball, basketball, football, gymnastics, hockey, soccer, softball, swimming and diving, track and field, volleyball, wrestling

Registration of Officials
-Fee: $16, plus $5 per sport
-Contact the WIAA for license information

Requirements for Officials
-Must be 18 years of age to officiate at the high school level; high school sophomores, juniors, and seniors can officiate contests up to and including the 9th grade level

Classification of Officials
-Levels are determined based on experience, sport meeting attendance, test scores and schedule of games:
Level 1
Level 2
Level 3
Level 4
Level 5
Master

Contact Information
Wisconsin Interscholastic Athletic Association
41 Park Ridge Dr.
P.O. Box 267
Stevens Point, WI 54481-0267
Phone: (715) 344-8580 Fax: (715) 344-4241
e-mail: refs@wiaawi.org

WYOMING HIGH SCHOOL ACTIVITIES ASSOCIATION

The Wyoming Sports Officials Association provides programs for its officials to promote uniformity in the mechanics of officiating. The WOSA strives to propagate competent young officials to replace retiring veterans; thus, a strong emphasis is placed on the recruitment of new officials.

Sports
Basketball, football, gymnastics, soccer, swimming, track, volleyball, wrestling

Registration of Officials
-Contact the WHSAA for an application
-First time fee: $20
-$48/$43 fee for initial sport; $20 fee each additional sport

Requirements and Classification of Officials
Registered
-Pay fees and complete open book exam
-Attend rules clinics, study clubs
Approved
-Must fulfill all requirements of a **Registered** official
-Must have served as a **Registered** official for two consecutive years
-Must receive a favorable observation
-Must score a minimum of 80% on a closed book rules exam
Certified
-Must fulfill all requirements of an **Approved** official
-Must have served as an **Approved** official for two consecutive years
-Must show evidence of working varsity level contests

Contact Information
Wyoming High School Activities Association
Wyoming Sports Officials Association
731 E. Second St.
Casper, WY 82601-2620
Phone: (307) 577-0614 Fax: (307) 577-0637
e-mail: coffey.com/~whsaa/sportsofficials.txt

Wyoming Sports Officials Association
President

Dale Micheli
P.O. Box 15
Ft. Bridger, WY 82933
Phone: (307) 782-3469

Wyoming Sports Officials Association
Area Representatives

Area 1
Tim Thompson
P.O. Box 1031
Big Piney, WY 83113

Area 2
Gene Hunt
650 Adams
Green River, WY 82935
Phone: (307) 875-6220

Area 3
Mike Harris
120 W. Bell
Riverton, WY 82501
Phone: (307) 856-5163

Area 4
Doug Morrison
623 Meadowlark
Worland, WY 82401
Phone: (307) 347-8322

Area 5
Moose Marosok
378 Idaho St.
Sheridan, WY 82801
Phone: (307) 674-7844

Area 6
Phil Marton
HC33 Box 5477
Casper, WY 82604
Phone: (307) 472-4123

Area 7
Rodney James
P.O. Box 727
Rawlins, WY 82301
Phone: (307) 324-2402

Area 8
Dave Williams
4209 Grays Gable Rd.
Laramie, WY 82072
Phone: (307) 721-8064

Area 9
Tony Crecelius
5204 Newland Ave.
Cheyenne, WY 82001
Phone: (307) 632-8508

Area 10
Marv Haiman
152 Hillcrest Dr.
Torrington, WY 82240
Phone: (307) 532-2306

Area 11
D.G. Reardon
1146 Almon Circle
Gillette, WY 82716
Phone: (307) 682-6925

Area 12
Butch Moretti
P.O. Box 223
Lyman, WY 82937
Phone: (307) 787-3171

APPENDIX I:
DIRECTORY OF
SPORTS ORGANIZATIONS

The following directory of sports organizations, associations, and regulatory bodies was compiled to assist prospective and active officials in locating specific sports organizations. This directory consists of three sections: education-based organizations, including interscholastic and college; community-based organizations; and sport-specific organizations. To use the directory, consult section one or section two for the names and addresses of organizations that pertain to your level of competition. Then proceed to the third section for a list of organizations specific to your sport.

The staff of LR Publishing strives for accuracy and thoroughness in its directory listings. Revisions, additions, and/or deletions to this directory can be fowarded to LR Publishing, Attn: Editor, 4555 Renaissance Pkwy., Suite 101, Cleveland, OH 44128, for inclusion in future editions.

⚫⚫⚫ denotes sports organizations with Olympic affiliation.

EDUCATION-BASED SPORTS ORGANIZATIONS

National Federation of State High School
Associations (NF)
11724 Plaza Circle
P.O. Box 20626
Kansas City, MO 64195
Phone: (816) 464-5400 Fax: (816) 464-5571
Internet: www.nfhs.org

National Association of Intercollegiate
Athletics (NAIA)
6120 S. Yale Ave., Ste. 1450
Tulsa, OK 74136-4223
Phone: (918) 494-8828 Fax: (918) 494-8841
Internet: www.naia.org

National Christian College Athletic Association
(NCCAA)
P.O. Box 1312
Marion, IN 46952-7712
Phone: (317) 674-8401 Fax: (317) 674-8487

National Collegiate Athletic Association
(NCAA)
6201 College Blvd.
Overland Park, KS 66211-2422
Phone: (913) 339-1906 Fax: (913) 339-1950
Internet: www.ncaa.org

National Junior College Athletic Association
(NJCAA)
1825 Austin Bluffs Pkwy., Ste. 100
Colorado Springs, CO 80918
Phone: (719) 590-9788 Fax: (719) 590-7324

NATIONAL OFFICIALS ASSOCIATIONS

National Association of Sports Officials
(NASO)
2017 Lathrop Ave.
Racine, WI 53405
Phone: (414) 632-5448 Fax: (414) 632-5460
Internet: www.naso.org

National Federation Interscholastic Officials
Association (NFIOA)
11724 Plaza Circle
P.O. Box 20626
Kansas City, MO 64195
Phone: (816) 464-5400 Fax: (816) 464-5571

COMMUNITY-BASED SPORTS ORGANIZATIONS

Amateur Athletic Union (AAU)
The Walt Disney Resort
P.O. Box 10000
Lake Buena Vista, FL 32830-1000
Phone: (407) 934-7200 Fax: (407) 934-7242
Internet: www.aausports.org

American Alliance for Health, Physical
Education, Recreation and Dance (AAHPERD)
1900 Association Dr.
Reston, VA 22091
Phone: (703) 476-3400 Fax: (703) 476-9527
Internet: www.aahperd.org

Boys and Girls Clubs of America
1230 W. Peachtree St., N.W.
Atlanta, GA 30309
Phone: (404) 815-5700 Fax: (404) 815 5799
Internet: www.bgca.org

Catholic Youth Organization (CYO)
1101 First Ave., Rm. 620
New York, NY 10022
Phone: (212) 371-1000 Fax (212) 826-3347

Jewish Community Centers Association
15 E. 26th St., Ste. 1417
New York, NY 10010-1579
Phone: (212) 532-4949 Fax: (212) 481-4174

National Association of Police Athletic Leagues, Inc.
618 N US Hwy. 1, Ste. 201
North Palm Beach, FL 33408-4609
Phone: (407) 844-1823 Fax: (407) 863-6120
e-mail: copnkid1@aol.com

National Congress of State Games
P.O. Box 7136
Billings, MT 59103-7136
Phone: (406) 254-7426 Fax: (406) 254-7426
Internet: www.stategames.org

National Exploring Division, Boy Scouts of America
1325 W. Walnut Hill Ln.
Irving, TX 75038
Phone: (214) 580-2423 Fax: (214) 580-2502
Internet: www.bsa.scouting.org

Native American Sports Council
1765 S. 8th St., Ste. T-6
Colorado Springs, CO 80906
Phone: (719) 632-5282 Fax: (719) 632-5614
e-mail: information@nascsports.org

National Senior Games Association
445 North Blvd., Ste. 2001
Baton Rouge, LA 70802
Phone: (504) 379-7337 Fax: (504) 379-7343

YMCA of the USA
101 N. Wacker Dr.
Chicago, IL 60606
Phone: (312) 977-0031 Fax: (312) 977-9063
Internet: www.ymca.org

YWCA of the USA
350 5th Ave., Third Fl.
New York, NY 10018
Phone: (212) 273-7800 Fax: (212) 465-2281

Disabled in Sports Organizations

U.S. Association of Blind Athletes
33 N. Institute
Colorado Springs, CO 80903
Phone: (719) 630-0422 Fax: (719) 630-0616
e-mail: USABA@iex.net
Internet: www.usaba.org

United States Cerebral Palsy Athletic Association
25 W. Independence Way
Kingston, RI 02881
Phone: (401) 874-7465 Fax: (401) 874-7468
e-mail: uscpaa@mail.bbsnet.com
Internet: www.uscpaa.org

USDA Deaf Sports Federation
3607 Washington Blvd., Ste. 4
Ogden, UT 84403-1737
e-mail: USADSF@aol.com
Internet: www.usadsf.org

Disabled Sports USA
451 Hungerford Dr., Ste. 100
Rockville, MD 20850
Phone: (301) 217-0960 Fax: (301) 217-0968
e-mail: dsusa@dsusa.org

Dwarf Athletic Association of America
418 Willow Way
Lewisville, TX 75077
Phone: (972) 317-8299 Fax: (972) 966-0184
e-mail: jfbda3@aol.com

Special Olympics International
1325 G St., N.W., Ste. 500
Washington, DC 20005
Phone: (202) 628-3630 Fax: (202) 824-0200
e-mail: specialolympics@msn.com
Internet: www.specialolympics.org

Wheelchair Sports USA
3595 E. Fountain Blvd., Ste. L-1
Colorado Springs, CO 80910
Phone: (719) 574-1150 Fax: (719) 5f74-9840
e-mail: wsusa@aol.com
Internet: www.wusa.org

SPORTS ORGANIZATIONS INDEXED BY SPORT

AKIDO

International Aikido Federation
c/o Dr. Peter Goldsbury
Uskita Hinmachi 3-29 4-Chome Higashi-ku
Hiroshima 732
Japan
Phone: (81-82) 211-1271
Fax: (81-82) 211-1955

Aikido World Headquarters
17-18 Watamatsu-cho Shinjuku-ku
Tokyo 162
Japan

ARCHERY

National Archery Association (NAA)
One Olympic Plaza
Colorado Springs, CO 80909-5778
Phone: (719) 578-4576
Fax: (719) 632-4733
e-mail: info@usarchery.org
Internet: www.usarchery.org

National Field Archery Association (NFAA)
31407 Outer I-10
Redlands, CA 92373
Phone (909) 794-2133
Fax (909) 794-8512
e-mail: nfaarchery@aol.com

Federation of Canadian Archers, Inc.
1600 James Naismith Dr.
Gloucester Ontario K1B 5N4
Canada

The National Crossbowmen of the USA
P.O. Box 1615
Easton, PA 18044

Federation Internationale de Tir a l'Arc
(FITA)
Avenue de Cour 135
1007 Lausanne
Switzerland
Phone: 41-21-614-3050
Fax: 41-21-614-3055
e-mail: fita@worldcom.ch
Internet: www.worldsport.com/sports/
archery/home.html

Internationale Armbrustschetzen Union (IAU)
Central Body
Scholsslirain 9
CH 6006 Luzern
Switzerland

AUSTRALIAN RULES FOOTBALL

Victorian Football League (VFL)
VFL House
120 Jolimont Rd.
Jolimont Victoria 3002
Australia

AUTO RACING

SCCA Pro Racing Ltd.
Subsidiary of Sports Car Club of America, Inc.
9033 E. Easter Place
Englewood, CO 80112
Phone: (303) 694-7223
Fax: (303) 694-7391
e-mail: scca@csi.com

U.S. Auto Club (USAC)
4910 W. 16th St.
Indianapolis Speedway, IN 46224
Phone: (317) 247-5151
Fax: (317) 247-0123

Federation International du Sport Automobile (FISA)
8 Place de la Concorde
75008 Paris
France

Union International Motornautique (UIM)
Nouveau Stade 11 2 Ave.
Prince Hereditaire Albert MC 98000
Monaco

BADMINTON

∞ USA Badminton
One Olympic Plaza
Colorado Springs, CO 80909
Phone: (719) 578-4808
Fax: (719) 578-4507
e-mail: info@usabadminton.org
Internet: www.usabadminton.org

Badminton Canada
1600 James Naismith Dr.
Gloucester Ontario K1B 5N4
Canada
Phone: (613) 748-5605
Fax: (613) 748-5695
e-mail: badminton@badminton.ca
Internet: www.badminton.ca

∞ International Badminton Federation (IBF)
Unit 4, Manor Park
MacKenzie Way
Cheltenham, Gloucestershire GL51 9TX
Great Britain
Phone: (44-1242) 23-4904
Fax: (44-1242) 22-1030
Internet: www.intbadfed.org

BANDY

Bandy Federation International
c/o Arne Giving, Secretary General
Elgfaret 23
Hosle N-1347
Norway
Phone: (47) 266-5800
Fax: (47) 266-5883

Svenska Bandyforbundet
(Kopmannagatan 19)
Box 78
S-641 21 Katrineholm
Sweden

BASEBALL

∞ USA Baseball
Hi Corbett Field, 3400 E. Camino Campestre
Tucson, AZ 85716
Phone: (520) 327-9700
Fax: (520) 327-9221
e-mail: usabaseball@aol.com
Internet: www.usabaseball.com

∞ International Baseball Federation
Avenue de Mon-Repos 24
Case Postale 131
1000 Lausanne 5, Switzerland
Phone: (41-21) 311-1863
Fax: (41-21) 311-1864
e-mail: iba@dial.eunet.ch
Internet: www.alpcom.it/digesu

American Legion
700 N. Pennsylvania
Indianapolis, IN 46204
Phone: (317) 630-1213
Fax: (317) 630-1369
e-mail: tal@iquest.com

Babe Ruth League, Inc.
P.O. Box 5000
1770 Brunswick Pike
Trenton, NJ 08638
Phone: (609) 695-1434
Fax: (609) 695-2505

Pony Baseball
P.O. Box 225
Washington, PA 15301
Phone: (724) 225-1060
Fax (724) 225-9852
e-mail: pony@pulsnet.com

American Amateur Baseball Congress
118-119 Redfield Plaza
Marshall, MI 49068
Phone: (616) 781-2002
Fax: (616) 781-2060

National Amateur Baseball Federation, Inc.
P.O. Box 705
Bowie, MD 20718
Phone: (301) 262-5005
Fax: (301) 262-5005

Major League Baseball (MLB)
245 Park Ave.
New York, NY 10167
Phone: (212) 931-7800
Internet: www.majorleague.com

National Baseball Congress
300 S. Sycamore
Wichita, KS 67213
Phone: (316) 267-3372
Fax (316) 267-3382
e-mail: wranglers@feist.com

National Association of Pro Baseball Leagues
P.O. Box A
201 Bayshore Dr. SE
St. Petersburg, FL 33731
Phone: (727) 822-6937
Fax (727) 821-5819
Internet: www.minorleaguebaseball.com

Brinkman/Froemming Umpire School
1021 Indian River Dr.
Cocoa, FL 32922

Harry Wendelstedt Umpire School
88 South St.
Andrews Drive
Ormond Beach, FL 32174
Phone: (904) 672-4879

Jim Evan's Academy of Professional Umpiring
12885 Research Blvd., Ste. 107
Austin, TX 78750
Phone: (512) 335-5959

BASKETBALL

Θ USA Basketball
5465 Mark Dabling Blvd.
Colorado Springs, CO 80918-3842
Phone: (719) 590-4800
Fax: (719) 590-4811
Internet: www.usabasketball.com

Θ Federation Internationale de Basketball
(FIBA)
Boschetsrieder Str. 67
P.O. Box 700607
81306 Munich, Germany
Phone: (49-89) 74-81-5800
Fax: (49-89) 74-81-5833

National Basketball Association (NBA)
645 Fifth Ave.
New York, NY 10022
Phone: (212) 407-8000
Fax: (212) 832-3861

Continental Basketball Association (CBA)
400 N. 5th St., Ste. 1425
Phoenix, AZ 85004
Phone: (602) 254-6677
Fax: (602) 258-9985
Internet: cbahoops.com

United States Basketball League (USBL)
46 Quirk Rd.
P.O. Box 211
Milford, CT 06460-3745
Phone: (203) 877-9508
Fax: (203) 878-8109

BIATHLON

Θ U.S. Biathlon Association (USBA)
29 Ethan Allen Ave.
Colchester, VT 05446
Phone: (802) 654-7833
Fax: (802) 654-7830
e-mail: usbiathlon@aol.com

Biathlon Canada
1600 James Naismith Dr.
Gloucester Ontario K1B 5N4
Canada
Phone: (613) 748-5608
Fax: (613) 748-5762
e-mail: rickn@biathloncanada.ca
Internet: www.biathloncanada.ca

⊗ International Biathlon Union (IBU)
Airportcenter-Postfach 1
A-5073 Wals-Himmelreich
Austria
Phone: (43-662) 855-5050
Fax: (43-662) 855-0508
e-mail: biathlon@ibu.at
Internet: www.ibu.at

Bobsled/Bobsleigh

⊗ U.S. Bobsled and Skeleton Foundation
(USBSF)
421 Old Military Rd.
P.O. Box 828
Lake Placid, NY 12946-0828
Phone: (518) 523-1842
Fax: (518) 523-9491
e-mail: info@usabobsled.org
Internet: www.usabobsled.org

⊗ Federation Internationale de Bobsleigh et
de Tobagganing (FIBT)
Via Piranesi 44B
20137 Milan
Italy
Phone: (39-2) 757-3319
Fax: (39-2) 738-0624
e-mail: fibtsecretariat@mail.asianet.it
Internet: www.bobsleigh.com

Boccie

International Boccie Association (IBA)
P.O. Box 170
Utica, NY 13503-0170

Federation Francaise du Sport Boules
11 Cours Lafayette
69006 Lyon
France

Bodybuilding

International Federation of Body Building
(IFBB)
P.O. Box 1490
Radio City Station, NY 10101
Phone: (914) 638-9290

National Physique Committee (NPC)
P.O. Box 3711
Pittsburgh, PA 15230
Phone: (412) 276-5027

Bowling

USA Bowling
5301 S. 76th St.
Greendale, WI 53129-0500
Phone: (414) 421-9008
Fax: (414) 421-1194
Internet: www.bowling.org

Federation Internationale des Quilleurs (FIQ)
1631 Mesa Ave., Ste. A
Colorado Springs, CO 80906
Phone: (719) 636-2695
Fax: (719) 636-3300

Boxing

⊗ USA Boxing
One Olympic Plaza
Colorado Springs, CO 80909-5776
Phone: (719) 578-4506
Fax: (719) 632-3426
e-mail: usaboxing@aol.com
Internet: www.usaboxing.org

USA Amateur Boxing Federation, Inc.
(USA/ABF)
1750 E. Boulder St.
Colorado Springs, CO 80909

⊗ Association Internationale de Boxe
Amateur (AIBA)
P.O. Box 0141
10321 Berlin
Germany
Phone: (49-30) 423-6766
Fax: (49-30) 423-5943
Internet: www.uni-leipzig.de/~iat/aiba1.htm

World Boxing Council
Geneva 33-DESP 503
Mexico D.I. 06600
Phone: (905) 525-3787
Fax: (905) 569-1911

CANOE/KAYAK

American Canoe Association (ACA)
7432 Alban Station Blvd., Ste. B-232
Springfield, VA 22150
Phone: (703) 451-0141
Fax: (703) 451-2245
e-mail: acadirect@aol.com
Internet: www.aca_paddler.org

⊛ U.S. Canoe and Kayak Team
421 Old Military Rd.
P.O. Box 789
Lake Placid, NY 12946
(518) 523-1855
Fax: (518) 523-3767
e-mail: usckt@aol.com
Internet: www.worldsport.com/sports/
    canoeing/home.html

Canadian Canoe Association
1600 James Naismith Dr.
Gloucester Ontario K1B 5N4
Canada
Phone: (613) 748-5623
Fax: (613) 748-5700

⊛ Federation Internationale de Canoe (FIC)
Dozsa Gyorgy ut 1-3
1143 Budapest
Hungary
Phone: (36-1) 363-4832
Fax: (36-1) 157-5643
Internet: www.worldsport.com/sports/
    canoeing/home.html

CRICKET

World Cricket League
301 W. 57th St., Ste. 5D
New York, NY 10019
Phone: (212) 582-8556
Fax: (212) 582-8531
e-mail: cricket@porus.com

CROQUET

British Croquet Association
Hurlington Club
Ranelagh Gardens London SW6 3PR
England

United States Croquet Association (USCA)
11585-B Polo Club Rd.
Wellington, FL 33414
Phone: (561) 753-9141
Fax: (561) 753-8801
e-mail: uscroquet@compuserv.com

CURLING

⊛ USA Curling
1100 Center Point Dr.
P.O. Box 866
Stevens Point, WI 54481-0866
Phone: (715) 344-1199
Fax: (715) 344-6885
Internet: www.usacurl.org

⊛ World Curling Federation (WCF)
81 Great King St.
Edinburgh EH3 6RN
Great Britain
Phone: (44-131) 556-4884
Fax: (44-131) 556-9400
Internet: www.worldsport.com/sports/
    curling/home.html

CYCLING

⊛ USA Cycling, Inc.
One Olympic Plaza
Colorado Springs, CO 80909-5775
Phone: (719) 578-4581
Fax: (719) 578-4596
Internet: www.usacycling.org

⊛ Union Cycliste Internationale (UCI)
Case Postale
1000 Lausanne 23
Switzerland
Phone: (41-21) 626-0080
Fax: (41-21) 626-0088

DARTS

American Darts Organization (ADO)
652 S. Brookhurst Ave., Ste. 543
Anaheim, CA 92804
Phone: (714) 254-0212
Fax: (714) 254-0214
Internet: www.infohwy.com/darts

DIVING

⚙️United States Diving, Inc. (USD)
Pan American Plaza, Ste. 430
201 S. Capitol Ave.
Indianapolis, IN 46225
Phone (317) 237-5252
Fax (317) 237-5257
e-mail: usdiving@aol.com
Internet: www.usdiving.org

⚙️Federation Internationale de Natation
Amateur (FINA)
Avenue de Beaumont 9
Rez-de-Chaussee
1012 Lausanne
Switzerland
Phone: (41-21) 312-6602
Fax: (41-21) 312-6610
Internet: www.fina.org

EQUESTRIAN

⚙️American Horse Shows Association
4047 Iron Works Pkwy.
Lexington, KY 40511
Phone: (606) 258-2472
Fax: (606) 231-6662
Internet: www.ahsa.org

U.S. Dressage Foundation (USDF)
P.O. Box 6669
Lincoln, NE 68506-0669
Phone: (402) 434-8550
Fax: (402) 434-8570

⚙️U.S. Equestrian Team
Pottersville Rd.
Gladstone, NJ 07934
Phone: (908) 234-1251
Fax: (908) 234-9417
Internet: www.uset.com

Canadian Equestrian Federation
1600 James Naismith Dr.
Gloucester Ontario K1B 5N4
Canada
Phone: (613) 748-5632
Fax: (613) 747-2920

⚙️Federation Equestre Internationale (FEI)
Ave. Mon-Repos 24
Case Postale 157
1000 Lausanne 5
Switzerland
Phone: (41-21) 312-5656
Fax: (41-21) 312-8677
Internet: www.worldsport.com/sports/
　　equestrian/home.html

FENCING

⚙️U.S. Fencing Association (USFA)
One Olympic Plaza
Colorado Springs, CO 80909-5774
Phone: (719) 578-4511
Fax: (719) 632-5737
Internet: www.usfa.org
e-mail: usfencing@aol.com

⚙️Federation Internationale d'Escrime (FIE)
Ave. Mon-Repos 24
Case Postale 2743
1002 Lausanne
Switzerland
Phone: (41-21) 320-3115
Fax: (41-21) 320-3116
Internet: www.fie.ch

FIELD HOCKEY

⚙️U.S. Field Hockey Association
One Olympic Plaza
Colorado Springs, CO 80909-5773
Phone: (719) 578-4567
Fax: (719) 632-0979
e-mail: usfha@usfieldhockey.com
Internet: www.usfieldhockey.com

⚙️Federation Internationale de Hockey (FIH)
Boite Postale. 5
1210 Brussels
Belgium
Phone: (32-2) 219-4537
Fax: (32-2) 219-2761
Internet: www.fihockey.org

FIGURE SKATING

ᛟᛟU.S. Figure Skating Association
20 First St.
Colorado Springs, CO 80906-3697
Phone: (719) 635-5200
Fax: (719) 635-9548
e-mail: usfsa1@aol.com
Internet: www.usfsa.org

Canadian Figure Skating Association
1600 James Naismith Dr.
Gloucester Ontario K1B 5N4
Canada
Phone: (613) 748-5635
Fax: (613) 748-5718
e-mail: cfsa@cfsa.ca
Internet: www.cfsa.ca

ᛟᛟInternational Skating Union (ISU)
Chemin de Primerose 2
CH-1007 Lausanne
Switzerland
Phone: (41-21) 612-6666
Fax: (41-21) 612-6677
e-mail: info@isu.ch
Internet: www.isu.org

FOOTBALL

Pop Warner Little Scholars, Inc.
586 Middletown Blvd. Ste. C 100
Langhorne, PA 19047
Phone: (215) 752-2691
Fax: (215) 752-2879

United States Flag Football League
5834 Pine Tree Dr.
Sanibel, FL 33957
(813) 472-0544

Arena Football League (AFL)
75 E. Wacker Dr., Ste. 400
Chicago, IL 60601
Phone: (312) 332-5510
Fax: (312) 332-5540

Canadian Football League (CFL)
110 Ellington Ave. W., 5th Fl.
Toronto Ontario M4R 1A3
Canada
Phone: (416) 322-9650
Fax: (416) 322-9651

National Football League (NFL)/
NFL Officials Association
280 Park Ave.
New York, NY 10017
Phone: (212) 450-2000
Fax: (212) 681-7599

NFL Europe
280 Park Ave.
New York, NY 10017
Phone: (212) 450-2107
Fax: (212) 681-7577

GOLF

United States Golf Association
P.O. Box 708
Far Hills, NJ 07931-0708
Phone: (908) 234-2300
Fax: (908) 234-9687

Professional Association of Golf Officials
1735 Market St., Ste. 3420
Philadelphia, PA 19103
Phone: (215) 979-3200
Fax: (215) 979-3201

GYMNASTICS
(ARTISTIC & RHYTHMIC)

ᛟᛟUSA Gymnastics
Pan American Plaza, Ste. 300
201 S. Capital Ave.
Indianapolis, IN 46225
Phone: (317) 237-5050
Fax: (317) 237-5069
Internet: www.usa~gymnastics.org

Federation Internationale de Gymnastique (FIG)
Rue des Oeuches 10
Case Postale 359
2740 Moutier 1
Switzerland
Phone: (41-32) 494-6410
Fax: (41-32) 494-6419
Internet: www.worldsport.com/sports/
        gymnastics/home.html

National Association of Women's Gymnastic Judging (NAWGJ)
Betty Sroufe, National Secretary/Treasurer
2096 Rolling Hills Blvd.
Fairfield, OH 45014
Phone: (513) 829-5671

HANDBALL

United States Handball Association
2333 N. Tucson Blvd.
Tucson, AZ 85716
Phone: (520) 795-0434
Fax: (520) 795-0465
e-mail: handball@ushandball.org
Internet: ushandball.org

ICE HOCKEY

USA Hockey, Inc.
1775 Bob Johnson Dr.
Colorado Springs, CO 80906
Phone: (719) 576-8724
Fax: (719) 538-1160
e-mail: usah@usahockey.org
Internet: www.usahockey.org

International Ice Hockey Federation (IIHF)
Parkring 11
8002 Zurich
Switzerland
Phone: (41-1) 289-8600
Fax: (41-1) 289-8622

American Hockey League (AHL)
425 Union St.
West Springfield, MA 01089
Phone: (413) 781-2030
Fax: (413) 733-4767

Hockey North America
11501 Sunset Hill Rd., 4th Fl.
Reston, VA 20190-4704
Phone: (703) 471-0400
Fax: (703) 904-7160
Internet: www.hna.com

International Hockey League (IHL)
1395 E. 12 Mile Rd.
Madison Hts., MI 48071
Phone: (248) 546-3230
Fax: (248) 546-1811
Internet: www.theihl.com

National Hockey League (NHL)
1251 Avenue of the Americas, 47th Fl.
New York, NY 10020-1104
Phone: (212) 789-2000
Fax: (212) 789-2020

United States Hockey League (USHL)
P.O. Box 1187
Hayward, WI 54843
Phone: (715) 634-6226
Fax: (715) 634-5755

JAI ALAI (PELOTA)

Federacion Internacional de Pelota Vasca Sede Central
Aldamar, 5-1 Dcha
San Sebastian, 20003
Spain
Phone: (34-4) 342-8415
Fax: (34-4) 342-8309

National Association of Jai Alai Frontons
Highway US-92
P.O. Box 2630
Daytona Beach, FL 32015

JUDO

USA Judo
One Olympic Plaza
Colorado Springs, CO 80909
Phone: (719) 578-4730
Fax: (719) 578-4733
Internet: www.usjudo.org

International Judo Federation (IJF)
Hortaleza 108
28004 Madrid
Spain
Phone: (34-1) 310-2618
Fax: (34-1) 319-0433

Judo Canada
1600 James Naismith Dr.
Gloucester Ontario K1B 5N4
Canada
Phone: (613) 748-5640
Fax: (613) 748-5697
e-mail: info@judocanada.org

KARATE

American Amateur Karate Federation
1930 Wilshire Blvd., Ste. 1208
Los Angeles, CA 90057
Phone: (213) 483-8261

USA Karate Federation
1300 Kenmore Blvd.
Akron, OH 44314
Phone: (330) 753-3114
Fax: (330) 753-6967
e-mail: usakf@imperium.net

USA National Karate-Do Federation, Inc.
8351 15th Ave., NW
P.O. Box 77083
Seattle, WA 98177-7083
Phone: (206) 440-8386
Fax: (206) 367-7557
Internet: www.usankf.org

World Union of Karatedo Organizations
Headquarters
Senpaku Shinko Building 1-15-16
Toranomon Minato-ku
Tokyo 105
Japan
Phone: (81-3) 503-6638

LACROSSE

U.S. Lacrosse
113 W. University Pkwy.
Baltimore, MD 21210
Phone: (410) 235-6882
Fax: (410) 366-6735
Internet: www.lacrosse.org

LUGE

U.S. Luge Association (USLA)
35 Church St.
Lake Placid, NY 12946-1805
Phone: (518) 523-2071
Fax: (518) 523-4106
e-mail: usaluge@usaluge.org
Internet: www.usaluge.org

Federation Internationale de Luge de
Course (FIL)
Rathausplatz 9
83471 Berchtesgaden
Germany
Phone: (49-8652) 699-60
Fax: (49-8652) 699-69

MOTORCYCLE RACING

American Motorcyclist Association (AMA)
13515 Yarmouth Dr.
Tickerington, OH 43147
Phone: (614) 856-1900
Fax: (614) 856-1920

Federation Internationale Motorcycliste (FIM)
19 Chemin William-Barbery
CH-1292 Chambesy Geneva
Switzerland
Phone: (41-22-75) 819-6061
Fax: (41-22-75) 819-2180

NETBALL

International Federation of Netball
Associations
99 Awaba St.
Mosman New South Wales 2088
Australia
Phone: (44-39) 428-2609

Paddleball

National Paddleball Association (NPA)
P.O. Box 712
Flint, MI 48501

Parachuting

Federation International Aeronautique
10-12 Rue du Capitaine Menard
Paris 75015
France
Phone: (33-14) 579-2477
Fax: (33-14) 579-7315

United States Parachute Association
1440 Duke St.
Alexandria, VA 22314
Phone: (703) 836-3495
Fax: (703) 836-2843
Internet: www.uspa.org

Star Crest Association
c/o Bill Newell, President
3418 Mona Way
Bakersfield, CA 93309
Phone: (805) 831-7771

U.S. BASE Association
321 W.Durian Ave.
Coalinga, CA 93210-1915
Phone: (213) 678-0163

Canadian Sport Parachute Association
4185 Dunning Rd.
Navan Ontario K4B 1J1
Canada
Phone/Fax: (613) 835-3731
e-mail: cspa@travel/net.com

Pentathlon:
Modern Pentathlon

U.S. Modern Pentathlon Association
7330 San Pedro, Box 10
San Antonio, TX 78216
Phone: (210) 528-2999
Fax: (210) 528-2992
e-mail: usmpa@texas.net
Internet: www.uspentathlon.org

Union Internationale de Pentathlon
Moderne (UIPMB)
Stade Louis II, Entrance E
13, Ave. des Castelans
Monte Carlo 98000
Monaco
Phone: (377) 9777-8555
Fax: (377) 9777-8550
e-mail: uipmb@image.dk
Internet: www.pentathlon.org

Polo

U.S. Polo Association
4059 Iron Works Pike
Lexington, KY 40511
Phone: (606) 255-0593
Fax: (606) 231-9738
e-mail: uspalexy@aol.com

Racquetball

International Racquetball Federation (IRF)
1685 W. Uintah
Colorado Springs, CO 80904-2921
Phone: (719) 635-5396
Fax: (719) 635-0685
e-mail: rbzine@interserve.com

Canadian Racquetball Association
2185 W. 14th Ave.
Vancouver, British Columbia V6K 2V8
Canada
Phone: (604) 734-6600
Fax: (613) 748-5644

Roller Hockey

Federation Internationale de Roller Skating
(FIRS)
Rambla Cataluna, 80 (piso 1)
08008 Barcelona
Spain
Phone: (34-3) 487-5348/5593
Fax: (34-3) 487-6916

Rowing

⚭ United States Rowing Association (U.S. Rowing)
Pan American Plaza, Ste. 400
201 S. Capitol Ave.
Indianapolis, IN 46225
Phone: (317) 237-5656
Fax: (317) 237-5646
e-mail: usrowing@aol.com
Internet: www.usrowing.org

⚭ Federation Internationale des Societies d'Aviron (FISA)
Case Postale 18
Ave. de Cour 135
1000 Lausanne 3
Switzerland
Phone: (41-21) 617-8373
Fax: (41-21) 617-8375
e-mail: fisa@ping.ch

Rugby

U.S. Rugby Football Foundation
One Beacon St.
Boston, MA 02108-3106
Phone: (617) 742-1510
Fax: (617) 431-0233

USA Rugby
3595 E. Fountain Blvd.
Colorado Springs, CO 80910
Phone: (719) 637-1022
Fax: (719) 637-1315
e-mail: usarugby@rmii.com
Internet: www.usarugby.org

Western Rugby Football Union of the United States
Dr. William L. Sexton, President
1405 E. Meadow Ln.
Kirksville, MO 63501-2635
Phone: (660) 626-2324
Fax: (660) 626-2965
e-mail: wls@fileserver5.kcom.edu

International Rugby Football Board (IRFB)
Huguenot House
35/38 St. Stephen's Green
Dublin 2
Ireland
Phone: (353-1) 662-54-44
Fax: (353-1)676-93-34
Internet: www.irfb.com

Sailing

⚭ United States Sailing Association
15 Maritime Dr.
P.O. Box 1260
Portsmouth, RI 02871-1260
Phone: (401) 683-0800
Fax: (401) 683-0840
Internet: www.ussailing.org

⚭ International Sailing Federation (ISAF)
Ariadne House, Town Quay
Southhampton SO14 2AQ
United Kingdom
Phone: (44-1703) 635-111
Fax: (44-1703) 635-789
e-mail: sail@isaf.co.uk
Internet: www.sailing.org

Shooting

⚭ USA Shooting
One Olympic Plaza
Colorado Springs, CO 80909-5762
Phone: (719) 578-4670
Fax: (719) 635-7989
Internet: www.usashooting.org

⚭ Union International di Tir (UIT)
Bavariaring 21
80336 Munich
Germany
Phone: (49-89) 53-4293 or 53-1012
Fax: (49-89) 53-9481
Internet: www.worldsport.com/sports/
                shooting/home.html

Shooting Federation of Canada
45 Shirley Blvd.
Nepean Ontario K1B 2W6
Canada
Phone: (613) 828-7338
Fax: (613) 828-7333

National Skeet Shooting Association
5931 Roft Rd.
San Antonio, TX 78253-9261
Phone: (210) 688-3371
Fax: (210) 688-3014
e-mail: nssa.nca.hdqtrs@internetmci.com

Amateur Trapshooting Association (ATA)
601 W. National Rd.
Vandalia, OH 45377
Phone: (513) 898-4638
Fax: (513) 898-5472

SKATING: ROLLER SKATING

USA Roller Skating
4730 South St.
P.O. Box 6579
Lincoln, NE 68506
Phone: (402) 483-7551
Fax: (402) 483-1465
Internet: www.usacrs.com

Federation Internationale de Roller-Skating
(FIRS)
Rambla Cataluna 80, piso 1
08008 Barcelona
Spain
Phone: (34-3) 487-5348 or 487-5593
Fax: (34-3) 487-6916
Internet: www.firs.org

U.S. Amateur Confederation of Roller Skating
P.O. Box 6579
Lincoln, NE 68506
Phone: (402) 483-7551
Fax: (402) 483-1465
e-mail: sk8sid@aol.com

SKIING

☾☾☾ U.S. Ski and Snowboard Association
1500 Kearns Blvd.
P.O. Box 100
Park City, UT 84060-0100
Phone: (435) 649-9090
Fax: (435) 647-2630
Internet: www.usskiteam.com or
www.ussa.org

Cross Country Canada
1600 James Naismith Dr.
Gloucester Ontario K1B 5N4
Canada
Phone: (613) 748-5662
Fax: (613) 748-5703
e-mail: xcski@cdnsport.ca

☾☾☾ Federation Internationale de Ski (FIS)
Blochstrasse 2
3653 Oberhofen Thunersee
Switzerland
Phone: (41-33) 244-6161
Fax: (41-33) 243-5353
Internet: www.worldsport.com/sports/
ski/home.html

SOCCER (FOOTBALL)

☾☾☾ United States Soccer Federation (USSF)
U.S. Soccer House
1801-1811 S. Prairie Ave.
Chicago, IL 60616
Phone: (312) 808-1300
Fax: (312) 808-9566
e-mail: socfed@aol.com
Internet: www.us~soccer.com

☾☾☾ Federation Internationale de Football
Association (FIFA)
Case Postale 85 (Hitzigweg 11)
8030 Zurich
Switzerland
Phone: (41-1) 384-9595
Fax: (41-1) 384-9696
Internet: www.fifa.com

Major League Soccer (MLS)
110 E. 42nd St., Ste. 1502
New York, NY 10017

Continental Indoor Soccer League (CISL)
16027 Ventura Blvd., Ste 605
Encino, CA 91436
Phone: (818) 906-7627

National Professional Soccer League (NPSL)
115 Dewalt Ave. NW
Canton, OH 44702
Phone: (330) 455-4625

SOFTBALL

⊕Amateur Softball Association (ASA)/
USA Softball
2801 N.E. 50th St.
Oklahoma City, OK 73111-7203
Phone: (405) 424-5266
Fax: (405) 424-3855
e-mail: info@softball.org
Internet: www.softball.org

⊕Federation Internationale de Softball (ISF)
4141 NW Expressway
Oklahoma City, OK 73116
Phone: (405) 879-2004
Fax: (405) 879-9801
e-mail: isfsoftball@accessacg.net

International Softball Congress (ISC)
6007 E. Hillcrest Circle
Anaheim Hills, CA 92807-3921
Phone: (714) 998-5694
Fax: (714) 282-7902

National Softball Association (NSA)
P.O. Box 7
Nicholasville, KY 40340
Phone: (606) 887-4114
Fax: (606) 887-4874

Pony Softball
P.O. Box 225
Washington, PA 15301
Phone: (724) 225-1060
Fax: (724) 225-9852

United States Slo-Pitch Softball Association
(USSSA)
3935 S. Crater Rd.
Petersburg, VA 23805
Phone: (804) 732-4099
Fax: (804) 732-1704

ASA National Umpire Schools
2801 N.E. 50th St.
Oklahoma City, OK 73111

SPEED SKATING

⊕U.S. Speedskating
P.O. Box 450639
Westlake, OH 44145
Phone: (440) 899-0128
Fax: (440) 899-0109

Amateur Speed Skating Union of the U.S.
(ASU)
1033 Shady Lane
Glen Ellyn, IL 60137
Phone: (630) 790-3230
Fax: (630) 790-3235
Internet: www.mit.edu/jeffrey/speedskating/
asu.html

Canadian Amateur Speed Skating Association
1600 James Naismith Dr., Ste. 312
Gloucester Ontario K1B 5N4
Canada
Phone: (613) 748-5669
Fax: (613) 748-5600
e-mail: ssc@speedskating~canada.ca
Internet: www.speedskating~canada.ca

⊕International Skating Union (ISU)
Chemin de Primerose 2
CH 1007 Lausanne
Switzerland
Phone: (41-21) 612-6666
Fax: (41-21) 612-6677
e-mail: info@isu.ch
Internet: www.isu.org

SWIMMING

ꕥ USA Swimming, Inc. (USS)
One Olympic Plaza
Colorado Springs, CO 80909-5770
Phone (719) 578-4578
Fax (719) 578-4669
Internet: www.usa~swimming.org

ꕥ Federation Internationale de Natation
Amateur (FINA)
Ave. de Beaumont 9
Rez-de-Chaussee
1012 Lausanne
Switzerland
Phone: (41-21) 312-6602
Fax: (41-21) 312-6610
Internet: www.fina.org

SYNCHRONIZED SWIMMING

U.S. Synchronized Swimming, Inc. (USSS)
ꕥ Pan American Plaza, Ste. 901
    201 S. Capitol Ave.
Indianapolis, IN 46225
Phone: (317) 237-5700
Fax: (317) 237-5705
e-mail: webmaster@usasynchro.org
Internet: www.usasynchro.org

ꕥ Federation Internationale de Natation
Amateur (FINA)
Ave. de Beaumont 9
Rez-de-Chaussee
1012 Lausanne
Switzerland
Phone: (41-21) 312-6602
Fax: (41-21) 312-6610
Internet: www.fina.org

TABLE TENNIS

ꕥ USA Table Tennis
One Olympic Plaza
Colorado Springs, CO 80909-5769
Phone: (719) 578-4583
Fax: (719) 632-6071
e-mail: usatt@iex.net
Internet: www.usatt.org

ꕥ International Table Tennis Federation
(ITTF)
53 London Rd.
St. Leonards-on Sea
East Sussex TN37 6AY
Great Britain
Phone: (44-1424) 72-1414
Fax: (44-1424) 43-1871
e-mail: hq@ittf.cablenet.co.uk
Internet: www.ittf.com

TAEKWONDO

American Taekwondo Association (ATA)
6210 Baseline Rd.
Little Rock, AR 72209
Phone: (501) 568-2821
Fax: (501) 568-2497

U.S. Taekwondo Union
One Olympic Plaza
Colorado Springs, CO 80909-5792
Phone: (719) 578-4632
Fax: (719) 578-4642
e-mail: ustumedia@aol.com
Internet: www.ustu.com

World Taekwondo Federation (WTF)
635 Yuksam-dong Kangnam-ku
Seoul 135-081
Korea
Phone: (82-2) 566-2505
Fax: (82-2) 553-4728
e-mail: wtf@unitel.co.kr
Internet: www.wtf.or.kr

TEAM HANDBALL

ꕥ U.S. Team Handball Federation
1903 Powers Ferry Rd., Ste.230
Atlanta, GA 30339
Phone: (770) 956-7660
Fax: (719) 956-7976
e-mail: info@usateamhandball.org
Internet: www.usateamhandball.org

Federation Internationale de Handball (IHF)
Lange Gasse 10
Case Postale 312
4020 Bale
Switzerland
Phone: (41-61) 272-1300
Fax: (41-61) 272-1344
e-mail: ihf@magnet.ch
Internet: www.worldsport.com/sports/
        handball/home.html

TENNIS

U.S. Tennis Association (USTA)
70 W. Red Oak Lane
White Plains, NY 10604-3602
Phone: (914) 696-7000
Fax: (914) 696-7167
Internet: www.usta.com

International Tennis Federation (ITF)
Palliser Rd., Barons Court
London W14 9EN
Great Britain
Phone: (44-171) 381-8060
Fax: (44-171) 381-5257
Internet: www.itftennis.com

Intercollegiate Tennis Association (ITA)
Lenz Tennis Center
P.O. Box 71
Princeton, NJ 08544

TRACK & FIELD

USA Track & Field
One RCA Dome, Ste. 140
P.O. Box 120
Indianapolis, IN 46206-0120
Phone: (317) 261-0500
Fax: (317) 261-0481
Internet: www.usatf.org

International Amateur Athletic Federation (IAFF)
17, Rue Princess-Florestine
Case Postale 359
98007 Monte Carlo
Monaco
Phone: (377-93) 10-888
Fax: (377-93) 15-9515
Internet: www.iaaf.org

TRIATHLON

USA Triathlon
3595 E. Fountain Blvd., Ste. F-1
Colorado Springs, CO 80910
Phone: (719) 597-9090
Fax: (719) 597-2121
e-mail: usatriathlon@usatriathlon.org
Internet: www.usatriathlon.org

International Triathlon Union (ITU)
1154 W 24th St.
North Vancouver British Columbia V7P 2J2
Canada
Phone: (604) 926-7250
Fax: (604) 926-7260
e-mail: ituhdq@axionet.com
Internet: www.triathlon.org

VOLLEYBALL

USA Volleyball (USAV)
3595 E. Fountain Blvd., Ste. I-2
Colorado Springs, CO 80910-1740
Phone: (719) 637-8300
Fax: (719) 597-6307
Internet: www.volleyball.org/usav

Federation Internationale de Volleyball (FIVB)
12 Ave. de la Gare
Case Postale
1001 Lausanne
Switzerland
Phone: (41-21) 345-3535
Fax: (41-21) 345-3545
Internet: www.fivb.ch

WATER POLO

⚙ U.S. Water Polo
1685 W. Uintah
Colorado Springs, CO 80904-2921
Phone: (719) 634-0699
Fax: (719) 634-0866
e-mail: uswpoffice@uswp.org
Internet: www.uswp.org

Water Polo Canada
1600 James Naismith Dr.
Gloucester Ontario K1B 5N4
Canada
Phone: (613) 748-5682
Fax: (613) 748-5777
e-mail: susanfh@rtm.cdnsport.ca

⚙ Federation Internationale de Natation
Amateur (FINA)
Ave. de Beaumont 9
Rez-de-Chaussee
1012 Lausanne
Switzerland
Phone: (41-21) 312-6602
Fax: (41-21) 312-6610
Internet: www.fina.org

WEIGHTLIFTING

⚙ U.S. Weightlifting Federation
One Olympic Plaza
Colorado Springs, CO 80909-5764
Phone: (719) 578-4508
Fax: (719) 578-4741
e-mail: usaw@worldnet.att.net
Internet: www.usaw.org

⚙ International Weightlifting Federation
(IWF)
Hold u.l
P.F. 614
1374 Budapest
Hungary
Phone: (36-1) 131-8153 or 153-0530
Fax: (36-1) 131-0199
Internet: www.worldsport.com/sports/
weightlifing/home.html

WINDSURFING

Canadian Yachting Association/
Windsurfing Canada
1600 James Naismith Dr., Ste. 504
Gloucester Ontario K1B 5N4
Canada
Phone: (613) 748-5687
Fax: (613) 748-5688
e-mail: sailcanada@sailing.ca
Internet: www.sailing.ca

World Boarding Association
Feldafinger Platz 2
Munchen 71 D-8000
Germany
Phone: (49-8) 978-1074

U.S. Windsurfing Association
P.O. Box 978
Hood River, OR 97031
Phone: (541) 386-8708
e-mail: uswa@aol.com

WRESTLING

⚙ USA Wrestling (USAW)
6155 Lehman Dr.
Colorado Springs, CO 80918
Phone: (719) 598-8181
Fax: (719) 598-9440
e-mail: usaw@concentric.net
Internet: www.usawrestling.org

⚙ Federation Internationale des Luttes
Associees (FILA)
Ave. Juste-Olivier
1006 Lausanne
Switzerland
Phone: (41-21) 312-8426
Fax: (41-21) 323-6073
Internet: www.worldsport.com/sports/
wrestling/home.html

U.S. Wrestling Officials Association (USWOA)
2612 Hamilton
Glenshaw, PA 15116
Phone: (412) 486-8997

YACHT RACING

U.S. Yacht Racing Union (USYRU)
8516 Sand Point Way, NE
Seattle, WA 98115

Canadian Yachting Association/
Windsurfing Canada
1600 James Naismith Dr., Ste. 504
Gloucester Ontario K1B 5N4
Canada
Phone: (613) 748-5687
Fax: (613) 748-5688
e-mail: sailcanada@sailing.ca
Internet: www.sailing.ca

International Yacht Racing Union (IYRU)
27 Broadwell
Waterloo, London SE1 9PL
Great Britain
Phone: (44-71) 928-4670
Fax: (44-71) 401-8304

APPENDIX II: OLYMPIC GAMES

In many sports, working the Olympic Games is considered the pinnacle of an official's career. Olympic officiating and judging positions are extended by invitation only to the best of the best. In most cases, Olympic officials are selected from the ranks of qualified and talented officials who are recommended by the regulatory body governing their sport. In addition, Olympic officials are drawn from each participating country to ensure fairness and reinforce the spirit of international cooperation that is the cornerstone of the Games.

While officials' pay at the Olympic level is not nearly as much many American officials make at the professional level, the prestige and responsibility of officiating Olympic competition is compensation enough for most officials. In addition, travel expenses normally are picked up by the organizing committee, and officials get to enjoy the world's largest sporting event from the best seat in the house.

Presented here is a complete roster of Olympic sports for both the Summer and Winter Games. Sports organizations and associations with Olympic affiliation are listed in the Directory of Sports Organizations which begins on page 441.

SUMMER OLYMPIC SPORTS

Aquatics
  Swimming
  Diving
  Water Polo
  Synchronized Swimming
Archery
Athletics / Track & Field
  Sprints / Distance
  Marathon
  Decathlon / Heptathlon
  Jumps / Vaults / Throws
  Race Walk
Badminton
Baseball
Basketball
Boxing
Canoeing / Kayaking
Cycling
  Mountain Biking
  Road
  Track
Equestrian
Fencing
Football / Soccer
Gymnastics
  Artistic
  Rhythmic
Handball
Judo
Modern Pentathlon
Rowing
Sailing
Shooting
Softball (Provisional)
Table Tennis
Taekwondo (Provisional)
Tennis
Triathlon (Provisional)
Volleyball
  Indoor
  Beach (Provisional)
Weightlifting
Wrestling

WINTER OLYMPIC SPORTS

Bobsleigh / Bobsled
Ice Hockey
Luge
Skating
  Speed
  Figure
Skiing
  Alpine
  Jumping
  Biathlon
  Nordic
Snow boarding

International Olympic Committee
Chateau de Vidy
CH-1007 Lausanne
Switzerland
Phone: (41-21) 621-6111
Fax: (41-21) 621-6216
Internet: www.olympic.org

Organizing Committees
1999 Winter World University Games
Slovakia University Sports Association
Junacka 6
832 80 Bratislava
Slovakia
Phone: (421-7) 5049-103
Fax: (421-7) 5049-571

1999 Special Olympics World Summer
Games
4000 W. Chase Blvd., Ste. 325
Raleigh, NC 27607
Phone: (919) 831-1999
Fax: (919) 835-4319
Internet: www.99games.org

1999 World University Games
Universiada Palma de Mallorca 1999
Camino LaVileta, 40
07011 Palma de Mallorca
Spain
Phone: (34-971) 45-7211
Fax: (34-971) 28-4180
Internet: www.uib.es/universiada99

1999 Pan American Games
433 Main St.
Winnipeg, Manitoba R3B 3B1
Canada
Phone: (204) 985-1999
Fax: (204) 985-4375
Internet: www.panamgames.org

Sydney Olympic Organizing Committee
for the Olympic Games (SOCOG)
Level 14, The Maritime Centre
207 Kent St.
GPO Box 2000
Sydney, NSW 2001
Australia
Phone: (61-29) 297-2000
Fax: (1-29) 297-2020
Internet: www.sydney.olympic.org

Sydney Paralympic Organizing
Committee
Level 7, The Maritime Centre
207 Kent St.
R383 Royal Exchange
Sydney, NSW 2000
Australia
Phone: (61-29) 297-2000
Fax: (61-29) 297-2020
Internet: www.sydney.paralympics.org

Salt Lake City Olympic Organizing
Committee
257 E. 200 South, 6th Floor
Phone: (801) 212-2002
Fax: (810) 364-7644
Internet: www.slo2002.org

Athens Olympic Organizing Committee
Zappio Megaro
Athens
Greece
Phone: (011-30) 1-324-0004
Fax: (011-30) 1-323-2004
Internet: www.athens2004.gr

APPENDIX III:
INTERNET RESOURCES
FOR OFFICIALS

A variety of resources for sports officials exists on the Internet. World Wide Web (www) sites are the most common, and these range from simple home pages to elaborate sites that allow users to ask technical questions and rules interpretation from veteran officials, link to other sites, or choose from a variety of sport or league-specific topics.

In a review of Internet resources conducted for this book, over 9,000 *hits* were generated by using *sports officiating* in the search field. Web sites included resumes of individual referees, officiating job postings, major officiating sites, and a host of regional and local officiating postings. A list of some of the major officiating sites is presented on the opposite page. However, due to the ever-changing nature of the Internet, readers are encouraged to conduct their own search queries in order to obtain the names of the latest sports officiating sites and current URLs.

Internet users may also wish to check in with one of the many sports newsgroups that addresses officiating. Common sports newsgroups are addressed as follows:

rec.sport.[insert sport name] example: rec.sport.baseball

In addition, there is one Newsgroup devoted exclusively to sports officiating. This may be found at: rec.sport.officiating. In this Newsgroup, officials share war stories, discuss rules changes and interpretations, and generally commiserate with one another.

SAMPLING OF WEB SITES FOR OFFICIALS*

Name: "The Referee/Umpire Home Page"
by Gary McGriff
URL: http://www.gmcgriff.com/refonline/
Remarks: A great general interest site for officials in all sports. Offers a variety of articles and information, along with access to the rec.sport.officiating newsgroup.

Name: "Because Refs Are People Too"
Sponsored by Roberto Alomar for *HuskyHoops Magazine*
URL: http://www.huskyhoops.com/officiat.htm
Remarks: Offers a series of links of interest to sports officials.

Name: "Sports Officiating Directory"
URL: http://www.ahandyguide.com/cat1/s/s983.htm
Remarks: A complete sports officiating directory, sports officiating guide, and index of links to a variety of sports.

Name: "Amateur Baseball Umpire Home Page"
URL: http://www.superaje.com/~brenmcla/
Remarks: Information for amateur umpires, including basic and advanced mechanics.

Name: "Ice Hockey Officials of Northern Connecticut"
URL: http://www.ihonc.com
Remarks: Provides articles and general information on ice hockey officiating.

Name: "Minnesota State Referee Committee"
URL: http://www.econ.umn.edu/~matheson/soccer/index.html
Remarks: An excellent resource for soccer referees with soccer articles, links and photos, plus links to other soccer sites.

Name: "Referee Magazine"
URL: http://www.referee.com
Remarks: The home page of *Referee Magazine*.

Name: "Sports Canada"
URL: http://www.cdnsport.ca
Remarks: The master site of Canadian Sports Federations includes sites for a variety of sports.

* List is by no means complete; this is merely a sampling of the sites available. A great many more resources exist, and readers are encouraged to conduct their own search queries for the latest information.

BIBLIOGRAPHY

John W. Bunn. **The Art of Officiating Sports.** Englewood Cliffs, NJ: Prentice-Hall, Inc., 1968

Edward F. Dolan, Jr. **Calling the Play: A Beginner's Guide to Amateur Sports Officiating.** New York, NY: Atheneum, 1982

_____. **Career Information Center: No. 11 – Public and Community Services.** New York, NY: Macmillan Publishing Company, 1993

Shelly Field. **Career Opportunities in the Sports Industry.** New York, NY: Facts on File, Inc., 1991

Marjorie Eberts & Margaret Gisler. **Careers for Good Samaritans & Other Humanitarian Types.** Lincolnwood, IL: VGM Career Horizons, 1995

William Ray Heitzman. **Careers for Sports Nuts and Other Athletic Types.** Lincolnwood, IL: VGM Career Horizons, 1991

Roy A. Edelfelt. **Careers in Education.** Lincolnwood, IL: VGM Career Horizons, 1993

Carolyn Simpson & Dwain Simpson. **Careers in Social Work.** New York, NY: The Rosen Publishing Group, Inc., 1992

Allen Richardson. **Careers Without College.** Princeton, NJ: Peterson's, 1993

Keith Bell. **Championship Thinking.** Englewood Cliffs, NJ: Prentice-Hall, Inc., 1983

_____. **Court and Field Diagram Guide.** Kansas City, MO: National Federation of State High School Associations, 1995

Tom Hammill. **The Football Official's "What If?" Answer Book: 96 Proven Performance Builders for Football Officials.** Franksville, WI: Referee Enterprises, Inc., 1988

Jerry Grunska. **Let's Make It Official: Practical Suggestions for the High School Official.** Kansas City, MO: National Federation of State High School Associations, 1995

Richard Clegg & William A. Thompson. **Modern Sports Officiating: A Practical Guide.** Dubuque, IA: WCB Brown & Benchmark, 1993

Joyce Hadley. **Part-time Careers.** Hawthorne, NJ: Career Press, 1993

Robert S. Weinberg & Peggy A. Richardson. **Psychology of Officiating.** Champaign, IL: Leisure Press, 1990

Robert W. Grant. **The Psychology of Sport: Facing One's True Opponent.** Jefferson, NC: McFarland & Company, Inc., 1952

The Diagram Group. **Rules of the Game.** New York, NY: St. Martin's Press, 1990

Bing Broido. **Spalding Book of Rules.** Indianapolis, IN: Masters Press, 1992

Tom Hammill & Dick Fredricks. **Take Charge Basketball Officiating.** Franksville, WI: Referee Enterprises, Inc., 1992

Kathy Davis. **Take Charge Volleyball Officiating.** Franksville, WI: Referee Enterprises, Inc., 1992

Luciano & Fisher. **The Umpire Strikes Back.** New York, NY: Bantam, 1892

John Hassan, editor. **1997 Information Please Sports Almanac.** New York, NY: Houghton Mifflin Co., 1997

ACKNOWLEDGMENTS

Many people contributed their knowledge and expertise to the compilation of this book. LR Publishing is indebted to the following:

Tom Blue, USA Volleyball rules interpreter; Bill Bupp, Supervisor of Officials, Michigan High School Athletic Association; Merle Butler, Director of Umpires, Amateur Softball Association; Dan Calandro, Director, Division I Men's Basketball Operations, National Collegiate Athletic Association; Dale Davidson, Ohio State Umpire-in-chief, United States Softball Association; Linda L. Lindeman DeCarlo, General Manager, Jet Media, Inc.; Fred Dubin, soccer official; Anneliese Eggert, swimming official and Secretary, U.S. Swimming Rules Committee; Richard Falk, Assistant Commissioner, Big Ten Conference; Sean Ford, Director of Basketball Operations, USA Basketball; Tim Gall, President, Eastword Publications; John Gillis, Assistant Director, National Federation of State High School Associations; Ron Hoyt, Athletic Director, Orange High School; George E. Killian, Executive Director, National Junior College Athletic Association; Mike Killpack, Director of Sports, Amateur Athletic Union; Jackie Kuhnert, United States Tennis Association; Mark Krzys, home plate umpire, Pony Tail Softball; Rick Laskey, volleyball referee; Tom Lepperd, Supervisor, Umpire Development Program; Missy Malool, Tour Director, United States Tennis Association; Barry Mano, President, Referee Enterprises, Inc.; Fritz McGinness, Assistant Executive Director, National Federation of State High School Associations; Jerry Meals, baseball umpire; Rob Miller, National Christian Collegiate Athletic Association; Fred Mosely, sports writer; Hank Nichols, National Coordinator for Men's Basketball Officiating, National Collegiate Athletic Association; David Parry, Supervisor of Officials, Big Ten Conference; Jerome Perry, track official; Julie Quickel, Public Information Assistant, National Collegiate Athletic Association; Robert Rice, Assistant Supervisor of Officials (retired), National Football League; Mark Riley, ice hockey official; Kathy Sellers, USA Track and Field; Dave Shatkowski, Director of Communications, U.S. Diving; Don Sparks, Executive Director, National Federation of State High School Associations; Betty Sroufe, national elite gymnastics judge; Donna Strobel, USA Wrestling; Robert Weinberg, Ph.D., Professor and Chair, Department of Physical Education, Health and Sport Studies, Miami University of Ohio; Dave Wester, Sports Information Assistant, National Association of Intercollegiate Athletics